ISBN 978-1-332-19697-5
PIBN 10296859

Forgotten Books is a registered trademark of FB &c Ltd.
Copyright © 2015 FB &c Ltd.
FB &c Ltd, Dalton House, 60 Windsor Avenue, London, SW19 2RR.
Company number 08720141. Registered in England and Wales.

For support please visit www.forgottenbooks.com

Similar Books Are Available from
www.forgottenbooks.com

Just Published,

BY BENJAMIN SMITH, 74, SOUTH CASTLE-STREET,

LIVERPOOL,

AND MAY BE HAD OF ALL THE BOOKSELLERS.

A NEW PLAN OF LIVERPOOL.

A NEW ILLUSTRATED PLAN OF LIVERPOOL AND ITS
SUBURBS, (on a Sheet) .... 0s. 9d.
DITTO, DITTO, (in Case, for Pocket) WITH
LISTS OF COACH FARES, HOTELS AND BANKS, 1s. 6d.

ALSO

A SERIES OF VIEWS

OF THE

PRINCIPAL

PUBLIC BUILDINGS

OF

LIVERPOOL,

CONTAINING

The New Assize Courts, and St. George's Hall,	Railway Station,
Town Hall,	Saint Luke's Church,
Custom House,	Great George-st. Chapel,
Apothecaries' Hall,	Saint James' Cemetery.
Royal Bank Buildings,	Plan of Liverpool 1650.
	View of Liverpool 1729,

On Enamelled Cards, price 4d. each, or 1s. 6d per Set of
six in a neat Envelope ;
And on Letter Paper, price 2d. each, or 3s. 6d. per quire.

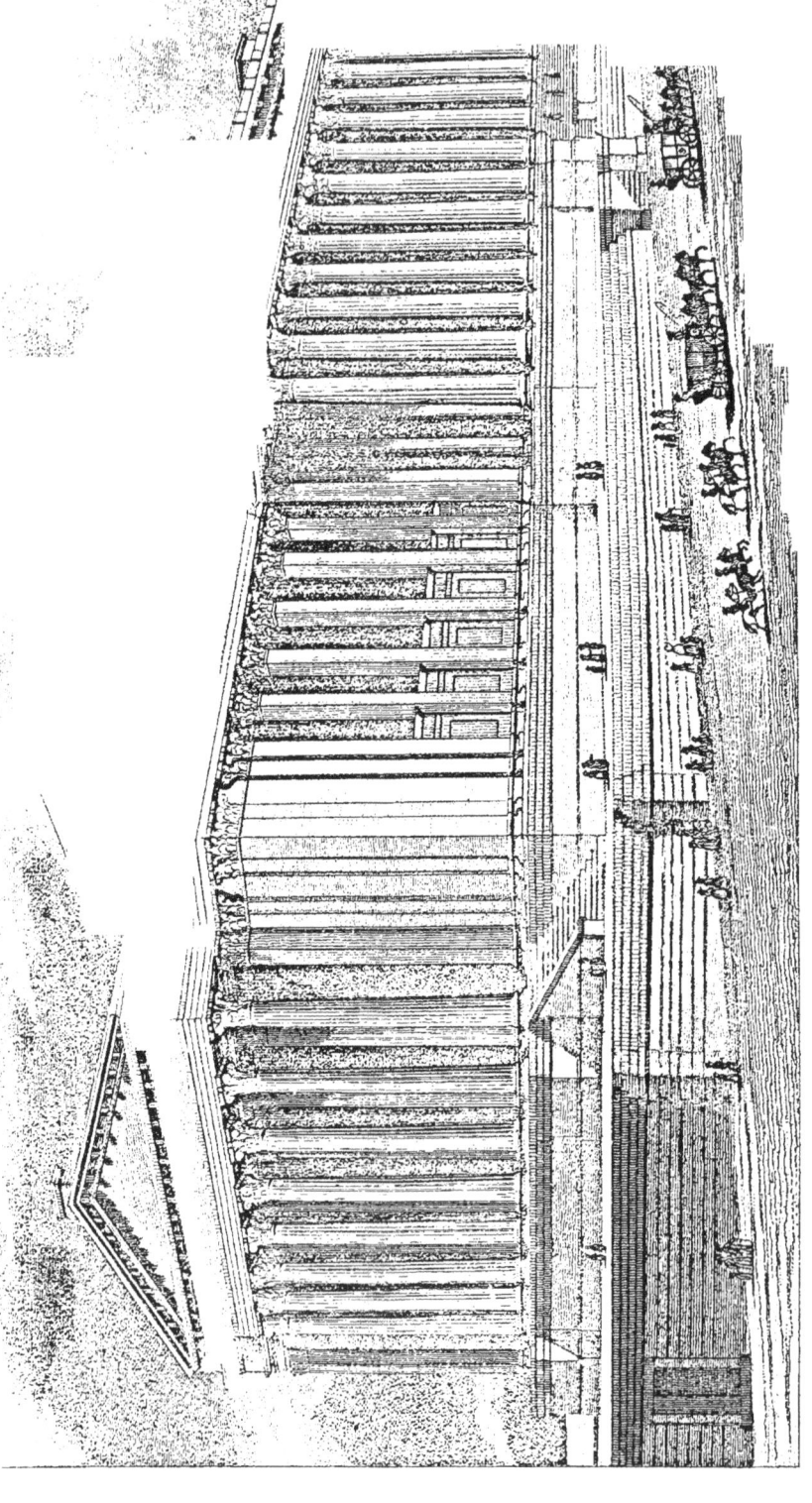

H LONSDALE ELMES ESQ

John Eldridge

SMITH'S

STRANGERS' GUIDE

TO

LIVERPOOL,

ITS ENVIRONS, AND PART OF CHESHIRE,

FOR

1843.

BY ALEXANDER BROWN, A. M.

Liverpool:

PRINTED AND PUBLISHED BY BENJAMIN SMITH,
SOUTH CASTLE-STREET.

PREFACE

The Publisher of the " STRANGER'S GUIDE TO LIVERPOOL"
trusts that the following pages will be found useful, not only as a
silent *cicerone* to the stranger, enabling him to spend, with pleasure and profit, a few days in this seat of commerce, but that they
will open up to the resident much that is interesting, as well as
new.

In compressing an account of *every* public building, institution, and object of note in Liverpool, into a space so small, as to
enable the work to be afforded at a moderate price, care has been
taken to omit nothing of importance ; and the arrangement which
has been adopted, is that best suited to the wants of the stranger.
For his special use an ITINERARY has been added, together
with an APPENDIX, containing such lists for reference as are most
required. In connexion with the descriptive matter, interesting
statistical information has been introduced whenever practicable
or useful. This department might have been extended, but while
we write the figures, the facts are changing, and it is, therefore,
needless to give numbers of only present value.

The Editor is aware that in the descriptions of *nearly five
hundred* of

——" the things of fame
That do renown this city"—

some errors may have found their way into his work, yet he hopes
they are both few and unimportant, and that he has delineated
faithfully, though briefly, the most prominent features of the objects constituting " the lions " of Liverpool; its sights, amusements, exhibitions, theatres, churches, courts of justice, prisons,
hospitals, monuments ; squares, streets, docks, warehouses, pub-

lic buildings, markets, shops; manufactures, railroads, steam-
boats, shipping; together with the manifold associations of civil
government, police, population, mortality, charities, industry,
wealth, education, literature, science and the arts.

To the kind patronage of the public, therefore, is committed
THE STRANGERS' GUIDE TO

LIVERPOOL,

"one of the finest towns in the world; the abode of industry
and of opulence; the home of commerce and magnificence,
familiar to those far sojourners who inhabit 'realms that Cæsar
never knew,' whose merchants are princes, and whose name is
borne in ocean leagues 'thrice form the centre to the uttermost
pole' by all the winds that blow—.

---

*The Publisher will feel grateful for information respecting
New Buildings, Institutions, Societies, &c.; or for suggestions of
any additions or alterations that may be desirable.*

LIST OF ILLUSTRATIONS.

INDEX.

Published by B. Smith

South Castle Street.

VIEW OF LIVERPOOL IN THE YEAR 1650.

HISTORY OF LIVERPOOL.

As is the case with all places which have slowly emerged from obscurity, the early history of Liverpool is very imperfect. It was not known by name previously to the year 1089, and it is not mentioned in Doomsday-Book, although the neighbouring villages of Everton, Formby, and Litherland, are enumerated. The derivation of the name Liverpool, has been frequently examined, but nothing decisive has been ascertained respecting it. The orthography has undergone many alterations, the name having successively been Lyrpul, Litherpul, Ly'rpole, Lyverpool, Lyverpol, Lurpole, Liverpol, Leverpool, and Liverpool.

In the year 1207 a charter was granted by King John to this embryo town, conferring on the inhabitants " all the liberties and free customs which any other free borough upon the sea hath in our territories." In 1227 the charter was confirmed by Henry III, who made the place a free borough for ever, for a fine of ten marks, and directed the formation of a guild, enacting that no person, unless of that guild, should " make merchandise," without the consent of the burgesses.

At various periods other charters were obtained, all of which appear to have been the means of bringing the town into notice, and of promoting its improvement and extension. In 1561 there were only seven streets, with 138 cottages and 690 inhabitants. They were Chapel-street, Bancke-street, (now Water-street), Moor-street, (now Tithebarn-street), Castle-street, Dale-street, High-street or Joggler-street, and Mylne-street, (now Oldhall-street).

In the year 1650 Liverpool had acquired considerable importance; and from that period may be dated the rapid progress of its prosperity, and the commencement of that commercial greatness which now renders it so conspicuous.

At this time the most prominent objects in the town were the Castle, the Tower, the Custom-house, and the Old Church. The Castle stood on the site of St. George's Church, and is supposed to have been built by Roger de Poictiers about the year 1076. It was intended to command the harbour, and was surrounded by a moat, into which the tide was admitted. It long stood the ravages of time, and the storms of political changes, and was only taken down in 1721. In 1420 its form was nearly rectangular, and it had four towers and battlements, with a large hall, and numerous apartments, and it enclosed an area about 49 yards square. Within the building was a well, brewhouse, bakehouse, and other conveniences. In digging the foundation for St. George's Church in 1826, the supposed south-west angle of the tower was discovered, and in 1828, when the Crescent was being built, a much larger portion of the ruins of the castle was met with.

The Tower was situated at the bottom of Water-street, on the north side; but it is not known at what period, or by whom it was erected. About the year 1360 the tower was the property of Sir Thomas de Latham, by whom it was presented to his son-in-law Sir John Stanley, along with several houses in the neighbourhood. In 1406 permission was obtained from Henry IV. to erect a spacious building on the former site, which received the same appellation, and it remained for some centuries in possession of the Stanley family. At a later period, prior to the middle of the 18th century, it was converted into an assembly room, and was subsequently occupied as a jail. In 1819 this relique of antiquity was pulled down and warehouses erected on its site.

The Custom-house was a small building on the margin of the river, at the bottom of Water-street.

The Old Church occupied the present site of St. Nicholas' Church; and the cemetery attached to it, being on the beach, was washed by each successive tide.

The Pool was a dirty swampy inlet, extending over the space now occupied by the Custom-house, along Paradise-street, Whitechapel, and Byrom-street, to Richmond-row, varying in width from about 1200 feet at its junction with the Mersey, to 150 or 200 feet at the bottom of Shaw's Brow, and being upwards of a mile in length. It was crossed by a bridge where Cooper's Row now is, by another at the end of Dale-street, and by a third, which was built by Lord Molyneux, at the bottom of Lord-street. It is not known at what period these bridges were removed. At the corner of Whitechapel and Sir Thomas' Buildings was a boat-house, with a ferry-boat for the convenience of passengers crossing the Pool; and there were sluices, or flood-gates, for the retention of the water, a little higher up. There was a stream proceeding from Mosslake fields, in a course along the present Pembroke-place, across London-road to the north end of Byrom-street, thence to the Pool, which was considered of great importance, as it served to cleanse the Pool when its flood-gates were opened.

The Harbour, till the construction of the first dock, was probably nothing more than a projecting pier, affording partial shelter to vessels lying within it. Where St. John's Church now stands was an extensive heath, which in 1743 was enclosed by order of the corporation, as a place for the inhabitants to dry clothes. Behind the present site of the Exchange was a hall belonging to the Moore family, where now stands the office occupied by Messrs. Barton, Irlam, and Higginson, and which gave name to Oldhall-street, in which it was situated.

In different parts of the town were crosses, none of which now remain, although the names of some of the streets may be traced to their proximity to them. The High Cross was situated where Exchange-street East now is. White Cross at the top of Chapel-street, St. Patrick's Cross in Tithebarn-street, and Townsend Cross at the bottom of Shaw's Brow.

It is pleasing to examine the ancient history of Liverpool, and to observe occurrences there noted, which we are now inclined to think strange, and to trace the rapid progress of the town as it rises from the condition of a fishing village to that of the second commercial seaport in the world : but the limits of this work do not admit of further detail. A notice of a few of the leading historical events may, however, be given :—

In 1338 King Edward the Third, in his expedition against France, required Liverpool to furnish one small vessel to be manned by six mariners, while Bristol had to provide 24, and Hull 16 vessels.

In 1563 the first prize ship taken by a Liverpool privateer arrived in the river, captured by a vessel of Sir Thomas Stanley's.

In 1644 the town was besieged by Prince Rupert, and was defended for a considerable time by Colonel Moore. At this period a high mud wall, with a ditch twelve yards wide and three yards deep, forti- fied the town from the east end of Dale-street to the river. It was also defended by the castle, which mounted a number of cannon, and a fort with eight guns, at the entrance of the harbour, which served not only to annoy the besiegers, but to protect the shipping. The head quarters of the Prince were at Everton, the camp being in the neighbourhood of St. Domingo; and the cottage in which he himself lodged is still remaining. After numerous unsuc- cessful attacks had been made on the town, it sur- rendered on the 26th June, and many of the inhabitants were put to the sword, while the remain- der were confined in the tower and St. Nicholas' Church. Shortly afterwards it was retaken by the par- liamentary forces; and in 1646 the walls were ordered to be repaired, and 500 tons of timber were granted for re-building the houses that had been destroyed by the troops of the Prince.

In 1648 Wallasey was considered a powerful rival to Liverpool, which now possessed 24 vessels of 462 tons, and 76 men.

In 1651 the town was visited by a dreadful plague,

which carried off 200 persons. For the purpose of preventing the threatened extension of the contagion, all who died of it were ordered to be immediately buried in Sickman's-lane, now Addison-street.

In 1715, on the advance of the Pretender's army, great preparations were made for the defence of the town. An intrenchment was thrown up, 70 pieces of cannon mounted, and one-third of the avenues laid under water. The shipping was so disposed that the rebels could neither plunder the town, nor make use of the vessels if they had so determined; and four of the rebels were executed in the neighbourhood of London-road.

During the rebellion in 1745, Liverpool raised an entire regiment, called the Royal Liverpool Blues, composed of 648 men, and five companies of volunteers, for the defence of the town. The expense, upwards of £6000, was defrayed by subscription, the corporation giving £2000. Active preparations were made for the protection of the inhabitants, batteries were erected, and the town was put in a complete state of defence.

Referring the reader who is desirous of studying more minutely the early history of Liverpool, to " Enfield's History," or " Gregson's Fragments of the History of Lancashire," we now pass on to the more recent statistics of the town.

The population of Liverpool in 1555 consisted of 138 householders, inhabiting 28 houses or cottages.

In 1700 there were 1,142 houses and 5,714 inhabitants.

„ 1720	2,367	11,833
„ 1742	3,600	18,000
„ 1760	5,156	25,787
„ 1801	11,784	77,708

In 1821there were 20,339 houses and 118,972 inhabitants.

„ 1831   27,361   „   165,221
„ 1841   „   „   224,954   „

The above statement gives the population of the parish only. From 1801 to 1811 the increase per cent. of inhabitants appears to have been nearly 23; from 1811 to 1821 it was 26 per cent.; from 1821 to 1831, 38¾ per cent.; and from 1831 to 1841 nearly 35 per cent.

In the parliamentary borough are included the townships of Everton, Kirkdale, West Derby, and Toxteth Park. The following exhibits the population of these townships at three decennial periods.

	1821.	1831.	1841.
Everton	2,109	4,518	9,148
Kirkdale......	861	2,591	3,779
West Derby ..	6,304	9,613	16,902
Toxteth Park..	12,829	24,067	41,180
	22,103	40,789	71,009

Taking the aggregate population of these townships, there appears to have been in the 10 years ending 1831, an increase at the rate of 84½ per cent., and in the 10 years ending in 1841, an increase of 74 per cent. By adding together the total population of these townships and that of the parish, we arrive at the actual population of the parliamentary borough, viz. 293,963, shewing an increase on the last ten years of 87,999 inhabitants. In addition to this there are upwards of 13,000 seamen belonging to the port, who are not included in the above return, which number must be added to the population of the borough to obtain the actual amount of the inhabitants in Liverpool. It is no exaggerated statement therefore, to say that the total population of Liverpool may be considered to be about 308,000.

From the general bill of mortality for 1841, it appears that the total number of burials in the parish of Liverpool, during that period was 5358, being a decrease of 691 on the amount of the previous year. The number of births during 1841, (as indicated by the baptisms,) was 10,223, and of marriages 3383, shewing an increase in births of 170, and in marriages of 242, since 1840. The total number of births, including those occurring in the suburbs, but within the Parliamentary borough, was 11,242; of deaths, 8520; and of marriages, 3687.

The following table distinguishes the ages of the deceased in the parish during 1841 :—

Under 2 years,	2010	Between 60 and 70 yrs.	297		
Between 2 and 5 yrs.	718	70 „ 80 „	224		
5 „ 10 „	252	„ 80 „ 90 „	76		
10 „ 20 „	203	„ 90 „ 100 „	13		
20 „ 30	408	100 & upwards	4		
30 „ 40	468				
40 „ 50	372	Total	5358		
50 „ 60	309				

From the Registrar-general's returns for 1840, a most extraordinary inference, on the subject of the mortality of Liverpool has been drawn by a recent writer, in a work entitled " *England in the 19th Century.*" It is there stated, from calculations erroneously made on the necessary data, that in Liverpool there are " *double the deaths* and marriages, and little more than half the number of births, averaged in the totality of England. * * * * This statement we submit with regret to the high-minded and public-spirited inhabitants of Liverpool, for they may, perhaps, probe the cause." It will be seen, however, by applying the Registrar-general's return of births, deaths, and marriages, to the total population of England in 1841, and the number of births, deaths, and marriages in Liverpool, to the population of the parish, that the very opposite is the case; and that Liverpool, so far from being an unhealthy town, is more salubrious than the majority of the larger towns in England. The following are the data on which this is grounded:—

	England.	L'pool parish.
Population in 1841	14,995,508	224,954
Proportion of Births to population	1 to 31	1 to 22
,, Deaths ,,	1 to $44\frac{1}{2}$	1 to 42
,, Marriages ,,	1 to $125\frac{1}{4}$	1 to $66\frac{1}{2}$
,, Births to Marriages	4 to 1	3 to 1

There are therefore, in the parish of Liverpool, *one half more births*, than the proportion averaged in the total population of England, nearly *the same number of deaths*, and *double the marriages*; which at once demonstrate the gratifying fact, that the climate of Liverpool is one of the most congenial in the kingdom.

COMMERCIAL HISTORY OF LIVERPOOL.

For part of the following history of the commerce of Liverpool, the author is in a great measure indebted to an able article on the subject, which recently appeared in the *Colonial Magazine*.

The naturally advantageous situation of Liverpool, rendered it at an early period, a place of some consequence, as the emporium whence the productions of the surrounding country were exported, and to which vessels in the coasting trade were accustomed to bring merchandise for the use of the interior. The sudden and extraordinary increase in the trade of the town, which has been apparent during the present century, has been chiefly commensurate with the manufacturing system, which sprung into existence in the latter part of the preceding century, converting villages into towns, with a rapidity only equalled in the fertile and virgin lands of the new continent. With the counties of York and Lancaster, Liverpool has long been connected, and by the numerous means of inland communication which they possess, it has become the port of the manufacturing districts, and almost the only place of transit for their raw material. It is also the chief port from which these materials are exported in their manufactured state to other countries, and so long as England maintains her proud pre-eminence as a manufacturing country, so long will Liverpool preserve its high prosperity.

So lately as the year 1648, the port was dependent

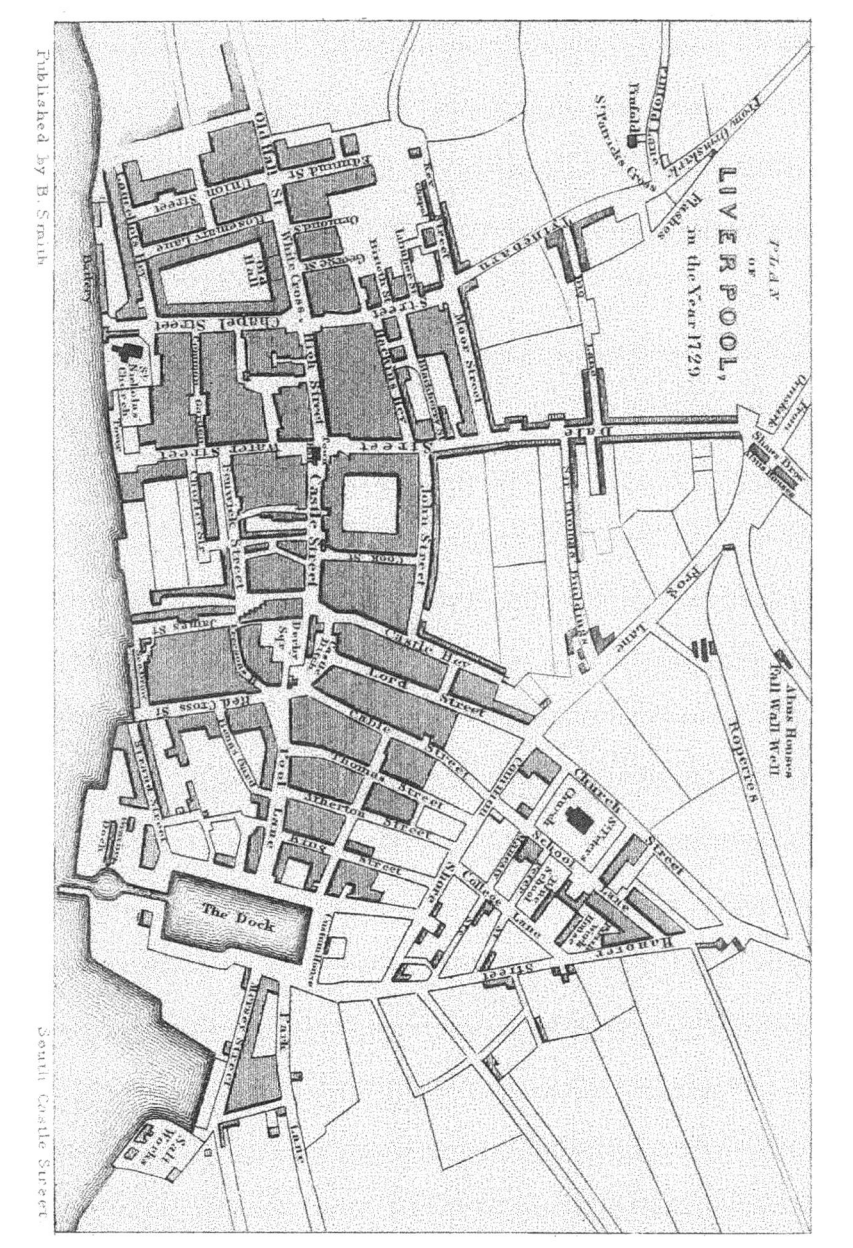

Published by B. Smith

on Chester, and had to make its returns of shipping to that place. A short time afterwards, we find Liverpool rated for shipping at £25, while Chester and Bristol are rated respectively at £26 and £1000.

The earliest traffic with foreign ports, consequent on the extension of the coasting trade, was chiefly with the northern parts of Europe, whence timber, iron, hemp, flax, &c., were imported, and shortly afterwards, a trade was opened with the south of Europe direct, instead of, as formerly, through the medium of Bristol and London. After the commencement of the West India and American trade, Bristol still maintained the superiority; and it was not until the manufactures of Manchester called for a large and constant supply of staple commodities, that Liverpool took the decided lead in commercial greatness which it still retains.

From 1722 to 1740, this port was engaged in the exportation of Manchester goods to Spanish America, to the amount of a million and a half sterling annually, supplying, by the co-operation of Spanish and West India traders, in an illicit manner, goods greatly lower than the price at which an exorbitant duty allowed them to be imported. When this trade was abolished by the British government, a new channel was opened, by means of which, Liverpool amassed enormous wealth.

With the West India trade sprung up, in violation of the principles of justice and humanity, that inhuman traffic, which has disgraced every nation ever engaged in it. In 1709, one vessel sailed from Liverpool for Africa, for a cargo of slaves, and in 1730, 15 vessels were despatched for the purpose of conveying slaves to the Spanish settlements in Jamaica. This attempt succeeded beyond all anticipation, and in 1765, no fewer than 86 vessels sailed by this route to the West Indies, conveying 25,720 slaves, and returning with 10,000 hogsheads and casks of sugar. London and Bristol now began to feel, by an abatement of the customs received, that a large amount of the trade was being transferred to Liverpool; for at this period, the port had more than one-half of the African vessels in the kingdom. When the slave trade was prohibited, the number of vessels had increased to 126, and although the African and West India trade consequently suffered some decline during the following years, yet it afterwards improved in a still greater ratio than before. The cessation of the slave trade has not, as might have been expected, seriously affected the interests of Liverpool; on the contrary, a succession of causes continually opened up fresh channels for enterprise, and gave increasing facility to mercantile operations.

The American trade, with the exception of the whale fisheries and the timber trade, is of recent origin. With the decay of the whale fisheries of the kingdom generally, the share of its prosperity which Liverpool possessed during its existence, was removed. In 1764 Liverpool had three whalers engaged; in 1788, when the trade was at its zenith, 21; and in 1823, when the last vessel was despatched, it ceased entirely. The timber trade is of more recent origin, and dates its prosperity from the year 1808, since which period it has become one of the most important branches of commerce connected with Liverpool. In 1841 the number of vessels with cargoes of timber from British America was 318, of 175,000 tons burden.

The intercourse between Liverpool and the Baltic, and north of Europe, was long of slow but steady growth, a circumstance to be attributed to the more favourable position of the ports of London and Hull, In 1770 the whole amount of imports from the Baltic was 621 bales and bundles of hemp, and 2 casks of tallow. In 1821 it had increased to 2530 tons of hemp, and 16,670 casks of tallow; and there were also imported 12,000 barrels of tar. In 1841 the amount of tallow from the Baltic was 18,000 barrels, and of tar 46,200 barrels. A considerable trade is carried on in Baltic timber, of which the cargoes of 40 vessels, amounting to 12,000 tons, were received during 1841. From the south of Europe and the Levant a large amount of produce is annually received in exchange for British manufactures, consisting chiefly of oil, grain, gums, madders, and dye-stuffs, fruit, valonia, &c.; and traders sail regularly from Liverpool to the different Mediterranean ports.

Outstepping the bounds of the European continent, the Liverpool merchants, at no very remote period, extended their traffic to the western hemisphere, embracing in their range the whole extent from the shores of Greenland to the extremity of Cape Horn. In 1764, 150 vessels were employed in the American trade; but this number declined during the war of independence. A mighty cause was however in operation, which soon produced an amazing effect, not only on the commerce of Liverpool, but on the traffic of the world. The steam engine and the spinning jenny were beginning to supersede hand-labour in

Britain; and at this juncture, with the means called into being of consuming an immensely increased supply of cotton, America discovered her capability of affording a supply of the raw material. As early as 1770 minute samples of the article had been brought to this country; but at a period even so recent as 1784, an American vessel was seized with eight bales of cotton on board, it being suspected that they were falsely entered. Since that time the ratio of increase in the amount of cotton imported has been as rapid as that of the manufacture. In 1790 the amount of imports into Liverpool was 50 bales, in 1800 it had increased to 29,138 bales, and in 1841 to the enormous amount of 844,601 bales from North America, and including the imports from Brazil, the East and West Indies, and Egypt, 1,161,949 bales. The exports of manufactures to North America are more than one-fifth of those to all parts of the globe; and of this part of the trade Liverpool has by far the greatest proportion. Upwards of ten packet-ships, as well as other vessels, and the line of steamers mentioned in a subsequent part of this work, sail regularly every month to the different ports in the States, and the Canadas.

With South America, the connexion of this port is not of very early origin. Although an illicit traffic with South America was previously carried on, a regular communication was not established until the present century. Since the commercial treaty with Brazil, cotton is now received directly from that country, to the extent of, in 1841, 89,534 bales. The quantity of sugar imported from the same quarter, during the same year, was 24,960 chests and barrels. The trade with Buenos Ayres, Monte Video, and Valparaiso, appears to have commenced with that to the Brazils, and since 1808, the amount of hides and tallow received thence, and manufactures exported in return, has been very considerable. In 1841, the number of hides imported into Liverpool, was upwards of 462,000. The number of vessels engaged in this trade is about 230, of 45,000 tons burthen.

The commerce with the East Indies, though extensive and valuable, has been carried on for scarcely more than 28 years; for until 1814, the monopoly of the East India Company prevented the merchants of Liverpool from embarking in this extensive field of enterprise. In 5 years they had 38 vessels engaged in the traffic, and they imported, besides other valuable produce, 62,000 bales of cotton. This branch of trade has since that period very rapidly increased, and during 1841, the imports amounted to 336,500 packages of sugar, 162,500 bales of cotton, 184,300 casks and bags of coffee, 476,000 hides, and 38,959 bags of saltpetre, besides a great variety of other valuable produce.

The opening of the trade with Canton, in 1834, was followed by the despatch of several vessels to China. In 1836, there were twelve arrivals, and in 1838, before the present interruption of that trade, the tea imported exceeded 4,000,000 lbs.

The intercourse with Australia is rapidly increasing; and since the wool of that country came into demand, the traffic has been considerable. During the past year, the number of bales of wool imported into Liverpool from Australia and Van Dieman's land, was 5,800, being an increase of 900 on the import of the previous year.

The Irish and coasting trades constituted the principal part of the limited commerce of the port, at a period when foreign intercourse was unknown. The earliest record of the actual traffic between Liverpool and Ireland, is of the date of 1759, when 327 vessels of 15,777 tons burthen arrived from Irish ports. In 30 years this amount was trebled; but the great era in this branch of trade, is to be dated from the introduction of steam navigation in 1820. In 1839, the cattle alone imported, amounted in value to £3,500,000, and numbered 964,000 head; and at present, with other articles, the trade cannot fall short of seven millions sterling per annum; it employs upwards of 400,000 tons of shipping, and from 30 to 40 large steam vessels.

The coasting trade is scarcely of less importance, though more limited in value. A large portion of it is with the Isle of Man, which has for many years contributed no mean share of domestic products. In the coasting trade, a large amount of shipping is engaged, in addition to the numerous steamers, exceeding in 1830, 5000 vessels; and the recent returns shew that this branch of home commerce is rapidly progressing.

The average number of arrivals from all parts of the world, now annually exceeds 16,000 vessels, of 2,400,000 tons, and the custom-house revenue at Liverpool, is nearly one-fourth of that of the whole kingdom; and of the total tonnage of Great Britain and Ireland, one-twelfth, or upwards of 10,000 vessels are connected by trade with Liverpool. The time is not far distant, when Liverpool, in its foreign commerce, will outvie the metropolis itself, for every circumstance conspires to extend its prosperity. Her physical resources are inexhaustible; and, had the limits of this work allowed it, a much more detailed account might have been given of her commercial prosperity, and of the particulars of commercial practice.

The above brief sketch of the trade in its different branches, will, however, give some idea of the extent and wealth of that seaport "whose merchants are princes," and whose fortunate position, as the outport of a country abounding in mineral fuel, places in her hands the sinews of that mighty power, which is extending its conquest over the wide world, walking the waters through storm and calm, and bridging the Atlantic itself, gliding over the plains of the old world, and through the eternal forests of the new.

PUBLIC AND COMMERCIAL BUILDINGS.

Although the public buildings of Liverpool appear to have been erected more for use than for ornament, on which account, until of late years, Liverpool could not furnish many specimens of architectural elegance, yet the taste of her inhabitants, keeping pace with the increase of their wealth, has latterly combined ornamental design with the mere substantialities of erection, and learned to appreciate architectural talent and genius.

THE CUSTOM HOUSE

deserves a prominent place among the public commercial buildings, as the magnitude of this simple and majestic pile of masonry, cannot fail to impress the stranger with an idea of the importance of that seaport which requires such an edifice for the transaction of its public business.

REVENUE BUILDINGS (the greater part of which is occupied by the offices of the customs, for which reason it is generally known as the Custom-house,) is situated on the site of the Old Dock, a little to the west of the old Custom-house. That small, inconvenient, and inelegant building had long been inadequate to the rapidly increasing trade of the port; and accordingly the interest of Messrs. Canning and Huskisson was employed in the negociation with government, on the subject of erecting a building

CUSTOM HOUSE.

FROM SOUTH CASTLE STREET.

which should afford accommodation for all the public offices. After a short period, a satisfactory arrangement was made, the government agreeing to pay £150,000, in annual instalments of £25,000, for the building, which was to be erected by the funds of the corporation, and on their land, and at the expiration of twenty years to be ceded to the crown. The plans of Mr. Foster, the corporation architect, were approved of by the Lords of the Treasury and the Board of Works, and the erection was commenced on the 12th August, 1828, the foundation stone having been then laid with great splendour by the mayor, Thomas Colley Porter, Esq. The building made rapid progress towards completion, and the greater part of it was opened for business in· 1839, the different portions of the work having been contracted for by the following gentlemen :—Messrs Tomkinson and Son, for the masonry; Messrs. S. and J. Holme, brickwork; Messrs. Foster and Stewart, joiners' and carpenters' work; Mr. R. M'Kee, slating and plastering; Mr. J. Knight, plumbing and glazing; Mr. J. Thompson, painting; Messrs. Mather, Dixon and Co., iron-work.

On the east and west fronts, as well as on the north side of the centre, are porticos, each composed of eight columns of the Ionic order, supporting an entablature and pediment, the former of which is carried round three sides of the building. The base of the columns of the east and west porticos, rest on platforms, ascended by flights of steps. Porticos slightly receding, formed by two Ionic columns, with corresponding pilasters, surmounted by a cornice, form the entrance to the north ends of both wings; and all the angles of the building, the lower part of which is rusticated, are ornamented by bold pilasters. The following dimensions will give some idea of the magnitude of this stupendous pile of masonry :—

The entire building covers 6700 superficial yards; the extreme length from east to west, is 466 feet 8 inches; the length of the centre portion, 252 feet 6 inches; the breadth of the centre, through the portico, 95 feet; the extreme length of the wings, 224 feet 7 inches, and their depth 94 feet 4 inches. The height of the columns, including the capital and base, is 50 feet 9 inches; that of the first or principal story, 20 feet; height of the second story, 21 feet 6 inches; and of the attics, 14 feet 8 inches. Total height from the plinth to the cornice, 66 feet 10 inches.

The basement is set apart for the reception of bonded and other goods ; the southern part of the east wing contains the Post-office on the first floor, on the second, the Excise and Stamp-offices. The north end of the east wing is appropriated to the offices of the Dock-trust, and the whole of the centre and west wing is fitted up for the accommodation of the various Custom-house officers. The long-room, which occupies the centre of the second story, is the greatest object of attraction. The total length of this splendid apartment is 146 feet, its width 70 feet, and height 45 feet ; and when viewed from either end, it has a noble appearance. The roof is supported by sixteen handsome Ionic pillars of stone, and corresponding pilasters, and it is surmounted by a magnificent cupola, containing the royal arms on four sides, and illuminated by twelve windows of stained glass. The ceiling of this room is divided into compartments, with handsome mouldings and carved work, and the apartment is lighted by 14 windows on the sides. The floor is flagged, and the desks and offices of the clerks, are in the recesses between the projections at the side of the room, which is heated by Price and Manby's patent hot air apparatus. The long-room is approached by a handsome staircase at each end, the landings of which are supported on eight Ionic pillars of stone and four pilasters. Each staircase has four flights of steps, two of which are on each side, and unite before reaching the ground floor. The passage opposite South Castle-street, supported on massive groupings of pilasters, with a groined roof, is under the long-room, and the passages to the right and left lead to the foot of the staircases already described.

THE POST OFFICE

occupies half of the ground floor of the east wing. The letter-boxes, paid-letter and registration windows, are under the portico on the east side, and a clock, which strikes the hours and quarters, is over the centre door leading to the ship-letter, money-order, &c., offices. A flight of stone steps at the south side, affords access to the delivery windows, in the numerous boxes of which are distributed the letters for the mercantile houses which prefer sending for them, to having them delivered by the letter-carriers, as well as to the strangers' window, which is on the right hand when entering the room. The offices of the post-master, and the other departments of the establishment are entered from the west side

of the wing. The internal arrangements of the establishment are of the most complete description, and
the regularity and despatch with which the entire
post-office business is conducted, do great credit to
Mr. Banning, the post-master. Particulars of the
despatch and arrival of mails, delivery of letters, receiving houses, &c., will be found in the Appendix.

THE EXCISE OFFICE,

formerly situated in Hanover-street, has been removed
to the portion of the building above the post-office,
and access to the various offices of this department,
is from the east staircase leading to the long-room.

THE STAMP OFFICE

is in the same portion of the building; and the principal part of the business connected with this department of the revenue is transacted here, although the
old stamp-office in the Old Church-yard, is still retained as a convenient place for the sale of stamps, &c.

THE DOCK OFFICE

is entered from the north side, and occupies half of
the east wing. On the landing of the staircase,
leading to the room in which the dock-committee
hold their meetings, is a handsome and very complete
model of a ship of war, an inspection of which may
be interesting to those who have seldom an opportunity of seeing a vessel fully equipped.

THE TOBACCO WAREHOUSE.

Although not worthy of notice on account of any
architectural elegance, the Tobacco Warehouse as

Kilpin

THE TOWN HALL.

Overton

connected with the Custom-house may here be described. It is situated on the west side of King's.
dock, and extends nearly the whole of its length, the
dimensions being 575 feet in length and 239 feet in
breadth. All tobacco coming to the port, is required
to be deposited here until the duty is paid; and on
this account, vessels discharging tobacco have generally a berth allotted them on the west side of the
dock. The building was erected by the corporation,
and is rented by government for the annual amount
of £4,200. Between the warehouse and the river
there is an agreeable promenade.

THE TOWN HALL.

When Liverpool was little more than a village, the
Town-hall was one of its most important buildings.
In the year 1350, it was denominated " *Domus beatæ
Mariæ.*" Several edifices in succession have been
erected on the same site, and removed to make way
for more modern structures. The foundation of the
present handsome erection, was laid in 1794, and the
building executed according to the designs of Mr.
Wood of Bath ; but the interior having been destroyed by fire, on the 18th January, 1795, considerable additions were made to it, and the whole finished
in its present form, at an outlay of more than £110,000,
under the superintendence of Mr. John Foster, the
town architect, and opened on the 4th June, 1797.
The whole of the basement is rusticated, and lighted
by windows with semicircular heads. The portico
on the south front, which harmonizes with the rest
of the structure, is of recent erection, and gives an
air of elegance and finish to the entire building. It

consists of a plain but bold pediment, with a balustrade, supported on six Corinthian columns, resting on the archways of rusticated stone, corresponding with the lower part of the building itself. At the angles and spaces between the windows, which are decorated with Corinthian pillars and friezes, are placed pilasters of the same order, between the capitals of which are emblematical tablets of bas-relief. The North front is composed of eight coupled columns in the centre, which stands a little forward, with corresponding pilasters resting on the rusticated basement, and finished with a pediment and balustrade, the latter being carried round the building. The east and west fronts have six three-quarter columns in the centre, and pilasters, between each of which is a segment-headed window. That portion of the building which was more recently added, recedes a little from the principal part, and on the east and west sides, the place of windows is supplied by niches, and ornamental work, between coupled pilasters. The dome, which is light and well proportioned, adds greatly to the elegance of the building. It is supported on Corinthian columns, between which are the long windows which illuminate the staircase in the interior, and it is surmounted by a colossal figure of Britannia. On the outside, above the columns, is a circular gallery, from which a splendid view of the town and surrounding country is obtained ; and the labour of ascending the staircases is well repaid by the magnificent prospect afforded on reaching the summit. Four clock faces are placed above the gallery, each of which is supported by a lion and unicorn, sculptured in stone. The interior of this

establishment may be viewed between ten and four
o'clock, by obtaining an order from the Treasurer's
office, on the west side, and no one will regret the
time occupied in the survey of what may be justly
called the finest building in Liverpool. The ground
floor is occupied by the council room, committee
rooms, and the mayor's, town-clerk's and other offices.
The suite of rooms forming the principal story, all
communicate with each other, and consist of a saloon,
two drawing rooms, two ball rooms, a banquet room,
refectory, and other apartments. The entire north
front of the building is occupied by a magnificent
ball room, 89 feet in length, 41 feet 6 inches in breadth,
and 40 feet in height. This splendid apartment is
fitted up in a most superb manner, and is lighted by
three massive gas chandeliers with 72 burners. The
sides of this, as well as the smaller ball room, are ornamented by pilasters of highly polished artificial
Scagliola marble, which in this room are surmounted
by richly executed Corinthian capitals. The smaller
ball room on the east side of the building measures
61 feet by 28, and has also a lofty ceiling. The
saloon opening from the grand staircase presents a
magnificent appearance, as its furniture is of the
most costly description. It contains full length
portraits of George III., by Sir T. Lawrence; of
George IV., when Prince of Wales, by Hopner; of
the late Duke of York, by Philips; and of William
IV., when Duke of Clarence, by Shee. The banquet
room is on the west side, and is used by the mayor
for the civic entertainments. Its length is 50 feet,
and breadth 30 feet. The refectory occupies the
centre of the building, and is entered from the stair-

cases and the small ball room. From the grand staircase at the door of the saloon, is presented one of the most imposing *coups d' œil* to be met with in modern architecture, as the interior of the dome, illuminated by a lateral light of peculiar softness, displays a richness and elegance of design, and taste in the execution, which is seldom to be met with, the pure Grecian style of architecture having been preserved throughout. The height from the pavement to the centre of the dome is 106 feet.

On the first landing of the staircase is a colossal statue of Canning, beautifully executed in marble, by Chantrey, delineating the features of the statesman at the moment when he had arrived at a great oratorical climax, standing in a graceful but commanding attitude, with his hands crossed upon his breast and resting on his right foot, watching with interest the effect of his oratory on his audience. The figure is gracefully wrapped in a Roman toga, and the mellow light of the dome falling on the brilliantly pure marble of which it is constructed, gives it an expression of exquisite finish, which can scarcely be equalled, even by the other works of that great sculptor.

EXCHANGE BUILDINGS.

So splendid a range of building as the quadrangle of the Liverpool Exchange, erected solely for commercial purposes, is perhaps not to be found in any other part of Britain. It is situated immediately behind the Town-hall, the north front of which forms one side of the square. The first stone was laid on 30th June, 1803, and the entire expense of the erection,

which amounted to £110,848, was defrayed by subscriptions of £100 per share. The structure was
nearly four years in building. The architect of this,
as well as of many other of our public buildings, was
Mr. John Foster, senior. The area inclosed by the
four sides is 16,848 square feet, and on three sides it
is surrounded by a piazza 15 feet wide, supported by
arches, which give the building a stately appearance.
The north side corresponds with the opposite front
of the Town-hall in its architectural arrangement,
the centre part of it projecting, and having eight
coupled Corinthian columns 25 feet in height, supporting an entablature similar to that on the Town-
hall. On this entablature are placed four emblematical figures, of stone, representing the four elements,
to correspond with the figures of the four quarters
of the globe on the opposite side. The entrance from
Oldhall-street is well deserving of notice. It is
through a spacious vestibule, divided into three
avenues by thirty-two coupled columns, supporting a
beautifully groined roof, and presenting a specimen
of architectural taste worthy of a more conspicuous
situation. The ground floor of the east side of the
quadrangle is occupied by the spacious newsroom,
subsequently described; and the second floor, by a
smaller room used by the underwriters. The remainder of the building consists of merchants', bro-
kers', and other commercial offices, and the upper
floors at the back comprise warehouses, &c., for the
reception of merchandise.

NELSON'S MONUMENT.

In the centre of the area is a magnificent monument,

cast in bronze, erected in memory of Nelson, by R. Westmacott, of London, from the design of Matthew Charles Wyatt, of the same place. The expense of its erection was entirely defrayed by public sub-scription, £9000 having been raised in a few days, and it was completed on 21st October, 1813. The principal figure is Nelson, who, resting one foot on a conquered enemy, and the other on a cannon, with an eye stedfast and upraised to Victory, is receiving from her a fourth naval crown upon his sword, which, to indicate the loss of his right arm, is held in the left hand. The right shoulder is concealed by the flag which Victory is lowering to him, under the folds of which death lies in ambush for his victim, indicating that he received the reward of victory and the stroke of death at the same time. The zeal of the navy, eager to revenge the loss of its gallant admiral, is represented by the figure of an enraged British seaman. Britannia in the back ground, with laurels in her hand, and leaning, regardless of them, on her shield and spear, describes the feeling of the country, fluctuating between the pride and anguish of a triumph so dearly purchased. Round the moulding of the pedestal are inscribed the memorable words of Nelson, "ENGLAND EXPECTS EVERY MAN TO DO HIS DUTY." At the base of the pedestal are four figures as captives in chains, emblematic of his four greatest victories, and on the sides are four fine bas-reliefs, executed in bronze, illustrative of the same victories, viz. St. Vincent, The Nile, Copenhagen and Trafalgar. The figures are all in the proportion of 7 feet, and the weight of bronze of which the monument is composed is upwards of 22 tons.

ROYAL BANK BUILDINGS.

DALE STREET.

Published By mi Smith, South Castle Street Liverpool.

THE CORN EXCHANGE

was erected in 1807, by Mr. Foster, and opened on 4th August, 1808, the expense having been defrayed by public subscription. It is situated in Brunswick-street, and has a plain stone front, in the Doric style of architecture. Its length is 114 feet, and breadth 60 feet.

THE BANKS.

The business hours of the majority, are from ten to three, except Friday, when they are closed at one.

The following are worthy of notice on account of their architectural elegance.

THE ROYAL BANK, AND BUILDINGS.

This extensive and magnificent range of buildings (situate at the west end of Dale-street,) was lately erected by the proprietors of the Royal Bank, from the plans of Samuel Rowland, Esq. The ground story is rusticated, and the centre part is lighted by a range of segment-headed windows. The wings, which are divided from the centre by two archways, are decorated with palladium windows of the Doric order. A facia and cornice finishes the ground story, and supports a range of lofty columns and pilasters of the Corinthian order. The centre of the upper part of the building consists of eight three-quarter columns, and two stories of windows and a string course; the wings, and the spaces over the arches, have two stories of palladium windows, three of the lower story of the Ionic order, with enriched friezes, decorated with elaborate and beautiful foliage. The entablature of the Corinthian order, in its full proportions and ornaments, is continued

along the entire front of the building, and is surmounted by a balustrade, in the centre of which a
pedestal supports the Royal Arms, giving an appropriate finish to the upper part of the edifice. At the
end of the enclosure is the Bank itself, which is of
chaste and elegant design. Four well proportioned
fluted Doric columns support a plain but hold cornice, on which rest four fluted Ionic columns, of
more slender proportions, finished with a rich entablature and a pediment. The lintels of the side doors
are handsomely ornamented by carved-work, and the
sides and angles of the building are further improved
by pilasters corresponding with the rest of the design.

The interior of the Bank, in elegance, almost sur-
passes the exterior. The ceiling is panelled with
gilded mouldings, and supported by columns of a
composition resembling marble.

The other parts of this extensive range of building
are occupied by private offices.

THE UNION BANK

Brunswick-street. This building, which is of recent
erection, has an exceedingly neat appearance, and is
constructed of Portland stone. Two fluted Ionic
columns support a pediment over the entrance, on
which is a scroll with the motto, " *Vis unita fortior.*"
A finely executed allegorical has-relief, carved from
one block of stone, is placed above the doorway, and
a balustrade finishes the side of the building, which,
with the exception of a bold cornice at the top, and
pediments over the windows, is very simple. The
interior is richly fitted up, and the ceiling is divided
into compartments by mouldings.

THE NORTH AND SOUTH WALES BANK,

situated at the corner of Derby-square and Fenwick-street. It was completed in 1841, and is built entirely of stone. It is surmounted by an exceedingly massive, but elaborately carved entablature, and the portico in front, is formed by two fluted Corinthian columns. The side in Fenwick-street, is adorned by Corinthian pilasters, with rich capitals, between which are placed the windows, those of the lower story having semicircular heads. The appearance of the building is somewhat injured by the awkwardness of the site which prevented the architect from making it rectangular, two of its angles being acute, and two obtuse.

THE BRANCH BANK OF ENGLAND

in Hanover-street, is a plain stone edifice, with a rusticated front, and is scarcely worthy of notice, on account of any elegance. It was opened in 1828, before which period, there was no Branch of the Bank of England in Liverpool.

THE BANK OF SAVINGS

is situated near the top of Bold-street, and, as its name implies, was instituted for the deposit of the savings of the humbler class of society, which are invested in the public funds. It is open for receiving deposits daily, and one week's notice is required previous to the withdrawal of money. The affairs of the bank are managed by twenty-one directors, five of whom are trustees, who meet on the first Friday and day following, of each month, to transact business, receive deposits, &c.

BANKERS IN LIVERPOOL.

Name.	Manager.	No. of Shares.	Amt. p Share.	Paid up Capital.	Address.	London Agent.
Bank of England (branch)	{ S. ... (Agent.) W. ...ber (sub-A.) }	—	—	—	52, Hanover street.	Bank of England.
Bank of Liverpool	J. Langton	50,000	£100	£476,825	5, Water-street...	Glyn, Hallifax and Co.
Israel Barned and Co.	—	Private	—	—	9, Lord-street....	...t, Son and Co.
A. Heywood, Sons and Co.	—	Private	—	—	9, Brunswick-s...t.	Denison, Heywood & Co.
Leyland and Bullins	—	Private	—	—	15, King-street....	Masterman, ...rs & Co.
L'pool ...	W. Wilson	20,000	20	8,050	14, South Castle-st.	Curries and Co.
Liverpool Borough Bank	J. Jerdein	50,000	10	445,050	3, Water-street...	Glyn, Hallifax and Co.
L'pool Commercial Bk.	J. Macgregor	5,000	10	8,400	1, High-street.	...s, Deacon & Co.
Man. and L'poo Dist. Bk.	Robt. ...ler	1,000	10	1,200	2, ...st.	Smith, Payne & Smiths.
Moss and Co.	—	Private	—	—	4, Dale-street.	Barclay, Bevan and Co.
...th and South Wales Bk.	—	40,000	10	215,200	1, Derby-square.	London and ... Bk.
Royal Bank of L'pool	J. Chaffers	2,000	1000	600,000	12, Dale-street....	Robarts, Curtis and Co.
Union Bank	J. Lister	3000	20	2,150	6, Brunswick-st.	Cunliffes, Brooks & Co.
Bank for Savings	—	—	—	—	93, Bold-street....	—

THE UNDERWRITERS' ROOM

is over the Exchange News Room, and is conducted on the plan of that at Lloyd's, in London. It is seventy-two feet long, thirty-six feet wide, and has a handsomely finished coved roof. It is fitted up with boxes and other conveniences for the accommodation of persons transacting business, and is provided with newspapers, shipping lists, &c., besides a considerable number of maps, charts, and books of reference.

THE COTTON SALES' ROOM

is above the last mentioned, on the upper floor, and is fitted up with a gallery and benches, with small sample-tables placed at intervals. Round the room, and at the upper end, are larger tables for the same purpose. It is frequently used as a place of meeting for commercial companies, &c.

THE DOCKS.

It is interesting to trace the history of a community striving with difficulties which nature has thrown in its way, yet gradually removing these obstacles apparently insurmountable, till, rising slowly, it at length attains the highest eminence that industry and perseverance have reached. Such a history may be found in the improvements which have been made

D

on the harbour accommodation of Liverpool; for before it acquired its present high reputation as a seaport, it had to struggle with natural inconveniences which render the enterprise and skill of its inhabitants in surmounting them, remarkably conspicuous.

Pier after pier of massive masonry has been erected to prevent the encroachments of the sea; and the space thus defended has been gradually excavated, to afford safety and accommodation to shipping, and secure it from the inconvenience of exposure on an open shore. From the simple accommodation afforded by the " Pool," as enclosed by gates in the year 1635, the Docks of Liverpool have been extended, till they are now superior in mangitude to those of any seaport in the world, London alone excepted, and are capable of receiving the largest vessels. The approaches to the harbour have been deepened, sand banks have been removed, and channels excavated, to render the port accessible; and these exertions have been amply repaid in the rapid acquirement of commercial greatness.

Extending along the east side of the Mersey for more than three miles, the marine wall presents an opposing front to the force of the waves, which cannot fail to strike the observer with astonishment; for although, on account of the flatness of the surrounding scenery, and the unusual length of the erections, it has not such a commanding effect as a stranger might be led to expect, yet, when its parts are examined separately, the magnitude will immediately become apparent.

The entire area of water in the several docks, and

the basins connected with them, at present amounts to one hundred and twelve statute acres, and they are provided with a total quay space upwards of nine miles in length.

In the neighbourhood of all the docks, although not immediately upon the quays, there are large piles of warehouses for the reception of produce, many of them, though massive, being handsome constructions; and along the side of George's and Salthouse Docks, they have been erected with a piazza or foot-walk on the ground story, for the convenience of foot-passengers. Handsome little edifices have been constructed on the piers of the new docks, for the convenience of the dock-masters, gatemen, and police; and the Customs are provided with dépôts at the principal import docks, for the temporary reception of goods for the purpose of examination, or ascertaining the tares, &c. of the packages. The passages between the several basins and docks are crossed by neat iron bridges, which open horizontally, to allow the ingress and egress of shipping at high water. The dock gates open inwards, are provided with sluices to regulate the depth of water; and on the top are narrow footways, with iron railings, for the convenience of pedestrians when the gates are closed.

The affairs of the dock estate are conducted by a committee of twenty-one members, thirteen of whom are elected from the town council, (who are the trustees,) and the remaining eight from the merchants and shipowners, who are rate payers. Three of the trustees retire annually, and their place is supplied by the town council, any of the retiring members being re-eligible. They are required to hold their

meetings at least once a week, and oftener if necessary; and seven members, including the chairman
and deputy-chairman, constitute a quorum, who
have full authority to act. The proceedings of the
committee are subject to the approval of the corporation.

The arrangement of the shipping is entrusted to
two harbour-masters, and eleven dock-masters, who
superintend the entire disposal of the vessels in dock,
allotting them berths, providing them in turn with
quay accommodation, and enforcing the regulations,
the observance of which is absolutely necessary to
prevent confusion. The minor affairs are managed
by dock-gatemen and police-officers, by the latter of
whom the property on the quays is as effectually pro-
tected from plunder, as if deposited in warehouses;
and they are ready to afford every information relative to the situation of vessels, &c., that may be
required.

Approaching Liverpool from the sea, the first Dock
in order, is the

CLARENCE DOCK.

This dock, with the half-tide basin adjoining, was
opened in 1830 and has since been entirely appropriated to the use of steamers. It was one of the
first erected under the able superintendence of Mr.
Hartley, Surveyor of the Dock Trustees, and being
constructed with granite piers, and the workmanship
being of the most substantial and elegant description,
it forms a specimen of mural architecture which is
rarely to be surpassed. It is entered from the half-
tide basin, on the west side, by a lock, and is en-

tirely surrounded by sheds for the protection of goods.

Connected with Clarence Dock, and erected at the same period, are two commodious Graving Docks, the mechanical structure of which, combined with the beauty of the workmanship displayed in their con-cave sides, cannot fail to excite admiration. The width of their entrances is forty-five feet, thus afford-ing sufficient room for the passage of vessels of large size; and the great number that have been repaired in these docks since their opening, shews how highly their conveniences have been appreciated.

TRAFALGAR DOCK

is contiguous to the above, and is entered by a pas-sage from Clarence Basin. It has been but recently opened, and is generally used by steam-vessels, chiefly such as are undergoing repair, or completing their equipment, for whose convenience the Dock Committee has provided a powerful crane on the north side. A small round building is between this dock and the basin, which has on the top a clock, with three dials, and a large bell for striking the hours.

VICTORIA DOCK

is situated between Trafalgar and Waterloo Docks, with both of which it communicates. It has also gates opening into the river, but they do not appear to be available to the extent anticipated, as they are frequently difficult of access, owing to the strong current of the tide, and the narrowness of the passage. This dock has been generally used by vessels laid up, or which have been some time in port.

WATERLOO DOCK

was opened on the 6th of September, 1834, since which period it has been used for the purpose of a general dock, but containing chiefly the larger vessels. It is, together with the two last-named docks, with which it communicates, entirely surrounded by a lofty wall. It is most accessible from Prince's Basin, which is at the south end.

PRINCE'S DOCK

is the next in order proceeding southward, after passing the basin, and its size and central situation render it the most important. After having been six years in construction, it was opened with much ceremony, on the occasion of the coronation of Geo. IV, 19th July, 1821. The expense of the erection, with the marine works attached, was estimated at £561,059. This dock is chiefly appropriated to the large vessels engaged in the American, East India, or China trade, the east side being set apart for vessels discharging, and the west for those loading. On the west, south, and east sides are spacious transit sheds. It is entered from George's Basin, at the south end, as well as from that at the north extremity, and the passages are closed by locks, the gates of which are forty-five feet wide, and thirty-four feet deep, and constructed so as to admit vessels at half-tide. Between the river and the west side of the wall surrounding the dock, is a splendid marine parade, 750 yards in length, and 11 yards in breadth, on the edge of which is a parapet about three feet in height, with steps at convenient distances, down to the river, for the landing of passengers. From this parade, known by the name of the Prince's Parade, may be obtained the finest views of the river, the shipping, and the increasing erections on the Cheshire side of the Mersey. The Seacombe, Egremont and New Brighton steamers sail from the south end of this parade.

GEORGE'S DOCK BASIN

is situated between Prince's and George's Docks, opposite St. Nicholas' Church, and is connected with them both. George's Pier, at high water, presents the liveliest scene to be found in the neighbourhood of the docks, as nearly all the steamers belonging to the port, as well as the numerous ferry boats, &c., make this pier, and the slips attached to it, their place of landing. Opposite the broad steps a floating landing stage is moored, which is connected with the pier at low water, for the convenience of passengers by the ferry and other steamers.

George's Baths, an account of which is to be found in a subsequent page, are situated on the piece of ground between George's Dock and the river, and the short parade in front of them is a place of much resort.

GEORGE'S DOCK.

In 1762 an act was obtained for the erection of this dock, which was completed at an expense of £20,000 in 1771. It is usually appropriated to vessels of the larger description, and the same regulations are observed respecting the sides of the dock on which they are loaded and discharged, as already noticed for Prince's Dock. At the south end is a large vessel fitted up as a church for the use of seamen ; but there is some prospect of its place being supplied by a substantial erection on land, in the immediate neighbourhood.

The Manchester New Quay Company's basin and sheds occupy the space next to George's Dock.

Still further south, and nearly opposite the Custom-house, is Canning Dock.

CANNING DOCK,

formerly known as the Dry Dock, was at no very distant period altered to a wet dock, since which time it has been chiefly frequented by coasting vessels, fishing smacks, and other small craft. Connected with it, and between the dock and the river, are three graving docks, to which access can also be obtained from George's Dock, by means of a passage between the two of considerable length. The act for its erection was obtained in 1738, and the materials of which it was constructed having gradually suffered considerable decay, it underwent a thorough repair some years ago. As it was not sufficiently deep to admit large vessels, it was recently deepened about eight feet. A pair of double gates, of the most improved construction, retaining the water in either direction, was also erected, with massive granite piers, in the passage between this and George's Dock.

The Old Dock, on the site of which the Custom-house now stands, entered from the east side of Canning Dock, and reached as far as South John-street in the eastward direction. It was closed in 1826, and the building of the Custom-house was commenced in 1828.

SALTHOUSE DOCK

is connected with the last-mentioned, and was made, at the same period. Its name was derived from the circumstance of there being at the bottom of Orford-street a saltwork, which is now removed to Garston, about six miles up the river. The shallowness of this dock rendered it unavailable for the larger vessels, and it was therefore appropriated chiefly to coasters and traders.

The alterations now in progress on Salthouse Dock and the adjoining land are very considerable, and are being executed according to the plans of Mr. Hartley, the dock surveyor; his proposals, after considerable delay and careful examination, having been considered the best adapted to the present circumstances of the port. They consist of the enlargement of Salthouse Dock northward, making it of a more rectangular form, and deepening it; and the erection of a commodious new dock, on the space towards the river, formerly occupied by warehouses, ship-building yards, &c.

THE NEW DOCK

will be of a rectangular form, entered from the present passage to Canning Dock, at the mouth of which gates will be placed, communicating also with Salthouse Dock, by a gate on the east side; the whole to be surrounded by warehouses on the quay, after the plan of those at the London docks, with a marine parade on the west side.

DUKE'S DOCK

is private property, belonging to the trustees of the

Duke of Bridgewater's estate, and surrounded by warehouses and sheds for the reception of goods discharged from the flats or barges. The construction of this dock is such as to afford a large amount of quay space; this being obtained by its formation with cuttings projecting from the main part in the shape of a cross.

KING'S DOCK

was erected at an expense of £25 000, and opened on the 3rd October, 1788. It is surrounded by sheds, and on the west side is situated the Queen's Tobacco Warehouse, which extends nearly the whole length of the dock. The proximity of the tobacco warehouse causes this dock to be frequented by all vessels from Havannah, Maryland, &c., bringing tobacco; and it is also the general place of discharge for vessels from the Levant, and European ports. King's Dock basin is provided with a stage on the bottom of the south side called a gridiron, on which vessels go at high water, and are left dry for the examination of their hulls, or for executing slight repairs. At the north-west corner of King's Dock lies the Floating Chapel for seamen, at which service is performed by ministers of various denominations.

QUEEN'S DOCK

is generally appropriated to the West India Baltic, and Dutch vessels, and was opened on the 17th April 1796, having cost in its erection £35,000. It is provided with sheds along a portion only of the east and west sides. For the convenience of vessels laden with timber, the quays towards the south end are sloped inwards at a considerable angle, by which means easy access is had to the cargoes. On the west side of Queen's Dock are two graving docks, opening from King's Basin, and extending parallel with the side of the dock about half its length. The space between the river and the south end of the dock is generally occupied by timber stores.

UNION DOCK

is connected with the south extremity of the above, and also communicates with the Brunswick and Coburg Docks. Till lately it was known as the Brunswick Half-tide Basin.

COBURG DOCK

formerly called Brunswick Basin, has undergone extensive alterations, to render it suitable for the reception of the ocean steamers. It opens directly into the river, and is connected by a passage with Union Dock. The entrance from the river is constructed of masonry of an elegant and substantial description, and is closed by gates 70 feet in width, which permit the introduction of the largest steam vessels.

BRUNSWICK DOCK

was erected under the able superintendence of the present Dock surveyor, and was opened on the 13th April, 1832. In the design and execution of the quays and other works, no ordinary amount of mechanical skill and ingenuity is displayed. It admits vessels of the largest tonnage, and is entirely appropriated by those in the timber trade, for whose convenience the quays are formed on an inclined plane, as above described, thus affording them greater facility in discharging. It is entered from Brunswick Basin, which lies on the west side of the dock, as well as from the Union Dock, and has the largest superficial area of any of the Liverpool Docks, although, on account of its width, it has not a proportionate amount of quay space. The depth of water in the river at the entrance of the basin has, by artificial means, been rendered equal to that of several of the north docks, notwithstanding its being so much further removed from the sea. Two graving docks are connected with the south extremity of Brunswick Dock, which is the last of the principal docks in a southward direction.

THE NEW SOUTH DOCKS.

They are—*Toxteth Dock,* which adjoins the graving docks mentioned above. It was opened in the beginning of the present year. It communicates directly with the river by gates 40 feet wide, constructed so that they can be readily altered to prevent the water entering the dock, in the case of repairs being required, and they are nearly as deep as the gates of Prince's Dock. It is intended chiefly for the small timber and Baltic vessels.

This dock is the termination, in the southward direction, of the Corporation dock estate. The extreme length of the river wall belonging to the dock estate is two miles and 1087 yards.

The following docks are private property.

The two *Harrington Docks* are the next in order southward, and are the property of a joint stock company, who purchased the land from the Earl of Sefton. The first, known as the Eagle Quay Dock, is closed by gates about the same width as those of the Toxteth Dock; but the other, which is similar in form, is merely a basin, left dry when the tide recedes. They are used by vessels employed in the inland navigation. On the east side of the dock are the works of the Mersey Steel and Iron Company, subsequently noticed.

The *Egerton Dock*, belonging to the trustees of the Duke of Bridgewater's estate, is of a rectangular form, smaller than the Toxteth Dock, and has the water confined by gates. It is appropriated chiefly by the craft employed by the trust, for the conveyance of timber, &c. to the interior.

The *Herculaneum Old Basin* is the furthest in the southward direction, and is at present undergoing alteration.

The following ... *he shews at one* 'iew, *the Dimensions of the* ... laipool *Docks.*

DOCKS.	Widths of Entrance. Ft. In. Pts.			Area of Water. Acres. Yds.		Total Acres.		Quay Space. Lin.Yds.	Total Space. M. ... Yds.	
DRY BASINS.										
Prince's Basin..........				4	1549			509		
Seacombe Basin..........				0	1805			188		
George's Basin..........				3	1852			455		
Old ... Gut..........				1	2897			447		
Queen's Basin..........				5	191			601		
George's Ferry Basin..........				0	1344			160		
South Ferry				0	2927	15	2885	205	1	805
WET DOCKS.										
Prince's Dock ......North Gates..	45	6	6	11	614			1187		
Locks..South ...es..	44	11	9	0	3275	11	3889	426	0	1613
George's Dock......Nth Gates..	41	1	9	5	154			645		
Passage ......South Gates..	36	3	6	0	2439½	5	2593½	356	0	1001
Canning Dock......	42	0	6			3	4575	.....	0	500
Old ... Passage......	35	5	6							
Salthouse Dock......	33	3	6	4	3152			666		
Passage......				0	513	4	3665	93	0	759
King's Dock.	42	0	6	7	3356			800		
Passage......				0	540	7	3896	75	0	875
Queen's Dock ......Nth Gates..	42	0	6	10	1853			1082		
Passages ......South	41	11	6	0	1248½	10	3101½	173	0	255
Union Dock......				2	2858			407		
Passages	42	0	0	0	647			...		

Old ... Passage LIN. YDS. — A. YDS. 3 1890 ...... 557 ; 0 675½ 90

NEW NORTH DOCKS.

	ft	in				Area					
Clarence Dock	47 0 0	5 0	3713	2198	740	0 0	9 4
Lock		0	1400		174		635
Half-Tide Basin	50 0 0			273			
By Graving Dock Basin	45 0 0	0 0	3572	5[?]0	224	0	29
Passage			500	4072	67		
[?]gar Dock	45 0 0	5 0	4280		727	0 0	1020
Half of Passage	45 0 0	0	266	2643	37		
Locks { North Gates } { South Gates }		0	2937		256		
V[?]tia [?]k.	42 0 0	5 0	3027		681	0	827
River Entrance	40 0 0	0 0	600	4159	72		
Passages		0	532		74		
[?]oo [?]k. ...North Gates..	45 0 0	5 0	2790		700	0	993
Lock. ...S[?]th Gates..	45 0 0	0	2937	1153	256		
Passage	40 0 0	0	266		37		

NEW SOUTH DOCKS.

	ft	in				Area					
Brunsw[?]ck [?]k...North Gates..	42 0 0	12 0	2120	2744	1005	0	092
Passage		0	624		87		
[?]k Half-Tide Basin...West Gates..	45 0 0	1 0	2071	3388	318	0	491
Passage ...East Gates..	42 0 0	0	1317		173		
South Bas[?]n .	40 0 0	1 0	367	469	377	0	393
Passage.		0	102		16		
Manchester [?]k ...[?]r Gates.	33 8 0						
...[?]r Gates.	32 10 0						
Duke's Dock.	28 10 0						
TOTAL		11	4691¼			9	628

GRAVING DOCKS.

						Yards.
Canning Dock ..	No. 1..........	34	6	6	137¾	
	No. 2..........	35	9	6	158⅔	
	No. 3..........	35	9	0	146	
						442⅓
Queen's Dock ..	No 1........	42	0	0	146	
	No. 2 { Bottom	42	0	0 }	145	
	{ Top...	70	1	0 }		
						291
Clarence Dock ..	No. 1..........	45	0	0	133½	
	No. 2..........	45	0	0	133⅓	
						266⅔
Brunswick Dock.	No. 1..........	42	0	0	133½	
	No. 2..........	42	0	0	133⅓	
						266⅔
Meas. at Bottom.	....	....			....	1266⅔

*The extreme length of the River Wall belonging to the Dock
Estate is 2 miles and 1087 yards.*

THE SHIPPING, &c.

The rapid increase in the amount of Shipping
belonging to Liverpool, has taken place almost entirely of late years, since the improvements in science
have given a new stimulus to commercial enterprise.
In 1540 Liverpool had only twelve vessels, of 177
tons burthen, and manned by seventy-five men, while
in 1840, after a lapse of three centuries, she could
boast of 15,998 vessels, of 2,445,708 tons, having
entered the port during the short space of one year.

The number of vessels in the port at one time, exclusive of those discharging or loading in part at
Runcorn, frequently amounts to upwards of 800.

The dock dues annually received average £180,000.
During one week in May of the present year, 1842,

£8400 were received for dock duties, which is the largest amount ever drawn in so short a period.

From a parliamentary paper, dated April 5th, 1842, it appears that the gross customs revenue received

at Liverpool during 1840, was	£4,607,326,	and in 1841,	£4,140,593
„ London	„	11,116,685,	„	11,757,262
„ Bristol	„	1,027,160,	„	1,046,800
„ Dublin	„	889,564,	„	977,718
„ Glasgow and Greenock		814,211,	„	949,635

As the American packets, and other large vessels most deserving of notice, generally lie in Prince's Dock, the stranger will be most interested by visiting the vessels there, although there are many other elegant ships, equally worthy of attention, in the other docks.

THE AMERICAN PACKET-SHIPS

have long been known for their superior accommo-dations and handsome equipment, and an inspection of their cabins and other conveniences, which the officers on board are at all times ready to allow, will afford ample gratification for the small trouble incurred.

These vessels are of very large size, most of them being about 1000 tons burthen, and they have ac-commodation for from twenty to fifty cabin passen-gers, as well as for a few in the steerage. They are generally punctual in sailing on the day appointed, or as soon after as possible. The average length of passage out to New York is about five weeks, and the homeward passage is generally accomplished in about three weeks. This differs but little from the time occupied in the passage to Philadelphia, Boston, &c.

E

STEAM VESSELS.

The number of steam ships belonging to Liverpool is rapidly increasing, and she can already boast of some of the finest specimens of this description of naval architecture frequenting the Mersey. The most deserving of notice, as being the largest and most important, are—

THE BRITISH AND NORTH AMERICAN ROYAL MAIL STEAM SHIPS.

These splendid steamers are appointed by the Admiralty to carry the mails to Boston, calling at Halifax, and are despatched twice a month in summer, and once in winter. They are the Acadia, Britannia, Columbia, and Caledonia, of 1200 tons, and 440 horses' power each, built on the same model, at different ports on the Clyde, with every part of their arrangements similar. The dimensions of the Britannia, which was the first on the station, will give an idea of the size of the others. They are,—length, from taffrail to figure-head, 230 feet; breadth of beam, $36\frac{1}{2}$ feet; depth of hold, $22\frac{1}{2}$ feet. Since the establishment of this line of steamers, in July, 1840, the time required for crossing the Atlantic can be known, with almost as much certainty as that of conveyance by land, the average outward passage requiring about fourteen days and a half, and the homeward eleven or twelve days. The shortest passage made since their commencement was by the Britannia, which arrived on the 9th July, 1841, from Halifax in nine days and a half, and from Boston in twelve days seven hours. This steamer has also made the longest passage, which occupied eighteen days and a half.

This line of steamers lie in Coburg Dock, and visitors are admitted on board by an order from Messrs. Mac Iver, the agents.

The Glasgow Steamers, lying in Clarence Dock, are deserving of notice on account of the superior manner in which their interior is fitted up, and the elegance and comfort of their entire arrangements. They each have accommodation for nearly one hundred cabin passengers. The usual length of their passage to Greenock is seventeen or eighteen hours, according to the state of the weather.

The Dublin Mail and Contract Steam Packets are vessels of the first class, and are well worthy of inspection. They are moored in the Sloyne, off Birkenhead, from which place the morning mails sail; but the contract mails are despatched in the evening from George's pier. Ten or twelve hours is the average length of passage from Dublin.

Several of the other large steamers, sailing coast-wise, to Ireland, Isle of Man, &c., are fitted up in a superior manner, and may be generally found in Clarence or Trafalgar Dock.

Of the River Steam Packets there is a large number, their average size being about 80 tons. The greater part of them sail half-hourly in summer, and hourly in winter, from George's Pier, but a few are despatched from the south end of Princes' Pier.

Not fewer than from fifty to sixty steamers sail regularly from Liverpool every week; and, including those lying in dock unemployed, the port has probably upwards of a hundred steam vessels connected

with it, many of which could, upon any sudden na.
tional emergency, be made available as vessels of war.

For particulars of the sailing of the Steam Packets
from Liverpool, see the appendix.

THE PILOT BOATS

are small sloops, of beautiful model and exceedingly
strong build, eleven in number; which cruise about
the channel for the purpose of furnishing pilots to
inward-bound vessels, and receiving them on board
when they have conducted outward-bound vessels
into the open sea and are about to leave them. The
crews of these boats are all men of experience, who
have a thorough knowledge of the approaches to
the harbour; and immediately on a pilot's boarding
a vessel, the master and officers resign the entire
control and responsibility to him, merely acting under his direction till he brings the vessel into dock.

THE LIFE-BOATS,

belonging to the harbour and bay of Liverpool are,
two at Liverpool, two at the Magazines, two at Hoylake, two at Point of Ayr, and one at Formby. The
Liverpool boats are kept at the boat-house on Canning,
or No. 2, pierhead, the keys of which are to be had at
the Custom-house or dock-office, and are manned by
a master and ten men. —The Steam-tug Company
have also a life-boat, kept at the south end of Prince's
Pier, the key of the building in which it is deposited
is to be found at No. 5, New Quay. The valuable
assistance rendered by these boats in cases of extreme danger has been very frequently displayed, and
the number of lives saved by the exertions of their

crews, affords the strongest evidence of their practical utility.

QUARANTINE.

The anchorage appointed for vessels from the Levant and other ports from which they are liable to bring infectious diseases, is opposite New Ferry. The hulks of several old men of war are there moored for the reception of cargoes which undergo fumigation &c., and for the accommodation of the crews of the vessels which have not a clean bill of health. The extreme rigour with which the quarantine regulations are enforced, seems almost unnecessary, as no symptom of infectious disease has appeared in any vessel from the usual plague ports for nearly 180 years; but it is better to submit to these precautionary measures for the public safety, than, by want of due care endanger the health of the community. A modification of the present quarantine system might be advantageous in a commercial point of view.

THE TELEGRAPH

is on the roof of a warehouse at the bottom of Chapel-street, and was erected in 1827 by the dock trustees, according to the arrangement of Lieut. Watson, and is now under the superintendence of Lieut. Lord, the marine surveyor. The communication with Holyhead, a distance of 72 miles, was opened on the 26th October, 1827, by the telegraphing of the American ship " Napoleon" in fifteen minutes to Bidston. The stations are eleven in number, and the time ordinarily occupied in communicating in-

formation is about five minutes, but it is very frequently performed in less than one minute.   The
shortest time in which a question has been asked at
Liverpool and an answer returned from Holyhead,
(a distance of 144 miles having been traversed), is
thirty-five seconds.   The whole arrangements are so
complete that its utility is considerably greater than
that of the government telegraph line between Ports-
mouth and London.   Information received by this
means is immediately communicated to the Exchange
News-room, and there made public.

THE LIGHT-HOUSES.

Of these there are several in the neighbourhood of
Liverpool.   The Rock Light-house is situated on a
rock on the west side of the entrance of the Mersey, and
is a very conspicuous object in approaching the town
from the sea.   The foundation of this elegant structure
was laid by Thomas Littledale, Esq., on the 8th June,
1827, and the building completed by Mr. Tomkinson,
from the design of Mr. Foster, in June, 1829, and
opened in March following.   Its height is ninety feet
above the level of the rock, and its form is such as is
best calculated to resist the fury of the waves.   The stone
of which it is built is of the hardest description, procured from Anglesea, and each block is dove-tailed in
to the other, and the whole united into one solid mass
by a liquid cement of volcanic origin, which, when
hardened, becomes even more durable than the rock
itself.   The expense of the erection, £27,500, was entirely defrayed by the Corporation, with a view to the
benefit of the commerce of the port.   The light exhibited at night is one of the most splendid in the

kingdom, being a revolving coloured light, which makes a revolution once in three minutes, and exhibits two brilliant white lights and one red light in succession. Each light attains its utmost luminous effect every minute, after which it becomes gradually less brilliant, till it appears to a distant observer totally eclipsed. In clear weather the light can be seen on the level of the sea, fifteen miles.

Bidston Light-house is in the form of a tower, on an eminence in Cheshire, at some distance from the shore, and shows a light only in a north-west direction, being masked to give a defined light in the Rock Channel. In connexion with this building is the first telegraph station on the Holyhead line, and immediately contiguous, on the ledge of the hill, are a number of private signal poles belonging to the different merchants and ship-owners in Liverpool, by means of which their vessels are reported.

Leasowe Light-house is a tall pile of building farther south on the Cheshire shore, and shows a masked light in the North Channel, but having nothing particularly worthy of notice.

Still farther south, and nine miles from Liverpool, are Hoylake upper and lower Light-houses, which are low buildings, exhibiting masked lights, the former to the northward, and both serving as a direction over Hoyle Bank.

On the Lancashire coast there are several light-houses, land-marks, and beacons, the chief of which are the Crosby Light, Bootle Land-marks, South-east Mark, &c.

There are three Light - Ships, the principal of which is

THE NORTH-WEST FLOATING LIGHT.

This is a large three-masted vessel, moored in Liverpool Bay about fifteen miles and a half from Liverpool, shewing three lights, which can be seen about ten miles in clear weather, and sounding a gong and bell alternately, when the atmosphere is thick. During the summer months some of the steamers sail regularly from George's Pier to this vessel and back, with passengers who are fond of a short but pleasant aquatic excursion.

FORMBY LIGHT-SHIP

has two masts, on which two lights are exhibited at night, and a red ball by day; and a bell is tolled in foggy weather. It is moored in Victoria Channel, about $9\frac{1}{2}$ miles from Liverpool.

CROSBY LIGHT-SHIP.

is a similar vessel, shewing one light at night, and a red ball by day, stationed in Crosby Channel, about $6\frac{1}{4}$ miles from Liverpool.

EMIGRATION.

The number of individuals emigrating from Liverpool is very great, as the convenience for procuring shipping to the United States and the Canadas, is greater at this than at any other seaport in the kingdom. For the purpose of giving information, and for the protection of emigrants, a government agent is appointed, to whom all enquiries should be addressed, unless the emigrant is willing to become the dupe of impostors, who hover about the docks, and are constantly entrapping the unwary.

The number of emigrants who sailed from Liverpool in the month of April, 1842, was

To the United States............ 13,056
To British Colonies, North Amer.. 1,945
_____
Total.. 15,001
_____

This surprising number exceeds the departures in April, 1841, by 8284.

CIVIL JURISDICTION.

Liverpool has been a corporate borough since 1208, (and probably earlier,) at which period it received a charter from King John, the original copy of which still exists. At various times further charters were granted by succeeding sovereigns, conferring several important privileges. It appears to have been represented in parliament since the reign of Henry II., in 1159, but the burgesses frequently neglected to avail themselves of the privilege of returning a member. Prior to the reform act, the two representatives were chosen by the burgesses or freemen, of whom there were about 5000, but the election is now conducted as in other boroughs. In 1841, the number of electors was 15,537, including 3903 freemen.

By the municipal act, Liverpool is divided into sixteen wards, each of which returns three councillors, and is also represented by an alderman, chosen by the council. The corporation thus consists of sixty-four members, one of whom, (John Shaw Leigh, Esq.) is the present mayor, (1842.) The council is formed into a number of committees, which attend to the particular interests of the docks, the corporation funds, the improvement of the town, lighting, watching, and cleansing the streets, the markets, schools, gaols, gardens, courts of law, &c., and their proceedings are periodically laid before the council, who are empowered to enact bye-laws.

The corporate estate of the borough of Liverpool is the most opulent in the kingdom, as it possesses an amount of property of not less value than £2,500,000, exclusive of the interest in leases. The income during the year ending 1st September, 1841, amounted to £249,216 2s 7d, of which £65,933 .18s 9d, were town-due receipts.

The chief borough officers are the Recorder, Stipendiary Magistrate, Town Clerk, Coroner, &c , all of whom have been some time in office.

The magistrates hold a court daily at the Sessions' House, for the trial of offenders, previous to their being passed to the sessions or assizes. The other courts, such as the Court of Requests, &c., are held in the same building, or at the office in High-street.

The government of the parish is invested in two churchwardens, four overseers, and other officers, with twenty-four guardians of the poor. There are twenty-four commissioners under the paving and sewerage acts, a number of whom are elected from the town council.

The Police establishment of Liverpool is exceedingly efficient, and consists of 619 men and officers, of whom about one-third are on duty during the day

ánd two-thirds during the night. They consist of
1 head constable, 1 commissioner of police, 7 super-
intendents, 41 inspectors and acting inspectors, 35
bridewell keepers, station-house clerks, &c., 534
constables, making a total of 619. About 60 of this
number are set apart for service at fires, and are distinguished by a different uniform. Since their establishment in 1836 they have proved of essential service to the town, in repressing vice, preserving the
peace, and affording a degree of protection to property, the advantage of which is only known to those
who experienced the working of the old constabulary
system. Officers on duty are distinguished by a strap
of blue and white on their left arm.

BUILDINGS CONNECTED WITH THE CIVIL GOVERNMENT.

THE NEW ASSIZE COURTS.

The foundation stone of a magnificent building, for
the purpose of holding the Assizes, Sessions, and
other courts, was laid on the 28th June, 1838, on the
site of the old Infirmary, near the Haymarket. The
following description, abridged from the *Companion
to the British Almanack,* is given, as the building is
not yet in a state of forwardness.

The order adopted is Corinthian, continued
throughout, and arranged so as to produce a very
rich *polystyle* composition, possessing more than an
ordinary degree of variety and contrast. The eastern

façade, or the longer side of the building, is 420 feet, the columns being 45 feet high, and 4 feet 6 inches in diameter. The south front, which, owing to the great fall of the ground at the end of the site, (about 16 feet), has the appearance of being raised on a terrace, and thereby acquires both additional dignity and picturesque effect, consists chiefly of a hexastyle monoprostyle portico, recessed within, to make its entire depth 24 feet. The columns are raised on a stylobate 10 feet high, and continued along the other fronts; and the height from the ground line to the apex of the pediment is 95 feet. This front alone would constitute an imposing piece of architecture; yet it appears little more than a subordinate portion, when compared with the eastern façade. Independently of its beauties of design, the latter has the merit of clearly expressing the general internal arrangement of the plan. The advanced or mono-prostyle colonnade in the centre is 200 feet in length, and being recessed, forms within an ample sheltered ambulatory 26 feet in depth; this corresponds with St. George's Hall, which comes in between the two Assize Courts, and defines itself externally in the composition, by being carried up higher than the rest. This division of the front consists of fifteen intercolumns, and the one on either side of it of five more. The north front presents a projecting hemi-cycle, in which the order is continued in attached columns; a very agreeable variety is thus produced, and the view of the building from the north-east differs considerably from that seen from the south-east. The northern portion of the plan will form a Concert-room, (subsequently noticed), and it makes the entire extent from north to south, including the steps leading up to the south portico, 500 feet. Taking into account its unusual altitude, the structure will, in point of magnitude alone, have few rivals in the kingdom. The two courts, which are lighted from above, are of similar dimensions, viz. 60 by 50 feet, and 35 feet high; and during the assizes, &c. the spacious hall between them will be opened to the public as the approach to both courts. The architect of this magnificent building is H. Lonsdale Elmes, Esq.

The entire building is to be heated and ventilated under the joint directions of Dr. Reid and the architect, the arrangements being such, that if necessary the whole effect of the apparatus can be directed to any one apartment.

SESSIONS HOUSE.

The Assizes, Sessions, and other Courts, have been, since 1828, held in the building in Chapel-street, erected for that purpose. It is a plain edifice, of the Grecian style of architecture, extending 174 feet south from Chapel-street, having principal entrances at each end, together with others on the sides. At the south end, a winding stair leads from the vestibule to the room above, which is fitted up in a handsome manner for holding the assizes, with convenience for the judges, magistrates, barristers, jurors, &c., and about one-third of the space gradually rising like steps from the front, is allotted to spectators. The prisoner's dock is about the centre of the room, from which a staircase proceeds, communicating by a subterranean passage with the

Bridewell opposite. At the north end is a larger apartment, 61½ by 39 feet, lighted from the roof, fitted up in a similar manner, and used as the Civil Court. In the centre of the building, between the two courts, are the magistrates', barristers', and other rooms. The expense of erection, amounting to £19,312 was defrayed by the corporation.

THE BOROUGH GAOL,

situated in Great Howard-street, was erected during the last century, on a plan recommended by the philan-thropist Howard, and from its open and rather elevated situation, is a healthy place of confinement for the unfortunate individuals incarcerated therein. Till 1811, it was occupied as a prison for French prisoners of war, since which period it has been used as the Borough Gaol. From the report of the Rev. T. Carter, chaplain of this gaol, it appears that during the year ending 30th September, 1841, there were committed 2,943 males, and 2,542 females, total 5,485. Of debtors, there were 366, viz., 342 males and 24 females, and the average daily number of all classes was 550.

HOUSE OF CORRECTION, KIRKDALE.

This spacious and well ventilated building, covers 28,648 square yards, and was built from designs by Mr. Wright, of Manchester, The front of the centre of the edifice is fitted up as the County Sessions-house, and is ornamented by an Ionic portico of eight columns, and the general form of the building is that of two semicircular wards, united at the ex-tremities. The governor's and turnkeys' apartments command a view of all the prisoners, who are employed in various trades, and on a treadmill capable of admitting 130 persons on it at one time. In the centre of the building is a commodious chapel, in which divine service is performed every Sunday. The prison is capable of containing 800 prisoners, who can be divided into 22 classes, and the arrangements for the separation and classification of offenders are very judicious.

BRIDEWELL

is a small and inconvenient structure, opposite the Sessions-house, with which it communicates by a subterranean passage, as formerly mentioned. Prisoners are seldom kept here longer than until they have been examined before the magistrates, when they are removed to the other gaols.

STATION HOUSES.

There are six smaller bridewells for the temporary reception of offenders, in Vauxhall-road, Rose-hill, Hotham-street, Brick-street, and at the Prince's and Brunswick Docks. In Seel-street and Rose-hill are commodious Police Stations, where the men are daily mustered and drilled between two and three o'clock.

THE FIRE POLICE STATION

is in Temple Place, Temple Court. Belonging to this establishment are fifteen powerful fire-engines, each of which has an ample supply of hose, fire-escapes, &c., six water carts, and two large tanks, which can be drawn by horses to the neighbourhood of a fire, each capable of containing seven tons of water. Several of the engines are distributed in different parts of the town. At the principal station, horses are kept harnessed night and day, in readiness for instant departure with the engines the moment an alarm of fire arrives.

THE PARISH OFFICES

in Fenwick-street, have a plain stuccoed front, and have been rebuilt since a considerable part of the street was destroyed by fire in 1831.

CLARENDON ROOMS

in South John-street, contain a number of apartments, generally used as the place of meeting of trustees, creditors, law-societies, &c., and here is deposited a library belonging to the gentlemen of the legal profession.

COMMERCIAL AND LITERARY INSTITUTIONS.

In a great commercial town, it is natural to expect to find a number of the former class of institutions; but Liverpool, while providing for her sons of commerce, has not been unmindful that commerce and literature ought to go hand in hand, and has therefore, at various periods, given birth to Literary Institutions, which in their respective characters may vie with any in the kingdom.

THE NEWS-ROOMS AND LIBRARIES

are worthy of a prominent place, as being both of a commercial and literary description.

THE EXCHANGE NEWS-ROOM.

To this elegant room strangers are admitted when introduced by a subscriber; and any one wishing to have an idea of the general appearance and business-looks of Liverpool merchants, ought to see them assembled in this spacious apartment, promenading the room, anxiously poring over a newspaper or shipping list, or clustering in groups; and undisturbed by the "busy hum of men," transferring property to the amount of millions. The length of the room is 130 feet, and breadth 52 feet. Twenty Doric columns, each of a single stone, support a coved and panneled ceiling, and form a magnificent colonnade in the centre of the room. Over the fireplaces, on the east side, are two emblematical tableaux in bas-relief, and the room is lighted by five large chandeliers. On a slate at the north end, is published the telegraphic intelligence, shipping arrivals, sailings, &c., and the tables are amply provided with London, provincial and foreign newspapers; shipping, share, and other lists, supplying every information necessary for the man of business.

THE ATHENÆUM,

the first institution of the kind in the kingdom, was erected in 1799 at an expense of £4000. It is a plain but well built stone edifice in Church-street, the news-room of which is well lighted, fitted up in an elegant and convenient manner; and supplied with

F

London and provincial papers, magazines, reviews, periodicals, &c. The number of proprietors is five hundred, whose annual payment is two guineas and a half. Above the news-room is a library consisting of about 16,000 volumes, many of which are exceedingly rare and valuable. None of the books are allowed to circulate; but a comfortable room is provided for individuals wishing to consult works in the library. Among other curious and ancient volumes may be mentioned a copy of the work of Henry VIII., which obtained for him the title of Defender of the Faith.

THE LYCÆUM

is a handsome edifice at the bottom of Bold-street, having on the Bold-street side a neat portico, supported by six Ionic columns. It was intended to enter from the Church-street side, but local circumstances caused the present entrance to be adopted. It was erected from the design of Mr. Harrison, of Chester, at an outlay of £11,000. The news-room is 68 feet long, and 48 feet wide, and has a coved ceiling 31 feet high. It is constantly supplied with newspapers, magazines, &c., and has six hundred subscribers; proprietors paying one guinea, and non-proprietors one pound ten shillings per annum each. The appearance of the library is striking; it is of a circular form, and lighted from the roof. A gallery surrounds the entire room, which is 135 feet in diameter, affording access to volumes on the higher shelves. This library, which is known as the "Liverpool Library," was originally established in 1758, for the purpose, as stated in the first " prospectus, of affording an ample fund of amusement and improvement in many kinds of useful and polite knowledge." The number of volumes then amounted to 450, and the library had 109 subscribers. In 1770, it had extended to 1600 volumes, since which period it has rapidly increased, and it now contains upwards of 34,000 volumes. As these works are allowed to circulate among 893 proprietors, it is consequently the largest circulating library in the kingdom. This library, to which the subscription is one guinea per annum, in addition to the purchase of a share, is daily increasing in value, as every standard work, and the popular literature of the day, are liberally supplied.

THE UNION NEWS ROOM

is a plain stone building, in Duke-street, so named from the circumstance of its being opened on the 1st January, 1801, the day on which the Irish Union took place. On the ground-floor is a large newsroom, provided with the usual Metropolitan and provincial papers, &c., and the adjoining apartments are occasionally used as exhibition rooms. The cost of erection, which was subscribed in shares, was was nearly £6000.

THE CLERICAL LIBRARY

was instituted for the use of the clergy of Liverpool, and is deposited at No. 93, Bold-street.

In addition to the above, there are several reading rooms and libraries connected with other institutions, which will be noticed along with the institutions themselves.

At the head of the Literary Institutions, as being the first established in Liverpool, is the

ROYAL INSTITUTION.

This is a plain brick building, in Colquitt-street, which was originally a private house, and was altered to its present form for the purposes of the institution. It was founded in 1814, under the auspices of the late William Roscoe, Esq., and other eminent literary gentlemen, £30,000 having been subscribed in shares of £100 each. As detailed in a report published by the first committee, its objects are, " to perpetuate in the town of Liverpool, an establishment for continuing and extending the acquisitions of early years to the subsequent periods of life, and forming that character of intellectual and moral improvement, without which, successful labour is only misapplied, and riches are of no real use to their possessor." Since its establishment, it has proved of essential service to Liverpool, in improving and ripening a literary taste, which is now every where fostered by the erection of kindred institutions. The public are admitted gratuitously on the first Monday of each month, and at any other time on payment of one shilling. When introduced by a proprietor or subscriber, strangers, not residing in Liverpool, are admitted free, and foreigners and travellers, though not introduced by a proprietor, are always admitted gratuitously. Hours of exhibiting from ten A.M., to four P.M. During the year ending Feb. 1842, 30,956 persons visited the museum, on free-admission days, without any injury having been done to the property of the institution; and in the previous year, 40,275 individuals availed themselves of the privilege. On entering the building, the first room on the left is the committee-room, which contains a small library of works of reference. At the end of the hall is the lecture-room, a commodious and comfortable apartment, capable of accommodating 500 persons. Behind the lecture-room is a laboratory with variou; conveniences. In the philosophical department, i; an excellent collection of apparatus and mechanical models. Above stairs is a variety of curiosities from the South Seas, many of which are extremely rare. The first room on the right contains the natural history specimens, comprising a great number of stuffed quadrupeds, &c. A small room on the left is devoted to antiquities, most of which, including several mummies, are from Egypt. The most elegant apartments are those containing the collection of birds, which are arranged in handsome glass cases round the rooms; and a very complete classification of minerals and shells occupies the tables in the centre of the room. On the higher floor is a further collection of fossils and minerals.

The schools of the institution are in Seel-street, and have a handsome stone front of the Doric style of architecture, consisting of a pediment supported by four beautifully proportioned columns. They are attended chiefly by the sons of the higher classes, who receive education to qualify them for the Universities, &c.

THE PERMANENT GALLERY OF ART

is in Colquitt-street, opposite the Royal Institution, to which it belongs. It was projected in 1840, and in May 1841, the plans of Mr. Cunningham were adopted, and the work contracted for by Mr. Beattie, for about £1450. The building is intended for the reception of casts and works of art; and the collection of casts from the Elgin, Ægina, Phygalian, and other ancient marbles, has been removed from the room in the Institution in which they were formerly deposited, to this more eligible situation, where are also models of the Laocoon, Apollo Belvedere, Venus de Medici, &c. The building consists of two stories, with one principal apartment in each. The lower one is occupied as the gallery of casts, and is lighted by a row of lateral windows on the north side. In the upper room is a series of very rare and antique paintings, chiefly of the old Italian school, from the collection of the late Mr. Roscoe, together with many which have been purchased or presented to the Institution. A splendid statue of Roscoe, executed in white marble by Chantrey, has, by the generosity of the committee, to whom it is entrusted, been added to this gallery.

Open from ten o'clock in the morning till six in the evening during summer, and in winter from ten o'clock to dusk. Charge for admission one shilling.

MECHANICS' INSTITUTION.

This is the most flourishing establishment of the kind in the kingdom, and is conducted in a manner eminently calculated to benefit all classes of the community. The building is in Mount-street, and has a massive stone front with a projecting portico, consisting of a cornice supported on four Ionic columns, erected from the plans of Mr. A. H. Holme, at an expense of upwards of £11,000, exclusive of £3000, the amount required to repair the damage sustained by fire immediately prior to its opening in 1837, and the cost of erecting the two wings, which have been recently added. The lecture-room is in the middle of the building, in the form of a horse-shoe, with the rostrum in the centre, and lighted from the roof, and it is capable of accommodating 1200 persons. Behind the lecture-room are apartments used as a laboratory and apparatus room, and the remainder of the ground floor is occupied by the library, board-room, school-rooms, &c. It is contemplated to erect an organ and orchestra at the back of the platform, in the lecture-room, in order to give additional effect to the musical performances. The second floor is appropriated to school-rooms, including the statue-gallery, which is used by the pupils of the drawing department. The space over the laboratory is elegantly fitted up as a museum, which promises at no distant period, to be of great interest and value. The walls of the passages above stairs are ornamented with several appropriate paintings, which have been presented by different individuals; and the niches on the staircases and in the lecture-room, are filled with busts and statues, some of which are executed in marble. The institution is open to visitors every Saturday morning, when the pupils are publicly examined; but the public are at any time at liberty to inspect the establishment. On Wednesday and Saturday evenings, lectures are given on popular and scientific subjects, to which non-members are admitted on payment of one shilling. During the year ending March, 1843, the number of members of the institution was :—

Life members	539
Annual members	1204
Quarterly Members	16
Sons of members	538
Apprentices of members........	273
Apprentices of non-members....	401
Ladies	404
Total...........	3375

The schools connected with the institution are in three divisions. The evening schools consist of twenty-five departments, conducted by thirty-one masters, and contain about 600 pupils, to whom · instruction is given in reading, grammar, composition, elocution, debating, geography, history, writing, arithmetic, and mathematics, book-keeping, chemistry, natural philosophy, mineralogy, astronomy; the Latin, Greek, French, German, and Spanish languages; figure, ornamental, landscape, perspective, mechanical and architectural drawing; naval architecture, painting, modelling, vocal music, dancing

and gymnastics.   The lower school has sixteen masters, and contains 576 pupils, who receive for £1 15s·
per annum, an excellent solid education.   The terms
of admission to the high school are £10 10s. per
annum for sons of members; and there are at present in this department 180 pupils, who receive instruction in every branch of education necessary for
a commercial or professional life, and have access to
all the advantages afforded by the institution.   The
library contains 11,011 volumes, in every department
of literature.   During 1842, 44,953 sets of works, or
68,603 volumes have been taken out by 2,805 readers.
In the months of June and July, 1842, an exhibition
of fine arts, manufactures, curiosities, &c., was held
in the institution, the receipts for which were about
£4,000.   During the thirty· six days which it continued open, it was visited by nearly 100,000 individuals.   About 20,000 pupils belonging to the different charity schools of the town were admitted
gratuitously, as were also the police and military
forces of the town, and 380 domestic servants.   The
whole of the privileges and advantages of the institution, including admission to several of the evening
classes, are obtained for £1 1s. per annum, and 5s·
for sons of members.

THE COLLEGIATE INSTITUTION.

The foundation stone of this elegant building was laid by the Right Hon. Lord Stanley, M.P., on the 22nd October, 1840, and it was publicly opened by the Lord Bishop of Chester, the Right Hon. W. E. Gladstone, M. P., and other distinguished individuals, on the 6th January, 1843. The object of the institution, as stated in the first prospectus, is " the education of the commercial, trading, and working classes, in which instruction in the doctrines and duties of Christianity, as taught by the United Churches of England and Ireland, shall for ever be communicated, in combination with literary, scientific, and commercial information." The building, which has been erected under the able superintendence of its talented architect, H. Lonsdale Elmes, Esq., is the noblest edifice erected for educational purposes in this part of the kingdom. The principal elevation faces Shaw-street, is of the Tudor style, 280 feet in length, collegiate in its aspect, and is consistently decorated throughout, with projecting centre and wings. A magnificent arch in the centre, over the principal entrance, together with colossal statues of Lord Francis Egerton and Lord Stanley, placed in richly carved canopied niches in the wings, add to the imposing effect. The lofty oriel windows carried up through two stories, give solidity and repose to the angles of the structure. The elevation consists of three tiers of windows, those of the two upper floors being combined together into a general composition, producing the effect of a single range of lofty windows. The highest floor is lighted

from the roof. The four stories comprise forty-eight apartments. Those on the ground floor are 14 feet in height, and consist of six school rooms, (two 25 by 20 feet, two 40 by 25 feet, and two 50 by 25 feet,) dining rooms, and keeper's rooms, besides vestibules, waiting rooms, and others of a subordinate nature. On the first floor are the board room, secretary's room, nine school rooms, (two 50 by 25 feet, three 40 by 25 feet, and four 25 by 20 feet,) lecturer's room, laboratory, &c., all 17 feet high. On the upper floor are several spacious apartments, used as a museum, picture and sculpture gallery, the latter of which is 218 feet in length, and access is to be had to each story by three separate staircases. The theatre is a spacious octagonal apartment, 50 feet high, capable of accommodating 2,300 persons, occupying a part of the first and second floors. It has an upper and a lower gallery, and behind the lecturer's platform is a music room, with rising seats for 300 performers, which is capable of being thrown open to the hall at pleasure. The monthly performances of the Philharmonic Society are held here, and their organ has been removed to this situation, till a more powerful one shall have been built for the institution.

The schools of the institution are in three classes. The upper school is under the superintendence of 12 masters, and the course of education comprises the classics, mathematics, chemistry, natural philosophy, writing, and book-keeping, the French, German, Italian, and Hebrew languages, drawing and vocal music. The middle school is conducted by 12 masters, and the lower school by 7 masters. In the evening schools are taught the following branches by 14 masters: navigation and nautical astronomy, algebra and geometry, English, arithmetic, writing; landscape, figure, and ornamental drawing and painting; mechanical and architectural drawing; modelling, and anatomical drawing, naval architecture, the classics, the German and French languages, vocal music, chemistry and natural philosophy. The terms are twenty guineas per annum for pupils of the upper school, ten for the middle school, and three for the lower school, with an annual subscription to the library and lectures. Lectures are delivered on Tuesday and Friday evenings, at half-past seven o'clock, on various interesting subjects, to which individuals are admitted, at 2s. for the lower gallery, 1s. for the body of the hall, and 6d. for the upper gallery. The Bishop of Chester is the visitor of the institution, Lord Francis Egerton the president, the Rev. Rectors of Liverpool the chairmen, and the principals are clergymen, graduates of the Universities of Oxford, Cambridge, or Dublin.

THE MEDICAL INSTITUTION

is a neat building, at the corner of Hope-street and Mount Pleasant, in the form of a segment of a circle, with a stone front, consisting of six Ionic columns and corresponding pilasters, forming an elevation 198 feet long and 35 feet high. The cost of erection was nearly £3,000, £1,000 of which was given, together with the land on which it stands, by the corporation, and the remainder was subscribed by the medical gentlemen of the town. The interior consists of a lecture room, lighted from the roof,

capable of accommodating 300 or 400 persons, a
library belonging to the members of the medical profession, a museum, and various other apartments.
The meetings of several philosophical societies are
held in this building. It was built from the plans
of Messrs. Rampling.

THE BROUGHAM INSTITUTE,

over the Arcade passage in Lawton-street, was established in 1836, for the purpose of providing instruction to the lower classes of society at a cheap rate,
and to give them an opportunity of holding meetings
for mutual improvement. Lectures are delivered on
Thursday evenings; discussions on questions of general interest take place on Tuesday evenings; and
there is connected with the institute a newsroom,
well supplied with newspapers, magazines, and periodicals. The subscription to the newsroom is 7s.
per annum, or 1d. for a casual visit. Open from
eight in the morning till ten at night.

THE MECHANICS AND APPRENTICES' LIBRARY

was established in 1803, chiefly through the exertions of the late Egerton Smith, Esq., and was latelv
removed to the Brougham Institute. Books are
allowed to be taken out by mechanics and others for
the small sum of 1d. a volume per week, on their
producing a recommendation from their employers.

CHARITABLE INSTITUTIONS.

THE proudest monuments of a nation's wealth are its Charitable Institutions; and in Liverpool the extent and utility of these establishments have uniformly kept pace with the wealth of the inhabitants

THE INFIRMARY,

situated in Brownlow-street, was opened for the reception of patients in 1824, having been erected from the designs of Mr. Foster, at an outlay of £27,000, in room of the old Infirmary in St. John's Lane, which was opened in 1749, and had become too small for the increasing population. Six Ionic columns, supporting a plain frieze and projecting cornice, (which is carried round the whole building,) form the portico at the front. The width at the back, including the wings which recede from the portico 82 feet, is 204 feet, and the depth from the front of the building to the back, 108 feet. Nearly twenty rooms on the ground floor afford accommodation for the officers of the Institution, committees, household, &c., except one large apartment in the left wing, which is fitted up as a ward-room for accidental cases. The upper stories are entirely appropriated for patients, and additions have been recently made to the establishment, by which more ample accommodation is afforded. Out of twenty wards, five, containing upwards of one hundred beds, are allotted to surgical cases, four to medical cases for men, and the remainder are set apart for women. In the centre of the

building is a steam engine which supplies the establishment with water, and with steam for cooking,
works a mangle, and is applied to other useful purposes. In the yard is an elevated erection, on which
is placed a clock, which can be seen from all parts of
the building, and strikes the hours and quarters.
The utility of this Institution is proved by the number and variety of patients who are annually admitted.
During 1841, 2186 patients were admitted, of which
number only 135 cases proved fatal, and 1375 were
cured. The average weekly number in the house
was 212. The affairs of this charity are managed by
a president, a committee of twenty-five, and the
other officers of the Institution are, a consulting
physician and two consulting surgeons, three physicians, three surgeons, a house surgeon, an apothe-
cary, and a matron.

THE LUNATIC ASYLUM

is connected with the above, and under the management of the same committee, besides a physician,
governor, and matron. It is situated in Ashton-
street, contiguous to the Infirmary, on extensive
premises, which are enclosed by a high stone wall.
The foundation-stone was laid in 1829 and the building was finished, under the direction of Mr. Foster,
at an expense of £11,000. The centre portion of the
structure recedes, the sides forming projecting wings,
and the walls, as high as the string sill of the upper
windows, are rusticated. The interior arrangement
provides every convenience to the unfortunate individuals requiring its restraint, affording a sufficiency
of light, air, and warmth. The wings are formed

into wards, with cells on each side, and the centre part is used as day-rooms, and as the keepers' apartments. Within this establishment patients of the more wealthy class of society receive all the attention, and experience all the comforts of a private asylum. During 1841 forty-three new patients were admitted in addition to forty-eight in the Institution on the 1st January, of which number twelve were cured and five died. The average weekly number in the house was thirty-four.

THE LOCK HOSPITAL

so named from the founder of such Institutions is under the same superintendence as the Infirmary and Lunatic Asylum, and is situated opposite the latter, on the east side of Ashton-street. The building was opened in 1834, is of simple construction, and affords accommodation to about 60 persons; 503 were admitted during the past year, of whom 400 have been cured. The average weekly number in the building was 42.

THE DISPENSARIES, NORTH AND SOUTH

are situated, the former in Vauxhall-road, and the latter in Upper Parliament-street. This Charity was originally instituted in September, 1778, at premises in John-st., and was afterwards removed to Church-st. and Marybone, and latterly to the present building in Vauxhall-road, which was occupied 1st Jan., 1831. The South Dispensary was established in 1822, in the building which it now occupies. The North Dispensary has a front, the centre of which consists of four Ionic columns, 30 feet high, supporting an entablature and battlement. The side parts project a little forward, and are ornamented by pilasters with Grecian capitals. The basement story is appropriated to the domestic arrangements of the establishment, besides having two bathing-rooms. On the principal floor are the Physicians' Hall, (39 by 20 feet), Surgeons' Hall, (22½ by 18 feet), with their examination rooms, the Secretary's office, laboratory, shop, waiting room, &c. On the second floor are the board-room, surgeons', apothecaries' and apprentices' rooms, library, &c.; and the upper floor is entirely occupied by sleeping apartments. Behind the main building are the bleeding and dissecting-rooms. The fact that upwards of 52,000 cases were relieved during the year 1841, at once attests the efficiency and utility of these institutions, which have, since their commencement in 1778, afforded relief to nearly 1,372,000 patients. During 1840 the total medical cases relieved at the North Dispensary were 17,569, at the South Dispensary 15,093, and surgical cases, 9125 and 8420 respectively; and of this number 19,262 were visited at their own houses, and supplied with medicine. The government of this charity is vested in a committee, which meets monthly, consisting of a president, two vice-presidents, a treasurer, two auditors, the churchwardens, and fifteen other governors, with a physician and surgeon from each Dispensary. Each Dispensary has a sub-committee of its own, which holds its meetings weekly, and whose decisions are under the control of the general board. Attendance is given daily, (Sundays excepted), at ten o'clock in the morning; and the only proper objects of this charity are the sick and poor, who are unable to pay for medicine.

EASTERN DISPENSARY.

In addition to the above long established institutions, the Eastern Dispensary was formed in 1838 for the convenience of the poor in the east district of the town. The building, which is No. 35, Islington, was formerly a private dwelling-house. The utility of this establishment may be seen from the number of cases relieved during the year 1841, which amounted to 6567, and 2204 were visited at their own residences. All patients require a subscriber's recommendation; and attendance is given daily at the Institution from eleven till one o'clock. The affairs of this charity are superintended by a president, four vice-presidents, a treasurer, a secretary, and a committee of twenty-four trustees. There are also connected with it three honorary medical officers, a consulting physician, and a house surgeon.

THE NORTHERN HOSPITAL

is a brick building, which was formerly a dwelling-house, situated at the end of Leeds-street, near the canal. The situation has rendered it of greater utility than it would have possessed had it been farther removed into town, as prompt assistance is now afforded in the case of the numerous accidents that occur in the neighbourhood of the docks. It is intended, as soon as the funds of the institution shall permit, to erect a more commodious building, as the present house is frequently so crowded, that cases even of extreme danger, have to be refused admittance. In

1841, 669 accidental cases, 507 medical, and 246 surgical patients were received, making with those in the establishment on the 1st January, 1,493 total patients; of this number 1,208 were cured, and 65 died. The direction of the affairs of this charity is vested in a committee, consisting of a president, vice-president, treasurer, two auditors, and twenty other trustees, who meet at least once a month, and oftener, if necessary. The medical officers are three honorary physicians, three honorary surgeons, and two house surgeons.

SOUTHERN AND TOXTETH HOSPITAL.

The first meeting of parties favourable to the formation of this institution, was held in the early part of 1838, when a subscription was commenced for carrying the plans of the projectors into effect. The corporation of Liverpool liberally presented 1,400 square yards of land, valued at £3,400, for the site of the hospital; and plans for the erection were gratuitously furnished by Mr. Cunningham. On the 2nd March, 1841, the foundation stone was laid by the mayor, and the building was completed on the 17th January, 1842, on which day it was publicly opened. The erection was contracted for by Mr. Bateman, for the sum of £3,925, which was raised by subscription. It consists of a handsome brick building, fronting Parliament-street, Flint-street, and Greenland-street. The principal front, which is in Flint-street, is two stories high, stuccoed, and has white stone facings. In the centre is a solid projection to relieve the uniformity of the appearance, and the building is entered by a plain portico, surmounted by a stone cornice, with an arched door way, and lighted by windows at the sides. The front part of the principal floor is occupied by the house-surgeon's and matron's private apartments, committee room, &c., A spacious corridor leads from the entrance hall along the entire length of the building, from which the wards on each side are entered, and it is terminated by the theatre, in which important operations are performed. This apartment is large, comfortable, and well lighted, and possesses conveniences for operation, equal to those of any similar institution in the kingdom. Adjoining it are baths and washing rooms. The remainder of the principal floor is occupied by the pupils' rooms, wards for male patients, the shop, nurses' rooms, and other conveniences. The whole establishment is ventilated and heated by Dr. Reid's apparatus, being the first hospital into which it has been introduced. There is a second floor over the front part of the building only, and this is entirely appropriated to the female patients, of whom about 15 can be accommodated. The entire building, which has in all nine wards, will contain from 50 to 60 patients, without crowding the apartments. Patients are admitted by a recommendation from a trustee; but cases of accident or extreme urgency are admitted at all times, night or day. The government of the hospital is vested in a committee, consisting of a president, vice-president, treasurer, two auditors, and fifteen other trustees, which meets monthly, and a sub-committee which meets every week. The medical officers are an honorary physician, three honorary surgeons, and a house surgeon;

and the domestic arrangements are superintended by a matron.

THE WORKHOUSE

was opened in 1772, and is situated on the space of ground between Brownlow-hill and Mount-pleasant; the front of the principal part of the building, before which is a large lawn, facing the former street. The interior accommodation is good; aged persons inhabiting apartments on the ground floor. Each individual is employed in some trade; the male adults as joiners, tailors, shoemakers, bricklayers, slaters, blacksmiths, spinners, &c., and the females as sempstresses, bonnet-makers, &c. Boys are instructed in various trades to fit them for becoming apprentices. The establishment is supported by the poor-rates, and is under the control of the parish authorities.

THE HOUSE OF RECOVERY

is a detatched building, in grounds contiguous to the workhouse, entering from Mount-pleasant, and it was opened in 1806. Patients are admitted to the benefits of this establishment when ill of fever, or any contagious disease, on the recommendation of a Physician, or of one of the officers of the Infirmary or Dispensaries. All due care is taken of the patients; and the judicious treatment here received, combined with the openness of the situation, is frequently the means of restoring the diseased to health and vigour, and of preventing the spread of epidemic diseases in the confined parts of the town.—Supported and governed as the workhouse.

SCHOOL FOR THE BLIND.

This institution is situated in London-road, at the corner of Hotham-street, has a plain stuccoed exterior, and extends in a long range of building as far back as Lord Nelson-street. A resolution has been recently made by the committee, that, "owing to the interruption which the pupils experience from the indiscriminate admission of visitors, non-subscribers cannot be admitted beyond the shop, without an introduction, either personally or by note, by a donor or subscriber." The institution is, however, with the above restriction, at all times open to visitors, who will derive most gratification from attending the school on Tuesdays and Fridays, at two o'clock, when there is a musical performance of the pupils. This establishment was founded in 1791, by a number of benevolent individuals, among the principal of whom was Pudsey Dawson, Esq., and it has since been very liberally supported. The inmates, of whom there are at present 107, are employed in various trades, such as weaving, spinning, rope and basket-making, the manufacture of mats, rugs, stair-carpets, floor-cloth, sash-line, shoe-making, &c., and the articles are sold for the benefit of the institution. During 1840, the amount disposed of was £1496 16s. 8d. Many of the pupils receive instructions in music, both vocal and instrumental, on the system of Dr. Bell, which has in other establishments been successfully introduced, and from this institution have emanated not a few talented musical performers. Particular care is paid to the religious and moral training of the inmates, as well as to their health; and inducements to proficiency and good conduct are held out to them, in the shape of gratuities on quitting the establishment, varying from £2 to £5, according to merit. From its commencement till 1840, 1062 have been received into the school, of whom 179 belonged to the parish of Liverpool, 241 to other parts of Lancashire, and 642 to other parts of the United Kingdom.

THE CATHOLIC BLIND ASYLUM,

situated at No. 16, Islington, was established in 1841, for the purpose of " affording to the Catholic blind an elementary education, and instruction in those branches of industry which shall be found suitable to each pupil's capacity, and of bringing them up in the principles of their religion." The government of the asylum is vested in a committee who hold quarterly meetings, and the institution is supported by subscription. Applicants must be above ten years of age, and have a recommendation from a subscriber; and a payment of two shillings a week towards the maintenance of each pupil, must be guaranteed, prior to his admission. There are at present eleven inmates in the establishment, which can accommodate sixteen, who are chiefly employed in basket and mat making, knitting, and in learning music. The institution is open to visitors at all hours of the day, and articles made by the pupils are exposed for sale.

SCHOOL FOR THE DEAF AND DUMB.

This institution, founded by William Comer, Esq., in 1825, was originally opened in Wood-street, and removed in October, 1840, to the present commodious premises in Oxford-street South, on the site of the entrance to the old Botanic Garden.

The principal object of the benevolent founder was to give to the institution more the character of a *seminary* than an *asylum*, by connecting with it a day school, the great importance of which is, as is shown in the report for 1829, " that attendance at a day school still leaves the pupils at liberty to participate in the exercise of those endearing relations, which it should ever be the object of christian charity to foster and promote;" and the system of day pupils allows, with a smaller outlay, the advantages of the institution to be afforded to a larger number of individuals, than if they were boarded in the establishment. The daily association of mutes, under the training of such an institution, with children of their own age, in possession of all their organs, must also be highly advantageous, as by imitation and example, faculties which would probably never be exercised in an asylum are here brought into play. This school is at present the only one in the kingdom open for the reception of day pupils, which is a matter of regret, as it appears from their last report, that in Great Britain there are 14,328 mutes, with only twelve institutions for their reception, at which no more than 745 are receiving the benefit of instruction. The school now contains 58 pupils, viz., 31 boarders, of whom 23 are boys and 8 girls, 22 day pupils, of whom 15 are boys and 7 girls, 5 private pupils who reside with the master. Of this number 52 are instructed *gratuitously*, and for all the children, a substantial dinner, (also gratis) is daily provided by the institution.

The foundation stone of the building was laid by the mayor, Hugh Hornby, Esq., on the 24th October, 1839, and the erection completed in one year. The building is of a plain Grecian character, the entrance front, which is of white stone, being relieved by a solid projection in the centre, surmounted by an entablature and pediment. A parapet or attic is carried round the principal fronts, and effectually hides the roof of the building. A portico of beautiful proportions, comprising two Ionic columns in *antis* approached by a broad flight of steps, forms the entrance to the principal floor, on each side of which are windows with moulded architrave. On entering the hall, which measures 18 feet by 18 feet, a painting by Illidge, of W. Comer, Esq., over the staircase, is the most prominent object. The principal floor has two private parlours for parlour-boarders, each 24 by 16 feet, private rooms for the master and matron, each 18 by 16 feet; an assistants' room, communicating with the school-room, 18 by 12 feet ; a spacious school-room, 40 by 33 feet, and a dining-room. Between the dining and school-rooms are sliding doors, by means of which the two can be thrown into one when more accommodation is necessary. The second and third floors are occupied by private bedrooms, and large and comfortable dormitories, capable of accommodating 100 *resident* pupils. The internal arrangement of the entire building is such, that each floor is divided into three compartments, by which means the boys' and girls' rooms are kept distinct from each other, as well as from the master's private rooms. The principal apartments are heated and ventilated by a simple but efficient apparatus, connected with a furnace in the yard. The basement story, the floor of which is only 1 foot 6 inches below the level of the street, contains spacious kitchens, store rooms, washing and bathing rooms for both boys and girls, &c.; and the part under the dining and school-rooms is open to the play-grounds, and fitted up as two separate gymnasiums. The entire building is the most complete of its kind in the kingdom, and reflects great credit on the skill of the architects, Messrs. Cunningham and Holme, and on the judgement of Mr. Rhind, the head-master, according to whose suggestions they acted. The structure was erected by Messrs. S. and J. Holme, at an expense of £5,938, the greatest part of which was defrayed by subscription. Visitors are admitted at any time by an order from a subscriber, but they are requested to attend, if possible, on Tuesdays, between the hours of ten and twelve, and two and four, in order that the arrangements of the school may not be interrupted. Every stranger who visits this interesting institution, cannot fail to be astonished at the proficiency which these unfortunate mutes exhibit in every department of study, and especially in the faculty of articulation, which has been most successfully introduced by Mr. Rhind, who shews that it is possible that *even the dumb may be taught to speak.*

THE EYE AND EAR INFIRMARY

was formed in January, 1841, by the Union of the Ophthalmic and Ear Institutions, the former of which had been in operation upwards of twenty years, during which period not fewer than 31,000 cases had been assisted, either with prescriptions or operations. The institution is near the bottom of Mount Pleasant, and has accommodation for eleven in-door patients, whose cases require peculiar care. The object of the charity is to afford *gratuitous* relief to the poor afflicted with diseases of the eye or ear, any person being eligible to assistance on the recommendation of a subscriber. It is open daily from eleven to twelve o'clock, and patients also receive occasional medical attendance at their own residences. During 1841, the number of patients relieved, or cured of the diseases of the eye, amounted to 2280, whose attendance amounted to 9000 visits. The number of patients relieved or cured of diseases of the ear, was 1879. The number of in-patients was 57.

THE ALMS HOUSES

in Cambridge-street, are a range of low buildings, in the form of three sides of a square, open to the front, built, as stated on the inscription, " By the Corporation of Liverpool, in 1787, in lieu of others formerly erected for certain charitable purposes."

THE SHIPWRIGHTS' ALMS HOUSES,

in Bond-street, have been erected by the Shipwrights, for the accommodation of decayed members of their Society.

THE BLUE COAT HOSPITAL,

in School-lane, consists of an extensive range of brick buildings, with stone ornaments, having a spacious area in front, enclosed by iron railings.

This institution was originally established in 1709, and consisted of a small building accommodating forty boys and ten girls, who received clothing and instruction gratuitously from the charity, but lived with their parents. In 1714, through the exertions of Bryan Blundell, Esq., a subscription was raised for providing an establishment in which the children should reside, and be entirely under the control of the institution. It was commenced in 1717, and completed in 1726. The object of this institution is stated in the inscriptions, " *Christianæ Charitati promovendæ inopique pueritiæ, Ecclesiee Anglicanæ principiis imbuendee Sacrum.*

ANNO SALUTIS, MDCCXVII.

Large additions have been subsequently made, nearly equal to the original building, the centre part of which is occupied by a large hall, over which is the Chapel. The wings are used as school-rooms, dormitories, and private apartments. 250 boys and 100 girls are boarded, clothed, and educated by this charity, the former of whom are instructed in reading' writing, arithmetic, grammar, geography, history, and occasionally geometry, and mensuration; and the girls are taught sewing, knitting, and domestic duties, in addition to the usual subjects. The Madras system is pursued, and the scholars are trained according to the principles of the established church. The age for admission of boys is nine years, and eight if they are orphans, and for girls eight years, all remaining till they are fourteen years of age.

Service is performed every Sunday afternoon, at half-past four, in the chapel of the institution, to which the public are admitted, on making a small donation at the door. One of the elder boys officiates as chaplain, and the whole of the children unite in singing and chanting the responses. About thirty of the boys and girls are then examined by another boy, on religious subjects, after which the service is concluded, and the pupils then proceed to the room below, where they have a substantial supper of bread and cheese, with a can of beer. The order, neatness, and ability of the scholars, reflect great credit on those under whose care they are placed. The charity has been very liberally supported, and many munificent donations have been made by benevolent individuals, some of whom have been educated in the institution.

FEMALE PENITENTIARY.

This institution was established in 1809 by a few benevolent individuals in premises in Edge-hill, and was afterwards removed to the more commodious building in Falkner-street, which can accommodate upwards of sixty individuals. The number of inmates during last year averaged fifty-eight, and the total number admitted since the institution was founded is 1092. It is supported by subscription, and has been successful in restoring to society more than one-third of the unfortunate females who have been received into the establishment. Previous to their being fully received to the benefits of the house, inmates undergo three months' probation.

CATHOLIC MAGDALEN ASYLUM.

The foundation stone of a building for this purpose

in connexion with a church to be also erected, was laid at Edge-hill 17th March, 1841. The expense to be defrayed by subscription.

PERMANENT NIGHT ASYLUM FOR THE HOUSELESS POOR.

This excellent institution, opened 25th December, 1830, is situated in Freemason's-row, Vauxhall-road, and has for its object to provide " an asylum during the rain and the chilling blasts of a winter's night, to the aged, the destitute, and the stranger in distress." This charity which owes its origin to the exertions of the late Egerton Smith, Esq., was the first of the kind established in the kingdom, and has during the first eight years of its existence afforded a comfortable shelter to individuals, occupying 122,736 berths. The actual number of persons admitted during that period was 42,266, shewing that the average stay of each individual was between two and three nights. The inmates sleep on sloping wooden beds, like those in a soldiers' guard-room, ranged against the wall in three tiers, and particular attention is paid to their cleanliness, and to the ventilation of the apartments. Over the entrance is the following inscription :—

ASYLUM FOR THE HOUSELESS POOR.

" Knock and it shall be opened unto you."

Luke, chap. 11, v. 9.

LANCASHIRE REFUGE FOR THE DESTITUTE,

in Roscoe-street, was opened in 1823, and is supported by voluntary contributions. The object of this charity is to afford a home, clothing, and maintenance to such of the female felons, liberated from the county jails, as shew signs of penitence and reformation, and it has been eminently useful in reforming the character and restoring to society many unfortunate females, who would otherwise have lived in a state of utter moral degradation. After a course of good conduct they are either reconciled and restored to their friends, or provided with situations as domestic servants.

LADIES' CHARITY.

This charity was established in 1795 for affording assistance and relief to poor but reputable married women, in child-bed, at their own houses, and providing them with the comforts which their situations require. It is conducted by a committee of ladies of the highest respectability, and a ball is annually held at the Town-hall, the proceeds of which are devoted to the objects of this charity. The number of cases relieved during 1841 was 1757, and the total number since the commencement exceeds 58,000.

DISTRICT PROVIDENT SOCIETY,

instituted in 1831, has for its objects " the encouragement of industry and frugality; the suppression of mendicity and imposture; and the occasional relief of sickness and unavoidable misfortune." The poor are encouraged to make small deposits, returnable with interest when required, and these in 1840-41 amounted to £12,818, received from 6,329 depositors. The number of families relieved by the charity during the same year, was 14,506, at a cost of £1,230. The total deposits with the society since its commencement have been £117,434. Office, Queen's-square.

STRANGERS' FRIEND SOCIETY,

Office in Benn's garden. This society originated with the Wesleyan Methodists in 1795, and has for its object the relief of poor strangers who have no claims for support on the parish of Liverpool. It is maintained by private subscription, and annually affords assistance to upwards of 16,000 individuals.

LIVERPOOL CHARITABLE SOCIETY

was established in 1823, and conducted on a plan similar to the above, chiefly by members of the established church.

SOCIETY FOR BETTERING THE CONDITION OF THE POOR.

The business of this Society, instituted in 1809, is carried on at the Saving's Bank, and is conducted on the principal that the best relief the poor can receive is that which comes from themselves. This is attained by the organization of Friendly Societies and Sick Clubs, to which small monthly contributions are made. With this society originated the

SOUP KITCHENS,

which are now supported by a distinct fund. These establishments are three in number, and their utility is apparent from the amount of wholesome food provided for the poor during periods of general distress. From 22nd December, 1841, to 7th February, 1842, were distributed,—at the Pickup-street Kitchen, 88,941 quarts. Flint-street Kitchen, 66,397 quarts. Gill-street, Kitchen, 59,301 quarts.—Total 214,639 quarts.

WELSH CHARITABLE SOCIETY,

was established in 1804, for the purpose of educating and clothing the children of Welsh parents in Liver-pool. The society supports large schools in Russell-street, which are attended by between 200 and 300 children, who pay one penny per week, and are taught the usual branches of plain education. They are conducted on the principles of the established church.

LIVERPOOL FEMALE ORPHAN SOCIETY.

The object of this institution, established 24th Aug. 1840, is to " relieve poor female orphans, belonging to Liverpool, deprived of both parents, exposed to the risk of want, the certainty of temptation, and the too frequent consequence of vice and misery; ' to bring them up in the principles of the established church, and qualify them for domestic service. The institution, which will accommodate from forty to fifty children, is at present situated in Upper Stan-hope-street; but it is contemplated to erect a more commodious building in Myrtle-street, near the new Haymarket, as soon as the funds of the institution are sufficient for the purpose. The age of admission is from eight to eleven, and the number of inmates in the establishment, on 28th February, 1842, was forty-two.

THE CATHOLIC ORPHAN HOUSE

is an institution of a similar nature in Mount Pleasant, established in 1819, in which about eighty girls are supported, who are admitted between the ages of six and eleven years.

H

CONVENT OF THE SISTERS OF MERCY.

A building for this purpose has been recently commenced in Mount Vernon-street, Edge-hill, the interior of which is to be on the plan of a similar establishment at Birmingham. The structure will be of the old ecclesiastical character, and will contain a chapel, cloisters, oratory, cemetery, sacristy, refectory, noviciate parlour, community room, work room, school room, twenty cells, a dining room for poor children, for whom there are also a dormitory and play room, and kitchen with other offices. To be erected by subscription, and from part of the funds left for charitable purposes by the late C. R. Blundell, Esq., of Ince.

THE CHARITABLE INSTITUTION HOUSE,

in Slater-street, is an institution peculiar to Liverpool, and was erected in 1819, at the joint expense of John Gladstone, James Cropper, and Samuel Hope, Esqrs., as a place of meeting for the committees of the charitable institutions of the town, who are accommodated without charge, on application to the trustees. A record office is attached to the establishment for the reports of all charitable institutions, and the lower part of the building is used as a depository for the Bible Society.

MARINE HUMANE SOCIETY,

instituted in 1823, for the laudable purpose of inducing seamen and others, by rewards and otherwise, to exert themselves in cases of shipwreck, danger, &c. for the preservation of life.

THE LIVERPOOL SHIPWRECK AND HUMANE SOCIETY.

is of a nature similar to the foregoing, and originated after the memorable hurricane which occurred in January, 1839. The objects of the society are, " the preservation of life from shipwreck,—providing relief for the immediate necessities of the unfortunate sufferers wrecked on the shores contiguous to the port of Liverpool, and the reward of persons instrumental in rescuing life from shipwreck." During the first two years of its existence, the society distributed £363 as rewards for saving life, and £113 as relief to sufferers from shipwreck.

SEAMENS' FRIEND SOCIETY, OR BETHEL UNION

was established for the purpose of improving the religious and moral condition of the seamen of the port, by procuring a suitable place of worship, establishing Day and Sunday Schools, circulating the scriptures and useful tracts, providing respectable lodging-houses for seamen, and encouraging among them habits of economy and frugality. The society has several meeting-rooms and libraries in the neighbourhood of the docks, and the Floating Chapel in King's Dock, is under their direction. The Bethel Union is chiefly supported by Dissenters.

MARINERS' CHURCH SOCIETY,

instituted in 1826, " for promoting the religious instruction of seamen, agreeably to the constitution of the established church." The Mariners' Church, in George's Dock, is under the management of this society, who have also recently opened a Mariners' Reading-room, at the south end of the dock. A

Sunday School is also supported by their funds, at present attended by about eighty children. Since its commencement, upwards of 14,000 tracts have been distributed by the society.

THE TOWN MISSION,

formerly called the Christian Instruction Society, was established in 1831, and has for its object the promotion of the religious improvement of the poor, by the employment of agents who visit them at their own houses, read the scriptures, converse on religious subjects, and endeavour to induce them to attend places of worship. Their efforts have been crowned with the happiest success. During 1841, 64,565 visits have been paid by the agents, who have held 3,152 meetings for prayer and expounding the scriptures, and have circulated 1,646 testaments, 1,715 religious books, and 68,000 tracts.

LIVERPOOL AUXILIARY OF THE BRITISH AND FOREIGN BIBLE SOCIETY

was instituted in 1811, has been well supported by persons of all denominations, and has provided thousands, who would otherwise have been without the blessing, with copies of the scriptures.

A LADIES' BRANCH SOCIETY

was formed in 1817, which has been carried on with a degree of zeal and energy, surpassing the most sanguine expectations of the founders. The bible depository is in Slater-street.

LIVERPOOL BRANCH OF THE NAVAL & MILITARY BIBLE SOCIETY.

established in November, 1831. An agent is employed by the society to visit outward-bound vessels, and supply the seamen with copies of the Bible at reduced rates. During the year ending May, 1840, 961 copies were thus distributed.

A LADIES' AUXILIARY

of the above society was formed in October, 1839.

LIVERPOOL CHRISTIAN KNOWLEDGE SOCIETY

is a district committee of the parent society, established 1815, which has a depository at 93, Bold-street, for the sale of bibles and other religious publications.

LIVERPOOL RELIGIOUS TRACT SOCIETY

has a depository at 50, Lord-street.

SUNDAY SCHOOL UNION.

Depository, 74, South Castle-street. This society has for its object the encouragement of the formation of Sunday Schools, and the elevation of the character of the teachers. A course of lectures is annually delivered to the teachers of the schools in the union, by ministers of various denominations.

In addition to the above charitable, benevolent, and religious societies, there are numerous others, which, though of minor importance, would have been here successively noticed, had the limits of the work allowed it.

EDUCATIONAL INSTITUTIONS.

Besides the Royal, Collegiate, and Mechanics' Institutions, which from their comprehensive nature, are classed with the Literary Institutions, Liverpool possesses many excellent schools adapted to the wants of the poorer classes.

THE CORPORATION SCHOOLS

are two in number, and from their respective localities, are denominated the North and South Schools; the former situated in Limekiln-lane, and the latter in Park-lane. They arose out of the Free Grammar School which was given up in 1803, and although its re-establishment was frequently discussed in council, no measure was adopted till 1825, when the present schools were erected, at an expense of £12,000. They were opened in 1827. The course of instruction consists of reading, writing, arithmetic, geography, &c., but the religious part of the education is a subject of constant dispute between the parties forming the town council. Connected with each school is a library. The number of children at present receiving education is—

N. School, 223 boys, 156 girls, 157 infants .. Total 545
S. School, 197 „ 126 „ 170 „ .. 493

Total 1038

THE CHURCH OF ENGLAND FREE SCHOOLS

are two in number, and were opened in 1837, in opposition to the Corporation Schools. The children educated in them receive the usual branches of education, with religious instruction in accordance with the principles of the Church of England. The North School is in Bond-street, and the South School is situated in Cornwallis-street, each of them having a boys', girls', and infants' school. Besides these two there are Free Schools connected with almost every Established Church in the town, and as they are all conducted on similar principles, it is unnecessary to enter into detail respecting them.

CHARITY SCHOOLS.

Hunter-street Charity School was established in 1793, by the late Stephen Waterworth, Esq., and endowed by bequest with the sum of £4000 from the late Mrs. Frances Waterworth, his sister, in 1800. The children are taught gratuitously on the National School system, and in conformity with the tenets of the Church of England.

Edge Hill Girls' Charity School was endowed by bequest of the late Miss Mason, in 1813. There are 40 girls on the books, who receive a useful education, and are partly clothed by the funds of the endowment.

Caledonian Charity School, erected in 1812 by subscription, for the education of children of Scottish parentage. The education is gratuitous, and the children are required to attend regularly some Sunday School.

Copperas Hill Charity School, erected by subscription among the Roman Catholics in 1806, and supported by subscription and donations. The system of instruction pursued is a modification of that of Dr. Bell.

Mr. Croppers' Orphan House, Toxteth Park, estab. lished in 1832, for boarding, clothing and educating indigent female orphans of all denominations.

Manesty-lane Charity School, is connected with Paradise-street Chapel, and was established by the late Mrs. Clough.

St. Patrick's Charity School, Toxteth Park, was established in 1807, by the Benevolent Society of St. Patrick, to provide instruction for the children of the indigent Irish of all denominations.

Hotham-street Day and Infant Schools are supported by members of the Society of Friends. The day schools were opened in 1819, and the Infant school was added in 1824. Connected with the Infant school is a soup establishment, at which from sixty to seventy children dine daily.

St. James' and St. Philip's Charity Schools, in St. James' Road, was originally established by the late Moses Benson, Esq., in 1802, who endowed the school with £1000, and by the congregation of St. James' Church. In 1825 the schools of the congregation of St. Philip's were united with those of St. James'.

National School, Edge-hill, was established in 1824 by voluntary contributions. Connected with the school is a library and a clothing society.

Girls' Charity School, Windsor, established by Miss Colquitt, in 1832, and supported by subscription.

Harrington Charity School was established in 1807, and supported by subscriptions and donations, aided by the payment of 1d. per week from each scholar.

Mr. Cropper's Charity School, Toxteth Park, was

established in 1830, and is principally supported by J. Cropper, Esq. There is a library, and a clothing society connected with the school.

Leeds-street Charity Day and Infant Schools, were established in 1815, in connexion with Leeds-street Wesleyan Chapel, and is supported by subscription.

Jordan-street Charity Day and Infant Schools. The former was opened in 1819 and the latter in 1821, and are supported by subscriptions chiefly among the Wesleyans.

In addition to the above there are charity schools connected with nearly all the places of worship in the town, which it is unnecessary to particularize, as they are chiefly supported by voluntary contributions from the members of the respective congregations to which they belong, and are conducted in a similar manner.

The state of Education generally, may be gathered from the following statement, founded on a " Report on the State of Education in the borough of Liverpool," compiled by the Manchester Statistical Society, in 1836, and read at the meeting of the British Association, at Bristol.

Of the total population of Liverpool it appears that $6\frac{1}{2}$ per cent. attend Sunday Schools; $1\frac{1}{2}$ per cent. receive Sunday School instruction *only ;* $12\frac{1}{2}$ per cent. attend Day Schools; $\frac{1}{4}$ per cent. attend Evening Schools; and $14\frac{1}{2}$ per cent. of the entire population are receiving instruction from all kinds of schools. This average must now be considerably greater, as since the period that the tables were compiled, numerous other educational establishments of all descriptions have sprung into existence.

PLACES OF WORSHIP.

The number of these erections is very considerable, and the style of architecture and internal arrangements of many, render them objects of interest.

ESTABLISHED CHURCH.

Till the year 1699, the town of Liverpool was merely a chapelry of the parish of Walton, and St. Nicholas, or the Old Church, was at that time the only ecclesiastical building in the town. So early as the year 1361, the Bishop of Lichfield, in whose diocese Liverpool then was, granted license to bury in the cemetery, attached to the chapel, which was probably erected about the period of the conquest. In 1565, the chapel was endowed by Queen Elizabeth, with the annual sum of £4 17s. 5d., for the support of the minister. The earliest parish records in Liverpool, are of the date of 1681, although there is in the Chester register office, a Liverpool register, dated 1624, from which it appears, that during that year, there were 21 burials, 4 marriages, and 35 christenings.

ST. NICHOLAS' CHURCH.

St. Nicholas', or the Old Church, is at the bottom of Chapel-street, and the present structure was erected in 1774, under the direction of Joseph Brooks, Esq., on the site of the former building. The old spire was, however, at that period left standing, and till 1810 was the only part of the Old Church remaining. Its entire removal was occasioned by its falling, on Sunday, the 11th February, that year, as the congregation were assembling for divine service. While the second peal was ringing, the whole of the spire, and the north and east sides of the upper part of the tower fell into the body of the church, burying beneath the ruins twenty-eight individuals, seventeen of whom were girls of the Moorfields School, at that moment proceeding up the aisle. This melancholy accident was attributed to the gradual decay of the arches supporting the spire, by the action of the elements, and the vibrations caused by the frequent ringing of the bells. The present handsome steeple was built in 1815, from plans by Mr. Harrison, of Chester, and consists of a tower of the Gothic style of architecture, surmounted by a beautifully designed open lantern, of a light and elegant form. The height from the base to the summit is 180 feet, 120 feet of which is the elevation of the tower, and it is provided with a peal of twelve bells. With the old spire were destroyed some of the few fine specimens of antiquity, of which Liverpool formerly boasted.

An image of St. Nicholas, the tutelar saint of the mariner, formerly stood in the church yard, at whose shrine sailors presented their offerings and vows. The church is 102 feet long and 70 feet wide, is well lighted by six windows on each side, has a gallery supported by short stone pillars, and has seat-room for 1322 persons. In the interior are several monuments, some of which are of considerable antiquity. One dated 1716, is in memory of William Clayton, Esq., who represented the borough in six different parliaments. Another marks the burial place of

Bryan Blundell, Esq., alderman, and one of the
founders of the Blue Coat Hospital. A third tablet
appears in memory of William Naylor Wright, formerly a captain, and once mayor of the town, erected
by an unknown individual, whose life he saved. An
elegant monument by Gibson, at one side of the
communion table, serves as a memorial of Mrs. Earle,
whose " innate goodness endeared her to her family
and connexions." The rectors of the parish are the
Rev. Jonathan Brooks, and the Rev. Augustus
Campbell.

ST. PETER'S CHURCH

situated in Church-street, is next in point of antiquity, and is supposed to be the first parish church
erected in Lancashire after the Reformation. It was
built by assessment in 1700, and was consecrated in
1704. The exterior is plain, of dark stone, and at
the west end is a tower 108 feet high, the upper part
of which is octangular, each angle being surmounted
by a pinnacle in the shape of a candlestick. The
clock is illuminated with gas, and there is in the
tower a peal of ten bells. Each of the four portals,
the designs of which were obtained from London, is of
a different style of architecture. The interior of the
church is plain, and has the appearance of considerable antiquity; the galleries being supported on oak
pedestals, richly carved, on each of which rests a
slender column supporting the roof. Behind the
altar is a piece of elaborate carving in brown oak;
and over it, in the altar window, a representation of
St. Peter. At the west end is an upper gallery, the
centre of which is occupied by the organ, and the

side parts are appropriated to the children of the Blue Coat Hospital. The principal monuments are, one at the south side of the church, in memory of Foster Cunliffe, Esq., who died in 1758; and another at the east end of the church, marked by costliness rather than beauty, in memory of William Lawley, Esq. The church is 86 feet 9 inches long, and 67 feet 2 inches wide, and will accommodate 1,287 persons.

ST. GEORGE'S CHURCH

at the top of Lord-street, was originally built in 1732, but, with the exception of the interior framework, was entirely rebuilt under the direction of Mr. Foster, in 1821. The walls of the building, (which is lighted by twelve segment-headed windows,) are rusticated and finished by a rich Doric entablature and em-panelled parapet. The spire is at the west end of the church, and the lower part, to correspond with the building itself, is rusticated and crowned by a similar entablature. From this base, which is 30 feet square, rises a square pedestal supporting an octagonal stylobate with Ionic columns $22\frac{1}{2}$ feet high, and $2\frac{1}{2}$ feet in diameter, at each angle. Between these columns are the belfry-windows and clock-dials. Eight Corinthian columns 21 feet high, of which the next tier consists, disposed round the centre part of the steeple, (which is here circular,) support a balustrade forming a passage round the steeple at the point whence the spire springs. The spire is octangular, and its total height 214 feet.

The interior of the church is very handsomely fitted up, and contains 817 sittings. In the chancel window is a beautiful painting of the crucifixion, by

Hilton. Below the church are vaults for sepulture, but there is no church-yard attached. The incumbents of this church succeed to the parish churches on the demise of the rectors.

ST. THOMAS'S CHURCH,

situated near the bottom of Park-lane, was consecrated in 1750. The body of the church is rusticated, and the interior is lighted by two rows of windows, between which are Ionic pilasters. On these rest an entablature and empanelled parapet, with vases above each pilaster. The spire was originally 240 feet high, but 20 feet of it was blown down on the 15th March, 1797, which was afterwards rebuilt. In 1822, considerable danger was apprehended from its having become insecure and vibrating during violent gales. It was accordingly surveyed, and ordered to be taken down. A short but handsome tower, with a square rustic basement now occupies its place. From this basement, a little above the cornice, the tower becomes octagonal, and has eight large belfry windows with circular heads and ornaments, and it is finished by a dome and cross. The interior of the church is plain, and will accommodate 1188 persons. The chancel is of a circular form, richly panelled and ornamented by fluted Corinthian pilasters. The galleries rest on eight pedestals, from which proceed Corinthian columns, finished by an entablature which supports the roof. At the west end is an upper gallery for the organ, &c.

ST. PAUL'S CHURCH

is situated in St. Paul's Square, and was consecrated

in 1769. The building has a rustic basement, and is of a soft stone, which in many places has suffered decay from the action of the elements. On the west side is a bold Ionic portico, consisting of a pediment projecting considerably, and supported on four columns, approached by a broad flight of steps. There are similar porticoes of three-quarter columns, on the north and south sides. The sides of the church are finished by a range of balustrades and plain vases. A handsome dome on an octangular base, crowned by a ball and cross, gives effect to the structure. This dome is supported internally by eight stone Ionic columns, reaching to the roof, which, from their heaviness, detract considerably from the appearance of the interior. The gallery, which is octangular, is placed behind these columns, and the altar is in an oval niche. This church will accommodate 1658 persons. In addition to the usual services, there is service in the Welsh language on Sunday evenings.

ST. ANNE'S CHURCH

in Great Richmond-street, was erected in 1772, at the expense of two private gentlemen, and will accommodate 864 persons. The building is of brick, stuccoed, of a plain appearance, and the principal entrance is at the south end, facing St. Anne-street. At the north end is a brick tower, the four angles of which are finished by small pinnacles. It is neatly fitted up, the gallery being supported on cast-iron pillars, said to have been the first of the kind used.

ST. JOHN'S CHURCH

in St. John's-lane, Haymarket, has seat-room for

1094, and was built in 1784, of yellow free-stone. The north and south fronts are each lighted by ten windows, with pointed arches, five in each story, between which are niched buttresses on each of which rests a pedestal and pinnacle. The tower is 123 feet high, rectangular, and finished at the top, with a number of small pyramids. The altar, over which is the organ gallery, is in a square recess at the east end. The lower part of the Church is free to the poor.

TRINITY CHURCH

in St. Anne street will accommodate 1188 persons. It was erected by a number of private individuals, and consecrated in 1792. At the west end of the Church, which is of stone, with a rusticated basement, is a square tower, which, towards the top, becomes ortagonal, with vases on each angle. It is lighted by two tiers of windows on each side; and finished by an attic demi-balustrade.

ST. STEPHEN'S CHURCH

is a small cemented building in Byrom-street, with seats for 497 persons. It was licensed as a Protestant dissenters' meeting-house of the Baptist denomination in 1722, and afterwards consecrated as a Church.

ST. MATTHEW'S CHURCH

is situated in Key-street, and accommodates 526 individuals. It was first licensed as a Protestant dissenters' meeting-house in 1707, and subsequently consecrated.

CHRIST CHURCH

is a handsome brick building in Hunter-street, ornamented with stone, capable of seating 2805 persons, erected at the sole expense of the late John Houghton, Esq., in 1797, and consecrated in 1800. On the north end of the building is a light cupola, in which is a commodious room with four large windows, commanding an extensive prospect of the town and neighbourhood. The top is surrounded by a circular gallery which may be ascended from this apartment. The interior of the church is handsome and commodions, with a light and airy appearance. It has a lower and upper gallery on three sides, besides an organ gallery on the south side over the altar. Four hundred of the sittings are free, and an endowment is provided for the minister, organist, clerk, and sexton, from the rents of several of the pews. The cost of erection of this church was about £15,000.

ST. JAMES' CHURCH,

in Upper Parliament-street, was erected by private proprietors in 1774. It is a plain brick building, with two tiers of circular-headed windows, and a square tower at the west end. The interior has recently undergone considerable improvement and decoration.

ALL SAINTS' CHURCH,

in Grosvenor-street, is a plain building, originally a tennis-court, which will hold nearly 2000 persons. It was built in 1798, and opened by license from the Bishop of the diocese in 1834.

ST. MARK'S CHURCH,

in Upper Duke-street, is a large brick building which had formerly a tower, the upper part of which has been removed. It was erected by subscription, licensed in 1803, and consecrated in 1815, having cost £10,000. It accommodates 1626 individuals, and has 300 free seats. The painting of the church window representing the "Ascension," is worthy of notice. The cost of this window was £700.

ST. MARY'S CHURCH,

Edgehill, is a plain but neat brick edifice, with a square tower at the west end, erected in 1813, by the late Thomas Mason, Esq. The interior is comfortable and convenient.

ST. GEORGE'S CHURCH, (EVERTON.)

This church, which was erected in 1814, on the site of the old beacon, is a handsome Gothic building of red sandstone. It is lighted by seven windows on each side, between each of which is an abutment terminating in a pinnacle. The whole of the window-frames, pillars, arches, groins, roof, &c. are of cast iron, giving the interior a light and tasteful appearance. In the church is a beautifully painted window, and at the other end of the church is a Gothic tower, 96 feet high, each angle of which is finished by a pinnacle.

ST. ANDREW'S CHURCH

in Renshaw-street, was built in 1815, at the sole expense of John Gladstone, Esq., at a cost of £14,000. It will accommodate 1650 persons, and has 400 free seats. The exterior is stuccoed, with stone ornaments, and it has a light turret steeple, surmounted by a dome and cross resting on eight columns.

ST. PHILIPS' CHURCH,

in Hardman-street, was built at an expense of £12,000, by Mr. John Cragg, and consecrated in 1816. It will accommodate 1000 individuals, and has 150 free seats. It is built of brick, plastered, in the Gothic style, and the frame work both internally and externally is of cast iron.

ST. MARY'S CHAPEL; OR, CHURCH OF THE SCHOOL FOR THE BLIND.

This beautiful building, situated in Hotham-street, (formerly called Duncan-street,) was erected by John Foster, Esq., who, after a long residence in Greece, was desirous of building in his native town, a church, the architecture of which should be a copy of some of the most perfect models of Grecian art, and at an outlay consistent with the resources of the charity. The foundation stone was laid on the 6th October, 1818, by the bishop of the diocese, and the church was opened by the same prelate on the 6th October of the following year. The architecture of the building is a peculiar species of the Doric order, and the portico of the west end is an exact copy of that of the temple of Jupiter Panhellenius, in the island of Egina. The church is capable of accommodating 1000 individuals, and one-half of the seats are appropriated for the use of strangers. With the school for the blind this building communicates by a subterraneous passage, through which the pupils enter

the church. Over the altar is a stained glass painting of the "Ascension," executed by Mr. Lyon, of this
town. Nearly behind the reading desk is an appropriate painting, by James Hilton, Esq., who obtained
for it the prize from the British Institution, the subject of which is "Christ restoring the blind to sight."
The picture was presented to the institution by
Henry Wilson, Esq. Over the vestry door, on the
north side, is a painting, by Haydon, purchased by
the institution, illustrative of the passage " Suffer
little children to come unto me." Within the church is
also a monument erected in memory of the late Pudsey Dawson, Esq., one of the founders of the charity.
A principal object in the erection of this elegant
church was to make it serve as an auxiliary for
supporting the benevolent institution with which it
is connected, on the plan of the Magdalen and
Foundling Hospitals of the Metropolis. Every
stranger, therefore, who attends divine service is
expected to contribute a small amount in silver
towards the charity; plates for receiving contributions being held at the door. The amount received
in this manner during 1840 was £756 2s. 8d. The
vocal part of the service is conducted by the blind
pupils, who are assisted by a powerful organ, built
by Gray, of London.

ST. MICHAEL'S CHURCH

is situated in Upper Pitt-street. The first stone was
laid on 24th June, 1816, and the parish expended
£35,000 on its erection, but it being still unfinished,
the corporation, in 1823 arranged for its completion,
which cost them £10,267. The church will accom-

modate 1306 persons, and has 520 free seats. It is
of the Corinthian order, having on the west side a
portico 61 feet 7 inches in length, consisting of ten
Corinthian columns 3 feet 2 inches in diameter, and
31 feet 8 inches high; the capitals of which are copied
from the remains of the temple of Jupiter Stator at
Rome, supporting an entablature, which is carried
round the building. The windows are circular-
headed, and divided into two by a panel. The pedestal, on which the steeple rests, is at the west end, and
supports sixteen Ionic columns 22 feet 6 inches high,
between which, are the belfry windows, with an entablature and balustrade. Above this is a pedestal carrying eight Corinthian columns and pilasters, forming
four projecting portals, and from this order sprang
an octangular spire, the total height of which was
201 feet from the ground. This part was struck by
lightning on the 24th August, 1841, and was so much
shattered as to require to be taken down.

ST. DAVID'S CHURCH,

near the bottom of Brownlow-hill, is a plain building,
98 feet by 52 feet, with a stone front, fitted up with
galleries on three sides, capable of accommodating
1200 persons, and having 300 free seats. It was
erected in 1827. Divine service is performed in
Welsh at nine and three o'clock, and in English at
eleven and half-past six o'clock every Sunday.

ST. MARTIN'S IN THE FIELDS.

This church is situated in Oxford-street (north) and
was erected by government in 1828, at an expense of
£20,000, from the designs of Mr. Foster, on land

given by the late Edward Houghton, Esq. The modern Gothic style of architecture is that adopted in the building, and at the west end is a tower, with octagonal turrets at the angles finished by pinnacles. From this tower rises an octangular spire crowned by a moulded cap and ornamental finial, the total height of which is 198 feet. It was shattered by lightning during the same storm by which St. Michael's spire was injured, but has been recently repaired. The Church, which is 97 feet by 69 feet, will hold 2000 persons, and has 1300 free seats. It is lighted by six lofty windows on each side, with pointed heads, and moulded traceries, and between each of which is a projecting buttress finished with a canopy and pinnacle. The interior is handsomely arranged; the gallery and a portion of the roof rest on iron pillars, from the top of which, spring 12 moulded arches, with a wall dividing the nave from the aisle. The parish authorities have purchased 10,000 square yards of land adjoining the church as a public cemetery, and surrounded it by a substantial stone wall.

ST. AUGUSTINE'S CHURCH,

situated on an eminence, in Shaw-street, Everton, was erected in 1830, at an expense of £5,000, on land given for the purpose by Thomas Shaw, Esq. The architect was Mr. John Broadbent, and the general design is Grecian. The details of the body of the church and the lower part of the tower are copied from the Choragic monument of Thrasyllus at Athens. The upper part of the tower consists of fluted columns, disposed round an octagonal centre, supporting an ogee dome, and is copied from the

St. LUKE'S CHURCH.

Published By Benj. Smith, South Castle Street Liverpool.

Ionic Temple on the Illissus. The pillars in the interior, supporting a gallery on three sides of the building, are continued to the roof, which is neatly ornamented. The church will seat 1500 persons, and has 250 free sittings.

ST. BRIDE'S CHURCH.

This church which is situated in Percy-street, Upper Parliament-street, was erected under the superintendence of Mr. Samuel Rowland, architect. It is capable of accommodating 1400 persons, 400 sittings being set apart for the poor, and was consecrated 29th December, 1830. At the west end is a bold portico of six Ionic columns, 29 feet 4 inches high, supporting an entablature and pediment. Six Græco-Egyptian windows on each side afford light to the interior, which is commodious and elegant. The gallery is supported on cast-iron pillars, and the ceiling is panelled.

ST. LUKE'S CHURCH,

at the corner of Berry-street and Leigh-street, forms a prominent object from the whole length of Bold-street. The foundation stone was laid in April, 1811, but owing to a variety of unavoidable circumstances it was not opened till 1831. The sum of £44,110 was expended by the corporation on its erection, from the design of John Foster, Esq. It is a beautiful specimen of the Gothic style of the fourteenth century, constructed entirely of white stone; and a considerable amount of ornament, both internally and externally, has been successfully introduced. The tower, which is at the west end, is 137 feet high, and has octagonal turrets at the angles, perforated by pointed loop-holes, with rich labels, and finished with embrasures. The beautiful proportions of the lofty windows add greatly to the appearance of the tower. The sides of the building are supported by buttresses, finished with pinnacles, and the windows between them are of three compartments, with tracery heads. The cornice is surmounted by moulded embrasures. The east window in the chancel has a pleasing appearance, and harmonises well with the richness of the panelling, the octagonal-headed turrets, and the open quatrefoil blocking at this end of the building. The interior is finished in a manner corresponding with the exterior of the edifice. There are no side galleries, and only a small one at the west end for the organ and choir. The ceiling is richly panelled in the centre, and groined at the sides, the intersections being filled up with foliage, drops, and open bosses. The ceiling of the chancel is also groined and divided from the body of the church by a bold arch. This church will accommodate about 2,000 persons in the area, including the chancel. The windows are ornamented with stained glass, and contain the armorial bearings of each member of the old corporation. The west entrances are approached by a broad flight of stone steps, and the church-yard is enclosed by handsome iron railings, with lofty pinnacled piers.

ST. JUDE'S CHURCH,

Low-hill. This church was erected by subscription, from designs by Messrs. Rickman and Hutchinson, of Birmingham, at an expense of little more than £6,000, and consecrated in 1831. It is built of brick, and cemented, with stone ornaments and facings, and the style of architecture is the Gothic of the thirteenth century. It has four large turrets with lofty pinnacles, and all the angles of the building are finished by smaller pinnacles. The principal entrance is a platform, approached by a flight of steps. The side windows are of the lancet form, having bold buttresses between them. At the east end is a large and richly filled circular window over the altar. The interior will accommodate 1,500 person, and it has 500 free seats ; it is handsomely arranged and decorated, and has galleries on three sides. The organ, the form of which harmonizes with the architecture of the church is placed over the altar. Below the church are commodious schools for the accommodation of about 400 children.

ST. CATHARINE'S CHURCH

forms the centre part of the east side of Abercromby-square. It was erected by subscription in 1831, by John Foster, Esq., at an expense of £10,000, and will accommodate 1,000 persons. The front has a portico of six Ionic columns, supporting an entablature with dentilled cornice, and a suitable pediment. The only light admitted into the interior, with the exception of that from the altar window, is by the cupola in the roof; this arrangement being necessary from the situation of the building. The galleries rest on square piers, which support Corinthian columns extending to the roof, and the ceiling is richly panelled.

ST. JOHN THE BAPTIST'S CHURCH,

situated in Park-road, is a beautiful specimen of the old English style of ecclesiastical architecture, and was erected in 1832. Its shape is cruciform, and it is built of red stone, finished on all the sides with a battlement, and pinnacles at the angles. The side aisles and angles of the building are supported by buttresses, which are also terminated by pinnacles with crockets and finials. The entrances at the north, south, and west ends, are plain, having above the door way circular windows, lighting the staircases within, and small niches on each side. The upper part of the building is lighted by numerous small lancet windows near the roof, but the lower ones are large and circular-headed. The steeple is at the west end, and consists of a square tower, with buttresses at the angles, terminating in pinnacles, with large belfry windows, above which are the clock faces and a battlement. From this springs a plain octagonal spire. The interior has a striking appearance, the lofty roof, in which the rafters are shewn, being supported on pointed arches, the piers of which are clustered. The aisles are separated from the nave by smaller stone arches, and the galleries are placed on cast iron pillars, at the extremities of the nave and transepts. The chancel window has three lancets, and before it is placed the pulpit, which is extremely light.

ST. MATTHIAS' CHURCH

is situated in Love-lane, Great Howard-street, and will accommodate 1,050 persons, having 500 free seats. It was opened in July, 1834, having been erected at an expense of £3,100, on land presented by the corporation. Under the church are two school-rooms, which will accommodate 500 scholars. The exterior is of brick, with a portico in front, supported by two massive Ionic columns.

ST. SIMON'S CHURCH

in Gloucester-street, was originally a Scotch Seces-sion chapel, and afterwards occupied by the Inde-pendents, from whom it was purchased. It was con-secrated in 1841, the congregation of the Hebrew church having removed from their former place of worship in Sir Thomas'-buildings.

ST. SAVIOUR'S CHURCH

is situated near Falkner-square, and was erected by subscription in 1839, from the design of Mr. Murray, of Dublin. It is of brick plastered, with a tower at the east end, the upper part of which is octagonal, com-posed of eight arches of brick-work, with four pedi-ments, and surmounted by a vase. The design of the front and tower was by Mr. Welch of this town, and not that originally intended. The interior is lighted by two tiers of windows, and the gallery is supported by neat cast iron pillars. The pulpit and desks are of massive oak and stand in the centre aisle.

ST. BARTHOLOMEW'S CHURCH

situated in Naylor-street, was opened on 6th Febru-ary, 1841, being the first erected by the Liverpool Church Building Society. It will accommodate from 1300 to 1400 persons, and half of the sittings are free. The architect was Mr. Clayton, of Ormskirk, and the expense of erection was £6000, inclusive of £2000, the price of the land. It is built of brick, of the Gothic style, with a neat spire from one of the angles; and its internal as well as external appearance impresses the spectator with the idea of an old ecclesiastical structure.

ST. BARNABAS' CHURCH

is situated at the bottom of Parliament-street, and was consecrated in June, 1841. It is built of red stone, and the workmanship is of a very superior description. It will accommodate about 1560 persons, and the interior is elegantly fitted up, with a due regard to convenience. The windows are of the lancet form, and between each of them, and at the angles are projecting buttresses, which are terminated by slender pinnacles. The steeple, which is 135 feet high, is at the south end, and the lower part is square, finished with pinnacles, cornice, &c., having a clock face and belfry windows above the door. From this tower, springs a slender spire with small lancet loop-holes. The principal entrance is at the south end under the steeple.

ST. SILAS' CHURCH

in Pembroke-place, was erected in 1841 by subscriptions and donations, chiefly raised by the congregation of St. Jude's Church. The front is of red stone, and the remainder of the building is of brick. The principal entrance is by a platform elevated a little above the level of the street. There is a plain Saxon spire, with a square base, projecting from the church. The building is well lighted by long lancet windows on each side. The interior is neatly arranged, with galleries on three sides, and upper galleries above the stair-case for the Sunday scholars. The roof is supported by rafters in the old Gothic style, which greatly improve its appearance. The chancel, which is in a square recess, is separated from the body of the church by a pointed arch, and is lighted by a small lancet window on each side.

ST. CLEMENT'S CHURCH,

Upper Stanhope-street, Windsor, is built of red sandstone, in the Saxon style, with a belfry at the east end. The principal entrance is at the north side, and the church is lighted by lancet windows. The appearance of the interior is striking, as it is low in the sides, and has a lofty pointed roof supported by oak rafters. The altar is in a projection at the east end, and there is a gallery carried round three sides of the building. Over the stair-cases are two small galleries for the Sunday school children, separated from the body of the church by arches. The whole of the interior is painted in imitation of black oak, and the design is exceedingly chaste and ornamental. The first stone was laid in May, 1840, and it was consecrated in June, 1841. £1500 of the expense was raised by subscription, and the remainder was defrayed by the Liverpool Church Building Society.

ST. THOMAS' CHURCH.

Warwick-street, near Brunswick Dock, is built of red sandstone, with a tower at the north end, the lower part of which is square, with pinnacles at the angles, and the upper part octagonal, finished with

a battlement and pinnacles, and having four belfry
windows. An inscription on the lower part of the
tower informs us that " *This church was built and endowed in* 1840, *by John Gladstone, Esq., of Fasque,
N. B., a merchant of Liverpool.*" The interior is plain,
with a gallery at the north end, and it will accommodate about 900 individuals. The pulpit and reading desk project on brackets from the wall on each
side of the altar, and enter by a door opening into a
staircase behind. The altar is lighted from the roof,
and the place of the usual chancel window is supplied by pannelling. Prayers are performed here
daily, at nine o'clock in the morning and at seven in
the evening, and on Sundays at three o'clock in the
afternoon, in addition to the usual services. In this
church, as well as in St. Silas', St. Clements, and
nearly all the new churches, there is not the usual
clerk's desk, the congregation being expected to join
in the responses.

ST. JOHN THE EVANGELIST'S CHURCH

is situated in Hope-street, and was opened as a
Church of England on 21st March, 1841, it having
been previously occupied as a place of worship by
a denomination styling themselves " *the* Christian
Society," who on that day, together with their pastor,
joined the established church. It is a plain stuccoed
building.

MARINER'S CHURCH.

This is a commodious place of worship for the use of
seamen, moored at the south end of George's Dock,
It was originally the " Tees," an 18 gun sloop, which

was granted by government for the purpose to which it is now applied. It is fitted up in the usual man. ner of a church, with galleries, &c., and the church of England service is regularly used.

Many of the churches in the suburbs are worthy of notice, some on account of their antiquity, and others for their architectural beauty. They will be pointed out in the Itinerary.

The hours of service and the clergymen of the different churches in Liverpool, are given in the Appendix.

CHURCHES IN CONNEXION WITH THE ESTABLISHED CHURCH OF SCOTLAND.

OLDHAM-STREET.

This is a large brick building without any architec. tural ornament; which was the first erected for the convenience of the Scottish inhabitants of Liverpool.

ST. ANDREW'S CHURCH,

in Rodney-street, was erected from the designs of Mr. Foster, and opened in 1824. It has a stone front with a lofty Ionic portico, very much enriched, sur- mounted by an entablature and balustrade. Over the stair-cases, which are at the angles, are two square turrets, composed of a square tower lighted by four windows, with eight isolated Corinthian columns, supporting an entablature, blocking, &c., and finish- ed by a cupola. The interior is handsomely fitted up with galleries on three sides.

ST. PETER'S CHURCH.

The foundation stone of a handsome building, to be styled St. Peter's Church, was laid a few month's ago, in Scotland-road, near St. Anthony's Chapel, and the building is rapidly progressing.

CATHOLIC CHAPELS.

ST. MARY'S, EDMUND-STREET.

A chapel erected on this site has existed from a very early period. About the year 1745, it was attacked by a mob, and burned to the ground, and soon afterwards the present one was erected. It is of very humble appearance, and though small, (measuring but 66 feet 6 inches, by 43 feet 8 inches,) will accommodate a large congregation in consequence of having two galleries, which extend far into the body, on all except the altar side. It is intended to be replaced by a magnificent chapel in the Gothic or ancient English style, the architect of which will be Welby Pugin, Esq. There are no schools attached to the present chapel, but it is intended to erect large, ones adjoining the new building. The clergy are monks of the order of St. Benedict.

ST. PETER'S, SEEL-STREET,

is a spacious building, (86 feet 4 inches, by 48 feet,) attended by a numerous congregation, and has in connection with it, schools for the education of 600 children, boys, girls, and infants. The clergy are Benedictine monks.

ST. NICHOLAS', COPPERAS-HILL,

is a large and elegant Gothic building, measuring 84
feet 3 inches, by 62 feet 6 inches, in which a beautiful
painted window, designed by W. Pugin, Esq., has re
cently been placed. It was erected by public subscription, and has attached to it schools, in which are
educated, 250 boys, and 230 girls. A convent,
(formerly noticed,) in connexion with this chapel, is
in progress of erection, in Mount Vernon-street.
The clergy are secular.

ST. PATRICK'S, PARK-PLACE, TOXTETH-PARK.

is a spacious brick building, the expense of which
was defrayed by subscription, on condition that the
ground-floor be for ever free to the poor. The front
is ornamented by a well-executed figure of St. Patrick,
presented by James Brancker, Esq., and the entrance
is from Doric porticos, at the north and south sides.
The schools educate about 450 children. The boys'
school is under the care of the religious brothers of
the christian schools. The clergy are secular

ST. ANTHONY'S, IN SCOTLAND-ROAD,

was erected in 1832, in place of a small chapel which
stood at the top of Dryden-street; it is a brick building in the Gothic style, designed by Mr. Broadbent,
and cost in erection about £12,000. Its extreme
length from east to west is 158½ feet, breadth 74 feet
and height 43½ feet. At the west end is a gallery extending 29 feet into the body of the chapel supported
on cast iron pillars. The ceiling is so formed as to
exhibit a nave and side aisles, and is pannelled and
enriched with bosses at the intersections. The cha-

K

pel will accommodate 1700 persons, and has 500 free seats. Attached to the building is a burying ground, and there are also upwards of 700 vaults for single interments, under the body of the chapel. The schools will accommodate about 1200 children. The clergy are secular.

ST. OSWALD'S, OLD SWAN,

is a handsome building in the old ecclesiastical style, the arrangements of which are faithfully revived from ancient authorities. The land on which it is erected was presented by Edward Challinor, Esq., of Oak Hill, and the funds for its erection were contributed chiefly by the late C. R. Blundell, Esq., of Ince. The clergy is secular.

ST. ANNE'S, CHATHAM-PLACE, EDGEHILL.

The first stone was laid on the 17th March, 1841. It is intended to be erected, as a church, in the Gothic style, and adjoining it, will be a convent for Nuns of the order of Sisters of Mercy. A Magdalen Asylum, for unfortunate females, will be erected at Aigburth, in connexion with it. The clergy will be Benedictine monks.

ST. FRANCIS XAVIER'S

is intended to be erected in the prevailing style (Gothic,) in Salisbury-street. The ground is already purchased. The clergy will be Jesuits.

CATHOLIC CHURCH.

THE CHURCH OF THE HOLY APOSTLES

is situated at the corner of Catherine-street, and Duke-street. This church, which has been already upwards of two years in progress, is built of white stone, in the florid Gothic style, with costly workmanship, and it is intended to be cruciform. The choir will be opened for service about the end of the present year, and the nave, tower, &c., will be afterwards added. The length of the entire building from east to west will be 129 feet, and breadth 57 feet; the height of the roof will be 60 feet inside, and the west window will be 30 feet high, richly embellished. A spire will be raised about 180 feet high, and the internal arrangements of the building will be strictly in accordance with old ecclesiastical architecture. The congregation, at present, meet in Pilgrim-street.

ORIGIN OF DISSENTERS IN LIVERPOOL.*

The dissenters in Liverpool are numerous, and highly respectable whether considered as to station, numbers, or character. It is probable that the ejection of the non-conformist ministers, in the reign of Charles II, under the act of uniformity, laid the foundation of the dissenting interest in this town, as it did in many other parts of the kingdom. The Rev. John Fog, of Liverpool, was among the ejected ministers, and the Rev. Joseph Thompson, of Sefton, a member of the University of Oxford, and the Rev. Thomas Crompton, M.A., of Toxteth-park, were also of the number. The original dissenting congregation in Liverpool, was a branch from the ancient chapel of some note in the annals of non-conformity, situated in the adjoining township of Toxteth-park. This

*From " Baines' Lancashire."

place was in the hands of the non-conformists at the time of passing the Bartholomew act, in 1662, and the Rev. Thomas Crompton was the minister. Immediately after the revolution in 1688, a chapel was built in Castle Hey, now called Harrington-street, which, in 1727, was removed to Benn's Gardens.

The original Baptist congregation was a branch of a society at Hill Cliffe, near Warrington, which came to Liverpool about the year 1700. In 1714, they erected a chapel in Everton-road, where their burial ground still remains.

The first Independent congregation was established in 1777, at Newington chapel, Renshaw-street, and was principally formed by seceders from Toxteth-park, and Benn's Gardens chapels.

The Scotch Presbyterians were established in 1793, and the Society of Friends since 1709. Methodism has existed since it became a distinct religious sect; and the establishment of the Roman Catholics is co-eval with the origin of the town itself.

***

INDEPENDENT CHAPELS.

GREAT GEORGE-STREET CHAPEL.

This beautiful edifice was erected from designs by J. Franklin, Esq., on the site of the former spacious chapel, which was destroyed by fire on the 19th February, 1840. It was opened on 21st October, 1841; is built of free-stone, of the description commonly known as "Park-stone," and is 127 feet in length, including the portico, and 66 feet in width. There is pew-accommodation for 1750 persons, be-

JOS. FRANKLIN ESQ.RE ARCH.T

sides the children's galleries. The site is at the junction of Great George-street, and Nelson-street, forming an acute angle; for which the former chapel,
being a parallelogram, was obviously unsuitable.
The present building is placed several yards backwards, thereby giving space for a circular vestibule,
of 25 feet diameter, fronting Great George-street.
The principal elevation consists of a portico of ten
fluted columns of the Corinthian order, after the elegant example of the temple of Jupiter Stator. The
height of the columns, including the plinth, base, and
capital, is 33 feet, the shaft being of *one stone*, a circumstance without precedent in this country. The
entire base of this front is approached by a flight of
steps corresponding in outline with the portico. The
columns are surmounted by an enriched entablature.
The circular part of the portico roof, is formed of
stone, in radiating courses, having moulded ribs and
terminals. Above this, is a continuation of the circular vestibule, the centre of which is enriched with
a continuous perforated quillochi to light the vestibule. Above the cornice is a trussed springer for
the dome, which is pannelled and ribbed, and surmounted by a carved finial. The flanks of the
building are decorated with pilasters, ten on each side,
with continued plinth and base-course, capitals, and
enriched entablature, corresponding with the front
elevation, these sides being terminated with an attic.
Between the pilasters are eighteen circular-headed
windows, with moulded architraves. The entrance
to the ground floor is through corridors leading from
the vestibule by a handsome double staircase, geo-
metrically constructed. There is a gallery round the

vestibule, under which is placed a monument of chaste design, opposite the entrance, in memory of the Rev. Thomas Spencer. The ceiling of the interior is panelled and enriched, with a circular centre part, deeply sunk, under which hangs a massive chandelier, by which the whole of the gallery, and middle portion of the ground floor are lighted for evening service. The pulpit is of elaborate design and executed in Dantzic oak. There is a gallery round the four sides of the building, and behind the pulpit is the organ, one of the largest in the town, built by Mr. Hill, of London. The design is elegant and greatly enriched. The corner towers are composed of Corinthian columns, with gilt pipes between, and the centre tower is three parts of a circle, composed of gilt pipes fifteen feet high, under a richly carved canopy; and the whole instrument, which is 25 feet high, is superbly carved and gilt. The whole of the aisles are covered with Brussels carpet. Below the chapel are two spacious schoolrooms and a lecture-room, to accommodate 450 persons; also, a library, vestry, and other minor apartments. A vestry at the rear of the building presents a front of four Ionic columns, supporting an entablature, the only relics of the former structure.

CRESCENT CHAPEL, EVERTON BROW,

is a handsome stone building with a portico of four fluted Ionic columns, in *antis*, supporting a pediment and cornice, and was opened on 23rd November, 1837. It was built by the congregation formerly worshipping at Bethesda chapel, Hotham-street, which was small and inconvenient. The chapel has accommodation for 1230 adults, and 260 children. Its extreme length is 92 feet, and it is 55 feet wide. The cost of the site and of the building was £9000. Architect, Joseph Franklin, Esq.

NEWINGTON CHAPEL, RENSHAW-STREET,

is a small brick building with a Gothic front. It was the place of the short ministry of the Rev. Thos. Spencer, a young man of extraordinary piety and talent, at the time when a melancholy accident deprived him of life, in 1811, shortly after the commencement of the erection of Great George-street chapel, which was intended for him.

HANOVER CHAPEL

is situated at the corner of Mill-street and Warwick-street, and is a plain brick building, opened for divine service on the 17th January, 1830.

The other Independent Chapels are plain in appearance, and do not require particular notice. They are to be found in the appendix.

BAPTIST CHAPELS.

The handsomest belonging to this denomination is

PEMBROKE CHAPEL,

which was opened 3rd July, 1839, and is situated at the corner of Pembroke-place and Crown-street. The front elevation has a projecting portico of four fluted Ionic columns, supporting a suitable pediment, and the whole of the building is of white sandstone. The interior, which is much admired for its con-

venience and simplicity of arrangement, is lighted by
two tiers of windows. A fine toned organ, the case
of which harmonizes with the architectural arrangement of the building, is placed in a gallery at the east
end, behind the pulpit. The number of sittings
amount to 1050, although 200 more may be added if
necessary, by altering the disposition of the aisles.
The cost of this edifice was about £9000, and the
architect, Joseph Franklin, Esq.

SOHO-STREET CHAPEL

is a neat and commodious building, recently erected
by the congregation formerly worshipping at Cock-
spur-street chapel.

BYROM-STREET CHAPEL

is a commodious building, with seat room for 936
persons. It is the oldest belonging to the Baptist
denomination in Liverpool.

LIME-STREET CHAPEL

is an old brick building, with accommodation for
579 persons. This chapel has been purchased by the
Corporation, being in the line of projected improvements, in consequence of which, it will shortly be
taken down, and a new one built in Hope-street.

SCOTCH SECESSION CHURCH,

situated at the corner of Great Orford-street, and
Mount Pleasant, is a plain and substantial structure
with stone front. The centre slightly recedes, and
the lower part consists of a portico with four Doric

columns, above which are the gallery windows. The interior is well arranged, and instead of the usual pulpit, there is a handsome platform formed by a continuation of the two stairs, supported on a massive pillar. Over this, is a canopy hung with drapery, and behind, it is painted in imitation of a circular recess. The chapel was erected by the congregation, formerly worshipping at Gloucester-street chapel, from the design of Mr. S. Rowlands, at an expense of £6441, and was opened 1st June, 1827. It will accommodate 1200 persons.

WESLEYAN CHAPELS.

MOUNT PLEASANT CHAPEL

is a plain brick building near the bottom of the street, with seat room for 680 persons.

PITT-STREET CHAPEL

is a spacious building, with a gallery of an oval form, surrounding the interior. It has a neat organ of good tone, and the pulpit, which is light, rests on fluted columns. Its dimensions are 74 feet 8 inches, by 63 feet 8 inches, and it holds 1300 individuals.

BRUNSWICK CHAPEL,

in Moss-street, has a handsome stone front, with a portico consisting of Ionic columns. It is of a horse-shoe form, disposed in the form of an amphitheatre, the seats rising as they recede from the pulpit. A small gallery is appropriated to the organ, the choir, and the children. The chapel will seat 1500 persons, and is 335 feet in circumference.

WESLEY CHAPEL,

in Stanhope-street, Toxteth-park, was opened in 1827. It has a stone front, and is surrounded by a spacious burial ground. The interior will accommodate 1500 persons, and has an organ by Bewsher and Fleetwood of this town.

GREAT HOMER-STREET CHAPEL,

is a handsome erection, with an elevation of the Grecian style, which is capable of accommodating 1300 persons. It was opened in 1839.

The other chapels of this denomination being buildings so plain as to require no description, will be seen on reference to the list of places of worship in the appendix.

WESLEYAN ASSOCIATION.

The principal chapel of this denomination is

PLEASANT-STREET CHAPEL.

This is a spacious building of brick, with stone ornaments and facings, measuring 75 by 57 feet, and capable of accommodating 1390 persons. It was erected from the designs of Mr. Duckworth.

METHODIST NEW CONNEXION.

This denomination occupy a handsome chapel in Park-place, connected with which are spacious school-rooms; and

HOTHAM-STREET CHAPEL,

(formerly called Bethesda,) which was purchased

from the Independent congregation, now removed to Crescent Chapel, Everton.

Their other chapel is in Bevington-hill.

SEAMENS' CHURCH

Rathbone-street, of the Independent Methodist denomination, is a large brick building, with stone ornaments, and an emblematical design, in relief, on the front, erected in 1835, for the convenience of seamen. It has accommodation for 1,000 persons, and it measures 51 feet by 50 feet.

WELSH CHAPELS.

The chapels in which the service is regularly performed in the Welsh language, are more numerous in proportion to the Welsh population, than those of any other description.

WELSH INDEPENDENT CHAPELS.

The oldest of this denomination is

THE TABERNACLE,

situated at the corner of Great Crosshall-street and Marybone. It was erected in 1817, and measures 60 by 48 feet.

BETHEL,

in Bedford-street, Toxteth Park, was erected in 1837, and is a neat brick building, with stone facings, measuring 54 by 42 feet.

SALEM,

in Brownlow-hill, is a handsome cemented building, measuring 57 by 45 feet, the interior of which is conveniently and tastefully arranged.   It was opened in 1841.

WELSH CALVINISTIC METHODISTS.

PALL MALL CHAPEL,

is the oldest Welsh place of worship in Liverpool, and was built in 1787.   It was afterwards rebuilt in 1816, and measures 57 feet by 46½ feet.

EBENEZER CHAPEL,

Bedford-street, was originally built in 1805, and rebuilt in 1840.   It is the largest place belonging to this body, and will accommodate about 2,000 persons.

The other chapels of this denomination are to be found in the list of places of worship in the appendix.

WELSH WESLEYAN CHAPELS.

CHESTER-STREET CHAPEL

was opened in 1837, and has a neat front, with two Doric porches.

BENN'S GARDEN CHAPEL,

which is at present occupied by this denomination, was the property of the Renshaw-street Unitarian congregation, who removed from it in 1811.   It was erected in 1727, for the convenience of part of the ongregation of Park chapel.

The Baptist and other Welsh chapels, being structures with no pretension to architectural design, it is, perhaps, unnecessary to notice individually. They will be found in the appendix.

UNITARIAN CHAPELS.

PARADISE-STREET CHAPEL

is an octagonal brick building, surmounted by an attic balustrade, and vases at the angles. Over the centre of the building is an octagonal lantern, which is a considerable ornament to the building. The pulpit is ascended by a double staircase, and is supported on columns; and the front of the galleries afford a specimen of rich inlaying and veneering with different kinds of wood.

RENSHAW-STREET CHAPEL,

is nearly opposite St. Andrew's church. It has a stone front, is well arranged in the interior, and has a large burial ground attached.

PARK CHAPEL,

in Park-road, near the Dingle, is the oldest Dissenters' chapel in Liverpool or the neighbourhood, having been occupied from the period of the act of uniformity in 1662, when its minister was ejected from the established church. It has frequently undergone extensive repairs.

THE FLOATING CHAPEL,

lies in the north west corner of King's Dock. It was originally a merchantman of 800 tons burthen, and now belongs to the Bethel Union, by whom it was purchased for £940. It is fitted up with a gallery, &c., in the form of a chapel, and will accommodate from 500 to 600 persons. Service is performed by the different dissenting ministers in the town, by rotation.

FRIENDS' MEETING HOUSE,

is situated in Hunter-street, and is a commodious but exceedingly plain brick building, capable of accommodating 2000 persons.

JEWS' SYNAGOGUE

in Seel-street, is a costly building with stone front, having four three-quarter Ionic columns supporting a pediment. Above the entrance is an inscription in Hebrew, and the date of erection, A.M. 5568, which, in the usual notation, is the year 1807. The interior is elegantly fitted up, the gallery being appropriated exclusively to ladies ; and at the north end of the building within an enclosed space, is the ark, containing the Law, &c.

The above description comprehends all the places of worship which are deserving of particular notice.

For the convenience of visitors, a list of all the places of worship in Liverpool and its neighbourhood, their ministers, and the hours of service, is given in the appendix.

Zepin
Overton

ST. JAMES' CEMETERY.

CEMETERIES.

Comparatively few of the places of worship have burial grounds attached, but their place is supplied by spacious cemeteries in different parts of the town and neighbourhood.

ST. JAMES' CEMETERY

is situated between Upper Parliament-street, and Duke-street, along the lower side of Hope-street. It contains 44,000 square yards of ground, which was originally a stone quarry, but was converted into a cemetery, and consecrated on 12th January, 1829. The land was given for the purpose by the Corporation, and the sum of £20,000 was raised by subscription to carry into effect the designs of a committee of management. It has the appearance of a narrow dell, the west side of which is covered with rich foliage, and the east side is arranged in inclined planes or terraces, cut from the solid rock, which, being without wood, have a very bare appearance. The catacombs or vaults, 105 in number, are hewn from the rock, and are entered from these terraces. The lower part of the cemetery is studded with graves tastefully arranged; and it is ornamented with serpentine walks, and shrubberies filling up the remainder; causing this mournful habitation of the King of terrors to have little of the gloominess which generally characterizes the abodes of the dead.

The oratory is placed on the edge of a perpendicular rock, at the north west corner, and is reached from the lower part of the cemetery by a small tunnel cut through the rock, leading to the platform on which the chapel is situated.　It is a fine specimen of the Grecian Doric architecture, and is a perfect model of a Greek Hypæthral temple.　It has a portico at each end, consisting of a pediment supported by six fluted columns, and is lighted from the roof. The floor of the interior is of mosaic work, and there are several well-executed busts ranged round the building.　Near the oratory, enclosed by a shrubbery, is the clergyman's house.

In the centre of the lower part of the cemetery is a circular mausoleum, similar to the lantern of Demosthenes, at Athens, consisting of a rustic basement, supporting ten three-quarter Corinthian columns, surmounted by a cornice and dome.　It was erected by public subscription in memory of William Huskisson, Esq., M.P., who was unfortunately killed on the day of the opening of the Liverpool and Manchester Railway, on the 15th September, 1830, by a locomotive engine passing over his body.　The light is admitted from near the roof, and falls with effect on the statue of the lamented Huskisson within.　The figure is standing erect, habited in the Roman Toga, with the arms folded on the breast.　The artist has happily caught an expression of countenance which the senator frequently exhibited, and has represented it with feeling and vigour.　The mausoleum was erected by Messrs. Tomkinson and Son, and the statue was executed by our townsman, Mr. Gibson.　Closer inspection of the figure may be procured by obtaining the key from the clerk, at the south end of the cemetery.

The number of interments at this cemetery during 1841, was 1074.

THE NECROPOLIS,

or " City of the dead," is a cemetery, opened in 1825, at the corner of Derby and Everton Roads, Low-hill. It was laid out from the design of Mr. Foster, at an an outlay of £8,000, and is the property of a number of proprietors. It occupies 24,000 square yards, and is tastefully arranged, the graves being placed at the north end, and beyond them, at the extremity of the ground, is a railed and covered space, appropriated to tombs with monumental tablets, &c. The house of the resident minister, and the chapel, are of the Grecian style of architecture, and separated by a lofty gateway on massive columns, the design of Mr. Foster. Parties interring are at liberty to avail themselves of the services of the resident chaplain, or of their own minister, and to use their own form of worship. During 1841, 1,797 burials took place here.

ST. MARY'S CEMETERY,

Kirkdale, covers three acres of ground, and has a handsome stone entrance, over which is the inscription " St. Mary's Cemetery, A. D. 1837." " *Mors Janua Vitæ.*" The architecture is Gothic, presenting an extensive and highly ornamented façade, finished by a battlement and pinnacles. The chapel, the interior of which is fitted up with oak carved work, is on the north side, and the house of the minister is on the south side of the entrance. Parties are at liberty to employ their own form of service, and their own minister, or to have the service performed by the resident chaplain.

PAROCHIAL CEMETERY.

In addition to that at St. Martin's church, there is a large burial ground in St. Mary's-lane, Abercromby-square, nearly opposite the Alms-houses, with a small chapel attached.

JEWS' BURIAL GROUND

was formerly in Boundary-place, but a new and more commodious cemetery was consecrated in September, 1837, in Deane-street, Kensington. It has a handsome cemented entrance, with a portico having two fluted Doric columns, under which is an arched gateway.

OLD BURIAL GROUND, EVERTON ROAD

nearly opposite the Necropolis, belongs to the Baptists, and was used when they were excluded from the parish grounds. It was the site of the first Baptist chapel erected in Liverpool.

RAILWAY STATION.

LIME STREET.

COMMERCIAL AND JOINT-STOCK COMPANIES

are exceedingly numerous, but it will be necessary to mention only a few of the most important.

THE RAILWAYS.

" In this wonder-working age," says a writer in No. 96, of the Quarterly Review, " few greater improvements have been made in any of the useful arts than in those applied to the system of travelling on land. Projectors and projects have multiplied with our years, and the fairy-petted princes of the Arabian Nights' Entertainments, were scarcely transported from place to place with more facility or despatch than Englishmen are in A.D. 1832. From Liverpool to Manchester, thirty-six miles, in an hour and a half !*   Surely Dœdalus is come amongst us again."

The Railway Station is situated in Lime-street, and occupies the whole of the space between Gloucester-street and Lord Nelson-street. The front elevation is a façade of white freestone, 330 feet in length, with thirty-six three-quarter Corinthian columns, supporting a suitable entablature. The ornaments are chaste and expressive, and relieve the heaviness which would otherwise characterize so extensive a range of building. The entrance is formed by two large archways, and two other blank doorways are added for the sake of uniformity.

* The journey is now performed in little more than an hour.

Smaller doors form the entrance to the booking and parcel offices. The total expense of this elegant erection was £7000, £2000 of which was handsomely granted by the Corporation; and it was built from the design of John Foster, Esq.

Behind the façade is a suite of spacious offices, occupied bv the Liverpool and Manchester, Grand Junction, North Union, and other railway companies. On entering the area, the feeling with which the spectator is impressed, is that of the strength, durability, completeness, aptitude and simplicity, of almost every thing he sees; and the order and regularity preserved, strongly displays the importance of method in such an establishment. The roof of the area is 70 feet in span, supported on massive beams and columns of iron, and lighted by numerous sky lights. From this point passengers are conveyed through a tunnel 2,230 yards in length, 25 feet in width, and 17 feet in height, which terminates a little above Edge-hill. At the Edge-hill station are two powerful steam-engines which draw the train, by means of an endless rope, up the tunnel from Lime-street; the carriages going down the declivity to Lime-street without any assistance. This tunnel, which is for passengers only, was opened in 1836.

Merchandise conveyed by the railway is deposited and received at the station, Wapping, near King's-dock, whence a large tunnel proceeds to within a short distance of the Edge-hill station, where the passenger tunnel ends. The length of this tunnel is 2,250 yards, and it is 22 feet in width, and 16 feet high, with a semicircular arch of 11 feet radius. It terminates at a spacious area, sunk 40 feet below the level of the ground, at Edge-hill, across which is stretched a Moorish arch, with towers on each side. Below are the boilers and engine houses, the former of which are used also for generating steam for the engines at Edge-hill station, a few hundred yards distant. A small tunnel proceeds from this area, upwards to Crown-street, where cattle, pigs, sheep, &c., are landed or shipped in the waggons. From the period of the opening of the railway, the passenger station was here, until the erection of the more convenient offices in Lime-street.

Although it is unnecessary, in this work, to enter into detail respecting the entire line, that having been already done in the numerous Railway Guides published in this and other towns; yet it will not be out of place to give a few of the leading events connected with the establishment of this railway, which was the first in the country, designed for the conveyance of passengers, and which now proudly triumphs as the great leader of a most important change in the national system of social communication.

The first meeting held for the proposal of establishing the railroad, was on 20th May, 1824, and on the 29th October following, the first prospectus of the undertaking was issued. In passing through parliament, the bill met with strenuous opposition from the proprietors of the various canals, and from local landowners, and it was ultimately lost in June, 1825. The application to parliament was afterwards renewed, and it was carried, on 26th April, 1826, after upwards of £70,000 had been expended in parliamentary proceedings. The work now commenced with spirit, under the superintendence of Mr. Stephenson,

Engineer, and in Sept. 1826, the first shaft of the tunnel was opened.   In 1829, a trial of the respective merits of several new locomotive engines was made, when Mr. Stephenson's engine, the Rocket, was declared the winner.   On the 1st of January, 1830, a line of rails was completed over the much-dreaded Chat-moss, and on the 15th September, the same year, this magnificent work of art was opened the entire distance from Liverpool to Manchester, with all the pomp and splendour, which titled visiters and wealth were able to display.   A deep gloom was thrown over the proceedings of that eventful day, by the melancholy accident which deprived the Right Hon. Wm. Huskisson, Esq., M.P. for Liverpool, of life.   The circumstances are too well known to require detail.   He was publicly interred in St. James' cemetery, and a splendid mausoleum was erected to his memory, as formerly noticed.   A marble slab at Parkside, marks the spot where the melancholy accident took place.

According to the statement of Mr. Pemberton, the original cost of construction of the Liverpool and Manchester Railway was £1,089,818 17s. 7d.

The amount of traffic on this railway is enormous, and it yields the proprietors a profitable return.

The Grand Junction, and other railways, need not be separately described, as they all unite with the Manchester line, a considerable distance from Liverpool.

THE CHESTER AND BIRKENHEAD RAILWAY

was opened in 1840. The terminus is at Grange-lane, Birkenhead, whence passengers are conveyed to Liverpool by steamers from Monks' Ferry. The establishment is very complete, and in its arrangements has profited considerably by the experience of the earlier constructed railways. The booking-office in Liverpool is at the corner of James-street.

LIVERPOOL AND HARRINGTON WATER-WORKS,

the principal office of which is in Hotham-street, were established in 1800, for the purpose of supplying the town with water. In 1826, an act was obtained empowering them to extend their supplies to the suburbs of Toxteth-park and Harrington. They now have pipes and mains for the supply of water in every part of the town, and spacious reservoirs at various places, which are supplied by steam-engines from several springs. A spacious reservoir, with a steam-engine and forcing pumps, &c., has recently been erected in Lodge-lane, Windsor.

LIVERPOOL (BOOTLE) WATER-WORKS

was established in 1799. They supply the town and shipping from springs at Bootle, a village about three miles north of Liverpool. The water is conveyed to the town, from reservoirs at the higher part of the town, to which it is pumped by powerful engines at the springs, through pipes 14 and 9 inches diameter. The reservoirs of this company, in different parts of the town, will contain about 5000 tons of water, and the extent of mains laid, is upwards of ninety miles. The principal office is in Manchester-street.

LIVERPOOL GAS-LIGHT COMPANY

was established in 1816, and was one of the earliest provincial gas companies. The works are situated in Dale-street and Vauxhall-road, the former building being of neat brick with the motto, " *Ex fumo dare lucem,*" inscribed under a Liver, at the front. The mains of this company, the largest of which are a foot in diameter, are upwards of 100 miles in length, and convey gas to the suburbs, as far as Seaforth, the Old Swan, Wavertree, and St. Michael's Hamlet, Toxteth-park. The gas is retained in nine gas-holders, four of sixty feet in diameter, and one of fifty-five feet; and the others will contain 139,000 cubic feet of gas. The gas works are at all times open to strangers on obtaining an order from the office.

THE LIVERPOOL NEW GAS AND COKE COMPANY

was formerly the Oil-gas Company. They have extensive mains laid from their works at Leigh-bridge, Vauxhall-road, to all parts of the town, and about 250 of the street lights at the docks are supplied by this company. The office is in Queen's-square.

In the town of Liverpool, there are 2700 street lamps and 350 at the docks; and, during winter, there is daily consumed not less than 1,000,000 cubic feet of gas; 650,000 feet of which is supplied by the former company.

THE BIRKENHEAD AND CLAUGHTON GAS AND WATER COMPANY,

on 1st January, 1841, opened works at Birkenhead,

Mᴿ ROBERT WINGATE, MANAGE

CUNNINGHAM & HOLME, ARCHITECTS

for supplying that populous neighbourhood with gas. The mains already laid are upwards of fourteen miles in length, and extend as far south as Rock Ferry. The gas-holder, in which the gas is retained, is 51 ft. in diameter, and will hold 35,000 cubic feet of gas. The company is at present engaged in opening the first shaft in the stratum, where they expect to obtain a supply of water.

THE APOTHECARIES' COMPANY

was established for the purpose of supplying medi- cine, and drugs, both wholesale and retail, free from adulteration. Their premises are in Colquitt-street, and consist of a spacious building of a most elabor- ate and unique design. The front is of freestone and has four pilasters on the lower story, between which, are the door and windows. Over each of them, are two beautifully carved oxen, bearing a heavy pedestal. Between the pedestals is a light balustrade, the whole forming a balcony. On the four pedestals are colos- sal figures of Galen, Hippocrates, Esculapius and Hygeia. The upper part of the building is finished by an enriched frieze and heavy dentilled cornice, with an attic balustrade at the top. The interior is fitted up in the same elaborate style as the exterior, with light carving and gilding, and mahogany carvings in the form of Sphynxes. The manufactory is behind, and is of a most complete description. The design was that of Messrs. Cunningham and Holme, and the erection cost £20,000.

THE STEAM-TUG COMPANY

are a joint-stock company, the proprietors of seven

powerful steamers, which are employed in towing vessels in or out of port during contrary winds. Four of these steamers are of one hundred horse-power The office is at 5, New Quay, opposite Prince's Dock.

THE ABBATOIR COMPANY.

The premises of this company are in Trowbridge-street, Brownlow-hill, and consist of extensive public slaughter houses, and places of accommodation for cattle, pigs, &c., which were erected by a private individual, assisted by the corporation, to prevent the nuisance being spread over the town.

PUBLIC ACCOMMODATIONS.

ST. JOHN'S MARKET.

This extensive building is situated in Great Charlotte-street, near Clayton and Williamson Squares,
and was erected from the designs of Mr. Foster, in
1822. It is built of brick, and is 183 yards long, and
45 yards wide, enclosing an area of 8235 square
yards. The roof is light and in five ranges, with side
lights, supported on 116 slender cast-iron pillars
twenty-five feet high, and the building is divided into
five avenues, extending the entire length. It is
lighted by 136 windows, and has numerous entrances.
The walls are lined by shops, and the sides of the
different avenues are occupied by stalls, on which
are offered for sale provisions of every description.
The total number of shops, stalls, and standings,
amounts to 669, which, in 1840-41, realized the sum
of £5,344 to the corporation as rent. Below the
south-west end of the building are a number of store
cellars. On entering this market the stranger cannot
fail to be astonished at the magnitude and lightness
of this extensive building; and at night, when lighted
by gas, it presents a brilliant appearance. It is
closed at eight o'clock every evening, except Wednesdays and Saturdays, when it is open till ten.

ST. JOHN'S FISH MARKET

is situated on the opposite side of Great Charlotte-
street, and was opened on 8th February, 1837. It
contains nineteen commodious shops, fifty-six stalls,

and twenty-two vaults underneath. The building has a handsome front which is rather elevated above the level of the street, and is entered by two flights of steps. It is entirely appropriated to the sale of fish, and the tables of the principal stalls are of white marble. The regulations regarding cleanliness are strictly enforced by the market constables, and from the lofty and airy construction of the building, the nerves of the most delicate need not be offended on entering this market.

THE PEDLERS' MARKET,

in Elliot-street, opposite the end of St. John's market, is appropriated to the sale of crockery-ware, baskets, shoes, pedlery, &c. It is of similar construction to those already described, but considerably narrower.

ST. JAMES' MARKET

is situated at the south end of Great George-street, near St. James' church. It was erected by the corporation at an expense of £13,662, and has recently been considerably enlarged. Its internal arrangement is similar to that of St. John's market, and it is appropriated to the sale of all kinds of provisions, butcher's meat, vegetables and fruits. The rent of the stalls in 1841, amounted to £1735.

ST. MARTIN'S MARKET,

situated between Scotland-road and Bevington-bush, was erected from Mr. Foster's designs, and opened in 1831, the cost of erection having been £13,000. It is 213 feet long and 135 feet wide, and divided into five compartments, with a lofty roof supported on cast iron pillars. The stalls are arranged so as to form a principal, and two smaller avenues at each side. The principal elevations in Scotland-road and Bevington-bush are of stone, in the Grecian-Doric style of architecture. The centre part forms a portico, which consists of four Doric columns supporting a pediment with an entablature and cornice. The entrances are approached by broad flights of steps.

THE HAY-MARKETS.

The hay-market was formerly held in Lime-street, but in 1841 it was removed to Crown-street, at the south end of the town, and Great Homer-street at the north. As the south hay-market, which occupies the site of the old Botanic Garden, is not sufficiently frequented, it is contemplated to remove it to a more central neighbourhood.

THE CATTLE MARKET

is at the Old Swan; Monday is the market day.

Other markets are held at Islington, Pownall-square, Cleveland square, &c., which are partly covered in.

A spacious general market is now in course of erection in Gill street.

The market days in Liverpool are Wednesdays and Saturdays, but every day the markets are well supplied. All the markets are the property of the Corporation, who derive from them an annual gross rental of £11,000.

THE ARCADE

enters from Newington, and is parallel with Bold-
street. It was erected by a company of proprietors,
and has a number of neat shops on one side, but the
situation has caused it to be a complete failure.

The new arcade near St. Luke's Church is a much
more handsome affair, but it extends as yet only a
few shops in length.

THE CORPORATION BATHS

were erected from Mr. Foster's designs at an expense
of £30,763. They are situated between George's
Dock and the river; are 239 feet in length, and 87
feet wide. The centre part of the principal elevation
projects, and on each side is a colonnade, formed by
coupled columns, eighty-six feet in length, and eight
feet wide. The gentlemen's baths are at the north
end. The principal bath is forty-five feet long by
twenty-seven feet wide, provided with numerous
comfortable dressing-rooms. Private tepid, vapour,
and shower-baths, are adjoining. The ladies' baths
are similarly arranged, at the south end of the
building. The water is received from the river, and
filtered till it is perfectly free from impurities, and a
fresh supply is constantly flowing into the baths.
The charges are very moderate.

THE FLOATING BATH

is in Summer moored opposite Prince's Pier, and
two boats are constantly plying between it and the
shore with visitors. It was launched in 1816. The
centre part is a large gentlemen's swimming bath,

with numerous dressing-rooms attached, and on the deck above is a delightful promenade. The charge, including the boat to and from the bath, is only sixpence.

THE CORPORATION WASH-HOUSE AND BATHS,

were opened in June, 1842, and are situated in Upper Frederick-street, a little above St. Thomas' church. It is a convenient brick building, with a large reservoir and boilers attached, fitted up with numerous apartments, in which are warm, cold, and shower baths, both private and public. The lower part of the building, and out-house, are occupied as wash-houses, and have large troughs with sloping sides, divided into compartments, ranged round the walls, as well as others in the centre of the room. Into these hot and cold water is admitted by pipes. The scale of charges is, for a warm bath, 2d.; private ditto, 6d.; and for the use of tubs, water, and drying in the wash-house, 1d. for not more than six hours; and it is expected that these extremely moderate rates, will induce the poorer classes to exercise the virtue of cleanliness, which is so essential to health. The hours of admission for men, are Tuesday, Wednesday, and Saturday, from six to nine, a.m., and six to nine, p.m.; Thursday, six to nine, p.m.; Sunday, six to eight, a.m. For women, Tuesday, Wednesday, and Saturday, from ten, a.m., to two, p.m., and four to five, p.m.; and on Friday, ten, a.m. to five, p.m.

MEDICATED AND VAPOUR BATHS.

Of these there are several. The principal are the

Victoria baths in Cases-street, Clayton-square, Great George-street baths, and Whitlaw's medicated baths in Renshaw-street.

BATHING MACHINES.

On the beach at the north shore, and at several of the ferries in Cheshire, there are bathing machines, for the convenience of those who prefer bathing in the open sea. They are only to be had during the flow of the tide, or about high water, as it is unsafe to bathe on the open beach of the Mersey when the tide is ebbing.

THE BARRACKS,

(formerly a private house,) are situated at the bottom of Duke-street.

HOTELS, &c.

The hotel accommodation of Liverpool is very ample, as those of the first-class and better description amount to nearly a hundred. Good Inns are to be found in the neighbourhood of the railway-stations and coach-offices.

There are also excellent commercial and private boarding-houses in various parts of the town, which have a very respectable character.

A list of the principal Inns is given in the appendix.

In the neighbourhood of the Exchange, there are numerous dining and coffee-rooms, and *restaurants*, as well as those attached to the hotels, where individuals may provide themselves at a moderate rate, with any meal, without having the trouble to proceed to their lodgings.

CONVEYANCES, &c.

of all kinds are very numerous. *Omnibuses* run at all hours to the suburbs from the neighbourhood of the Exchange, and from the principal hotels to the railway station, and the steamers. The hours of starting are given in the appendix.

Coaches, Cars and Cabs are to be had at a reasonable rate at any of the car stands and livery stables. The list of coach fares, &c., is in the appendix.

Luggage Porters are not numerous in Liverpool, it being generally cheaper, as well as more agreeable to hire a car than to engage a porter, if luggage is to be conveyed any distance. Porters are to be found principally in the neighbourhood of the docks, but the stranger must be on his guard against imposition.

M

PLACES OF
RECREATION AND AMUSEMENT.

THE BOTANIC GARDEN,

is situated in Edge-lane, about half a mile beyond Edgehill church. It is the property of a company of proprietors, who have arranged with the corporation for gratuitous admission to the public on Mondays and Fridays, from one to eight p.m. Strangers are at other times admitted gratuitously, by an order from a proprietor, or on payment of one shilling, between the hours six a.m. and nine p.m. The Botanic Garden was originally in Oxford-street, but the increase of buildings in the neighbourhood, rendered a new site necessary. The present premises occupy eleven statute acres, and are tastefully arranged. The conservatory which is 240 feet in length, contains many rare botanical specimens. The entrance lodge is built of stone in the chaste Grecian style of architecture.

THE ZOOLOGICAL GARDEN,

was opened on 27th May, 1833, and is the sole property of Mr. Atkins, who formerly possessed an excellent travelling menagerie. They are delightfully situated on a plot of ground singularly irregular, in Derby-road, a little beyond the Necropolis, and cover upwards of ten acres. No expense has been spared by the spirited proprietor in the arrangement and

construction of the establishment. Nothing has been
omitted in the way of ornament; the trees, the shrubs,
the flowers, are manifold in their varieties, and group-
ed with judgment; and the rustic and playful designs
of the houses and enclosures of the animals, add
much to the picturesque effect. The collection of
animals is very extensive, and constant additions are
made to the already valuable stock; as the position
of Liverpool, as a sea port, gives the proprietor great
advantages over inland towns, in making his selec-
tions. To give a list, even of the most interesting
animals, would be impossible in this work; the
stranger can only appreciate their interest after having visited the establishment. The gardens acquire
additional interest from the fêtes and galas which are
frequently given during the summer season. Imposing representations of Mount Vesuvius and St. Jean
D'Acre, accompanied by pyrotechnic displays, formed
the principal attraction during the last seasons. The
season of 1842 opened with a scene of still greater
magnificence, representing the city of Rome on the
night of the grand festival of St. Peter. In front of
the spectator, who is kept at a distance by a sheet of
water, the bridge of St. Angelo spans the river Tiber
which is crowded with vessels. On the right is the
tower of St. Angelo, and in the back ground the vast
edifice of St. Peter's, towering above the city. The
Vatican and Pontificial palace are conspicious objects;
and even when viewed by day light, the scene has all
the appearance of reality. As evening closes in, St.
Peter's and the habitations in the city are illuminated,
and every detail of that *chef d'œuvre* of modern architecture shines forth in lines of light. The display of

fireworks produces a gorgeous effect; but it must be seen to form an idea of its splendour. The gardens are open from nine in the morning till dark, and the charge for admission is one shilling.

PUBLIC PARKS.

The construction of Public Parks in the neighbourhood of the town was agitated in the town council for a considerable period, and a committee was chosen to make the necessary arrangements; but the difficulty of procuring a proper situation, and the diversity of opinion as to its utility, have for the present caused the project to be laid aside. Since the plan was relinquished, Richard Vaughan Yates, Esq., has in the most public-spirited manner, purchased, at an expense of £47,000, from the Earl of Sefton, forty-three acres of land in the vicinity of the Dingle, Toxteth Park, two-thirds of which are to be immediately converted into a public park, and the remainder is to be appropriated as sites for villas. The Earl of Sefton has generously contributed £1000 towards the expense of laying out the grounds.

The property is delightfully situated; and the inhabitants of Liverpool will thus, through the munificence of Mr. Yates, in a short time, enjoy all the advantages of a public park, without any expenditure of the public money.

THE DINGLE

is a sweet romantic dell, in the neighbourhood of the above, and is the property of Joseph Brooks Yates, Esq., who in the most generous manner opens it to the public on Wednesdays and Thursdays, from twelve to eight p.m., during the summer. It is a delightful retreat, extending to the river, having all the diversity of hill and dale, wood and grove, tastefully laid out in shady and winding walks, with numerous arbours and rustic seats. Few persons in Liverpool are aware of the beauty of this romantic spot, which is certainly a rare acquisition for the neighbourhood of a large town. Admission is gratuitous, visitors being only required to enter their names in a book at the lodge, to prevent improper persons gaining access to the grounds. The Dingle, in Park-road, is two miles from the Exchange, and is passed by an omnibus from town eight times a day.

ST. JAMES' WALK

is a pleasant promenade beside St. James' Cemetery, at the top of Duke-street, with an extensive shrubbery attached to it, which is at all times open to the public. It was erected during a period of public distress, about the year 1767, at the expense of the Corporation, who in this way afforded work to many individuals who were unemployed. On an elevated part of the grounds is a neat stuccoed building, formerly an observatory, now fitted up with apparatus for taking photogenic portraits. The specimens of this description of likenesses taken by the action of light on a prepared metallic plate, are worthy of examination, and will be readily shewn by the proprietors of the establishment.

One or two humorous anecdotes connected with this garden, shew that the Mount has contributed indirectly as well as directly, to the amusement of the

inhabitants.   The place was at first known as
" Quarry Hill," but, on its being ornamented, it received, with the sanction of the civic dignitaries, the
appellation of " Mount Zion."   This name was the
source of annoyance to a certain class of individuals,
and as is usual in such cases, poetical satire became
the channel by which they expressed their sentiments.
Among several other effusions, the following lines,
part of a long poem, ascribed to a Welsh clergyman,
were the means of causing its name to be altered:—

Fond of impiety, behold a shrine
They've dedicated to the God of wine,
And to excite our admiration more,
See " Bottled Beer " recorded on the door !

But thou who hear'st the poor man's prayer,
Protect the innocent, and guard the fair,
And if thou can'st forgive, forgive the Mayor.

The Rooks of the Mount Gardens have been long
known as a kind of interesting curiosity, as they had
taken up their abode among the dwellings of men.
Their history, like that of many families, which have
been equally looked up to, is hallowed by a legend
which accounts for their origin; like many such tales
it is at once marvellous and apocryphal.   It is said
that a certain gentleman who took great delight in
walking in the gardens early in the morning, once
upon a time, spied a magpie and his lady perched on
one of the trees, enjoying sweet converse among the
leafy boughs.   Though unacquainted with the language of birds he saw enough to convince him that
they were conversing on the important subject of a
future location.   The result showed that they came
to the conclusion, that they might fly further and
fare worse, for they forthwith commenced building
a nest.   A bright thought struck the gentleman, which

was the parent of a resolve, and that resolve was, that the magpies should become the parents of a rookery. He forthwith substituted rook's eggs for those of the magpie; and, in due time, the spurious brood came forth. Both foster parents performed the duties of father and mother with affectionate zeal, and thus became the founders of the colony. The poor magpies dreamt not of the future, and knew not the destiny of their illustrious family.

THEATRES.

THE THEATRE ROYAL,

in Williamson-square, is the only patent theatre in Liverpool, and therefore the only one in which the legitimate drama can be performed. It has a semi-circular stone front, with a rusticated basement, and the upper story is ornamented by coupled Ionic pilasters, bas-reliefs, &c. It was erected in 1772, at an expense of £6000, and has had additions subsequently made to it. The interior is very commodious, elegantly finished, and well adapted to the purpose for which it is intended. The present conductors are Messrs. J. H. Anderson, (the "Wizard of the North,") and J. Hammond, by whom the Metropolitan system of *half-price* has been adopted. Connected with the early history of this theatre is an incident, which, at the period of its occurrence, produced a great impression on the public mind. On the 2nd August, 1798, during the play of "The Stranger," Mr. John Palmer, of the London stage, suddenly dropped down and expired after having uttered the words,—

" There is another and a better world."

The spectators thinking that it was an incident in the play felt no alarm. The body was removed from the stage, but all attempts to restore animation were fruitless. When the announcement was made, an intense sensation, which it is impossible to describe, prevaded the audience, who slowly and silently retired. A few days after the interment a benefit was given for the widow and family, the prologue of the play having been written for the occasion by Mr. Roscoe. By this means upwards of £400 was collected in a single evening.

THE LIVER THEATRE,

is a small, but well arranged, and appropriately decorated building in Church-street, conducted by Mr. Raymond and a respectable company of performers. During the winter months, this establishment presents a great variety of attractions, and is a formidable rival to the Theatre Royal.

THE AMPHITHEATRE,

is the largest building of this description, and is open during the winter months for the performance of equestrian feats, pantomines, &c. The building, including the circle, which is very commodious, has frequently contained nearly 5000 persons, when assembled at a public meeting. It is situated in Great Charlotte-street, opposite St. John's Market.

THE WELLINGTON ROOMS

were erected in 1815, by subscription, according to the design of Mr. Edmund Aikin, of London, for the purpose of holding public assemblies, balls, &c. The building is situated at the corner of Mount Pleasant and Great Orford-street, and it has a stone front without windows. The centre has a circular portico supported by four Corinthian columns. The interior is tastefully arranged, and contains a ball-room, 80 feet bv 37 feet; a card-room 44 feet by 25 feet; a supper-room 50 feet by 25 feet, and other apartments.

THE ROTUNDA

is a circular building situated in Bold-street, near the Lycæum, elegantly fitted up as a billiard and club-room, and frequented by a select number of subscribers of the higher class of society.

THE PALATINE CLUB-HOUSE

is on the same side of Bold-street, a little higher up. Its interior is finished in a superior style, and it is conducted on the plan of some of the numerous clubs of the metropolis, and frequented by the most fashionable circles.

THE RACE-COURSE.

Although Aintree Race-course is five miles distant from the town, it still claims a place under the head of Liverpool Amusements. The Maghull Race-course, seven miles from Liverpool, was projected by the late Mr. Francis Bretherton, and on the 25th July, 1827, the first Liverpool races were run on that course. It subsequently passed into the hands of a committee, but on the opening of Aintree Race-course, shortly afterwards, its popularity declined, till it was finally deserted, and rich crops of corn now wave on the spot once marked by all the fun, frolic, dissipation and extravagance of a race meeting. The funds necessary for the establishment of Aintree Race-course were provided by the munificence of Mr. Lynn, who had warmly supported Maghull course, till its affairs were mismanaged. A short time ago he disposed of a portion of the concern in shares of £25 each, to proprietors, who have free admission to the grand stand. The grand stand has ample accommodation, the course is convenient, the ground is well chosen, and the races are well attended. Aintree (or Liverpool,) races are run in July and September, and the Steeple Chase is in March.

ST. GEORGE'S HALL.

This building will form the centre part of the splendid structure of the new Assize Courts, described in the early part of this volume. As regards the interior, St. George's Hall, measuring 161 by 75 feet, will be further extended along the upper part of its sides, by a series of recesses 13 feet deep, covering over the corridors which surround this part of the interior, and both separate it from, and connect it with the law courts. On the west side of the hall the light will be admitted laterally, through windows within these recesses, and on the opposite one through small domes, one in each recess. During the assizes this spacious hall will be open to the public, as the approach to both courts; at other times it will be appropriated at the discretion of the council to public or private meetings.

THE EXHIBITION ROOMS,

are situated in Post-office Place, Church-street. In these apartments there is held an annual exhibition of paintings during the autumn months; and through-

out the season there are frequently collections of
paintings, engravings, &c., exhibited here.

PLACES OF MEETING, &c.

THE MUSIC-HALL,

Bold-street, entering from Concert-street, is a spa-
cions apartment, much used for holding public meetings, *soirées*, &c.

THE ROYAL ASSEMBLY ROOMS

are situated in Great George-street, and were, until
lately, called the Templars'-hall. The apartments
are used for balls, lectures, &c. The building has a
neat front of stuccoed brickwork.

THE NELSON ASSEMBLY ROOM,

formerly called the Hall of Science, was erected and
occupied by the Socialists, until the period of their
extinction in Liverpool, a few months ago, when it
was purchased by a building-society, and is now ad-
vertised to be let for any moral and legal purpose,
and is licensed as a place of public worship. It is a
large, plain brick building, with cemented front,
and numerous apartments, situated in Lord Nelson-
street.

THE PORTICO,

Newington, is a small building erected for a pano-
ramic exhibition, but now made use of as a concert
or lecture room.

During the winter season, concerts, *soirées musi-
cales*, and other musical entertainments, are to be

met with at one or other of these rooms, nearly every evening. In summer they are less frequent.

GYMNASIUMS.

That of Mr. Huguenin in Cook-street, and Mr. Harrison in Colquitt-street, are worthy of inspection. The former is very commodious, and is fitted up with a more complete and extensive set of gymnastic apparatus, than any other establishment in the kingdom. It is open at all hours of the day, and the proprietor permits visitors to inspect his premises.

THE CHURCH-STREET BAZAAR,

the property of Messrs. Promoli and Hausburg, shews the rapid strides which wealth, and its attendant desire for the luxuries, elegancies, and refined necessaries of life, have made in this great commercial town. The front of the shop measures 60 feet, and it extends backwards 125 feet. Within this immense space, and in three stories of the building, are ranged on marble slabs and pedestals, with a great degree of taste and care, a magnificent and costly stock of every description of manufactured articles from all parts of the world. To describe the variety of articles exposed would be impossible; every description of clocks and watches, jewellery, antique urns, vases, casts, writing-desks, and costly articles of furniture and luxury constantly meet the eye. The proprietors invite the visit of strangers, who receive polite attention from the assistants, and are shewn through the entire premises, without it being expected of them to make a purchase.

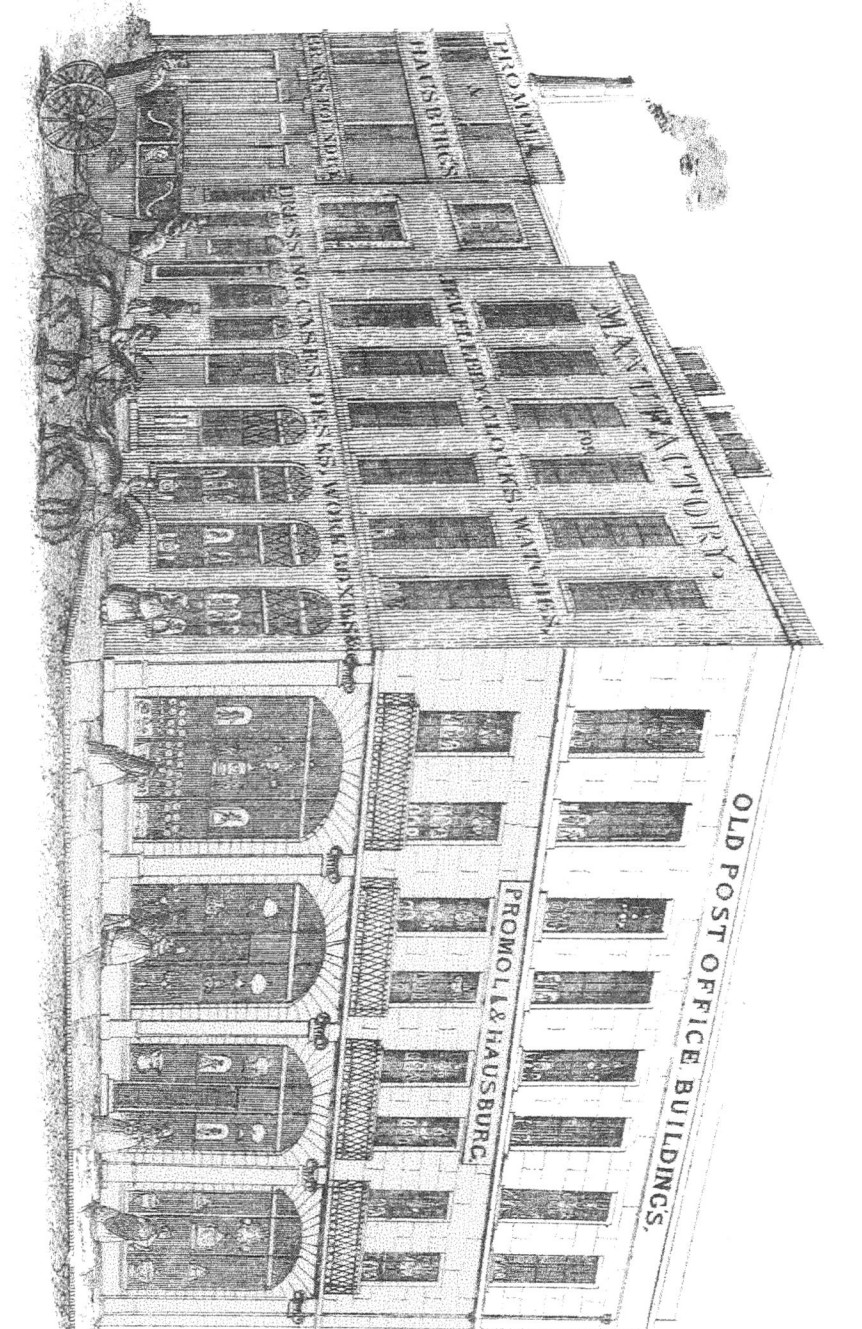

THE COALBROOKDALE IRON WAREHOUSE,

is a handsome building in James'-street, with a stone
front in the Grecian style.   The splendid show rooms
of this establishment are, at all times, open to visitors,
who will be interested by the extent of the premises,
and the beautiful specimens of iron manufacture.
Chimney and table ornaments, casts, vases, chandeliers, ornamental tables, grates, fenders, fire-irons,
and articles of taste and elegance, are here displayed.
The upper rooms, about twelve in number, contain
a vast variety of the more common cast-iron articles.
The visitor is lost among the endless ranges of fire
grates and stoves, beds, garden chairs, pans, boilers,
&c., thousands of which are piled up together.   The
works are at Coalbrookdale, in Shropshire.

MANUFACTURES.

Liverpool is not to any great extent a manufacturing town, and the few manufactures which do exist, are incidental to the traffic of the port, or arise from the domestic necessities of its large population.

The most important are the Steam-engine and Boiler Manufactories. The following description of Messrs. Fawcett and Preston's establishment * which is the largest in this neighbourhood, will be sufficient to give an idea of the other numerous engineering works.

MESSRS. FAWCETT AND PRESTON'S WORKS,

are situated in York-street, and cover a very extensive piece of ground. The principal object of this establishment is the construction of marine and other steam-engines, mill machinery, pieces of ordnance, &c. One department is devoted to the founding and boring of cannon. The guns are cast solid and afterwards bored, the cannon revolving horizontally on the boring machine, which gradually moves forward as the work proceeds. The operation is repeated till the aperture is of sufficient calibre; and the bore produced is as true and smooth as that of a rifle.

In the Foundry department, castings are made, the single pieces of which frequently weigh twenty tons. The detail of operations is similar to that adopted in smaller establishments.

* Abridged from the *Standard.*

The Smithy is one of the most extensive portions of the building. With the exception of the largest marine shafts, which are made at the Mersey Iron Works, all the malleable iron is worked on the premises. The dusky visages of the athletic workmen, the incessant hammering, and the constant roaring of the fires, remind the visitor of the description of the workshop of the Cyclops. Here, however, " bolts," are " forged," of which neither Jove nor his armourer, Vulcan, could have formed any notion.

In the Planing-machine room, are a number of machines, for planing and smoothing metal plates with mathematical accuracy. That the machine is nearly perfect is shown by the fact of two plates adhering when their surfaces have been smoothed by this apparatus.

In the Turning room are powerful lathes in which steam-engine shafts, cylinders, &c., are turned. The shafts of the *President* (steamer,) which weighed ten tons each, were manufactured here. Another description of lathe is employed in turning the tops or lids of the cylinders, and has turned the cylinder tops of the same vessel's engines, 80 inches in diameter.

The Pattern Makers' and " Fitting-up " shops are interesting on account of their magnitude.

In the Model room are hundreds of models of all possible parts of machines, many of which are of great value.

In the spacious sheds there are generally several powerful engines in the course of erection, and some of the largest ever manufactured have been produced from these premises. The frame work of the larger description of engines is most stupendous, and is

generally of elegant architectural design, and is frequently of such magnitude as strongly to resemble a
handsome Gothic church.   Some of the dimensions
of the engines of the ill-fated *President* will show
what has been executed at their works:—Diameter
of Cylinder 80 inches; Stroke of Engine 7 feet 6 inches; Weight of Cylinders 11 tons; Beams, (four of
them) upwards of 5 tons each; Condensers about
10 tons; Gothic Pillars, (four pairs) each 11 tons 7
cwt.; Paddle shaft 9 tons; Boilers, each, 30 tons;
Two Bed Plates, each in one casting, 15 tons.

The hoisting tackle used in setting up these engines
is worthy of notice.   By means of scaffolds and railways, any portion of a machine may be lowered per-
pendicularly over any spot of the building.

Not the least interesting department of their works
is that appropriated to the boiler-making, situated
in Oil-street.   The plates of which the boilers are
composed are rivetted together by red hot bolts which,
by contracting when cold, draw the plates together
with a force that could not otherwise be obtained.

The whole establishment, at which upwards of
700 men are employed, is a world of mechanism in
itself; and a visit to the extensive works, when per
mitted by the kindness of the proprietors, is one of
the most interesting that can be well imagined.

The premises of Messrs. Forrester and Co., at Vaux-
hall Foundry, and the Clarence Foundry belonging
to Messrs. E. Bury and Co., as well as the works of
Messrs. Mather, Dixon, and Co., are also very extensive.   At the former were manufactured the engines
for the steam-frigate " Guadaloupe," launched 12th
April, 1842.

THE MERSEY IRON AND STEEL WORKS,

are situated at the south end of the town beside Harrington Dock.   In these works old and scrap iron is
forged into bars, shafts, &c. and a considerable quantity of steel is manufactured.   In the former process
huge hammers worked by steam are employed, which
effectually unite the masses of heated metal.   The
largest piece of malleable iron manufactured at these
works was a paddle shaft for the Great Western
Steam Ship Company, Bristol, measuring 17 feet 6
inches in length, and 7 feet in circumference; and
weighing 15 tons, 15 cwt., 2 qrs., and 20 lbs.   The
two crank pins for the same engine were the largest
ever constructed, and together weighed 3 tons.

MR. LAIRDS' IRON SHIP-BUILDING YARD,
AND PATENT SLIP,

are situated in North Birkenhead, Cheshire.   From
these extensive premises have been launched, nearly
all the large iron steamers that have already been
constructed.   The Guadaloupe, a steam frigate of
800 tons, launched on 12th April 1842, is the eighth
iron war-vessel which Mr. Laird has built; they all
carry pivot guns, fore and aft.   Four of them, the
Nemesis, Phlegethon, Ariadne, and Medusa, are at
present in the China seas, and have proved the utility
of iron vessels for naval purposes.   The Guadaloupe,
(with the exception of the Hindostan, launched a few
days afterwards,) is the only large vessel of war,
which has been built in this port since the "Havannah"
Frigate in 1809.   Her dimensions are, length on deck
190 feet; beam 30 feet; and she will carry two
sixty-eight pounder pivot guns, one fore and one aft.

A visit to these works, is as interesting as any that can be obtained in the neighbourhood of the town. The Patent Slip is used for the purpose of hoisting vessels out of the water, and affording all the advantages of a graving-dock, without the loss of time caused by docking and undocking.

MESSRS. WILSON AND CO'S SHIP BUILDING YARDS.

On this side of the river, near Clarence Dock, are the ship building yards of Messrs. Wilson and Co., whence several large iron as well as wooden steam-ships have been launched. By these gentlemen were built the Oriental steamer, now carrying the mails between this country and Egypt, and the Hindostan, launched April 26th, of the present year, which will be fitted out as a vessel of war, with sixty-four pounders. Her dimensions are, length of keel 230 feet; length from taffrail to figure-head 250 feet; breadth of beam, exclusive of paddle-boxes 39 feet; depth of hold from the upper deck $30\frac{1}{2}$ feet; burden 2,000 tons; power of engines 500 horse.

There are a number of anchor-smiths and chain-cable manufacturers, as there is a good demand for such articles in the port.

There is only one Cotton Factory in Liverpool. It is a very extensive building, in which the spinning department is carried on, situated on the canal bank, at the north end of the town.

Soap Manufactories are numerous, and exceed those of the metropolis, or any other provincial town.

ALBION OIL MILLS.—In these mills, which are situated in Pembroke-street, powerful machinery is employed for compressing oil from seeds, by means of stamping engines, rollers, &c.

The Oil Mills of Messrs. Earle and Carter, Oil-street, are also of considerable extent.

There are several Veneer Mills in different parts of the town, where the finer descriptions of wood are cut by circular saws, into boards almost as thin as a shaving. The steam saw mills, of which there are four or five, are worthy of notice.

The principal remaining manufactures, are those of glass at the Olive Mount bottle-glass works; sugar-refining; ship-bread baking, by machinery; comb-making, coach-building, fringe-making; brewing and distilling; organ-building; printing of paper-hang-ings; and the manufacture of files, tools, watches and their movements.

BIOGRAPHICAL SKETCHES OF

EMINENT PERSONS,

CONNECTED WITH LIVERPOOL EITHER BY BIRTH OR

RESIDENCE.*

SIR WM. DE LA MORE was created a knight ban-
neret by Edward the Black Prince, for his valour at
Poictiers. *Thomas De La More* was twelve times
chosen mayor of Liverpool, towards the close of the
14th century, an office which was afterwards held by
ten or twelve branches of the same family. The renowned ballad of the "Dragon of Wantley," had its
origin in one of the Mores of this family.

JEREMIAH HORROX, a celebrated astronomer, was
born at Lower-lodge, Toxteth-park, in 1619. At an
early age he manifested a desire to become acquainted with the science of astronomy, and in 1633 he entered Emanuel College, Cambridge, where he became
acquainted with Wm. Crabtree, of Manchester, who
was engaged in similar pursuits. The genius of
Horrox overcame every obstacle which poverty and
other circumstances threw in his way, and on the 24th
Nov. 1639 he made an observation of a transit of Venus, which, from his own calculation, he ascertained
would then occur. Part of the works of Horrox

* The earlier part of these sketches is collected from " Smither's
Commerce and Statistics of Liverpool."

have been collected by his biographer, Dr. Wallis, a copy of which is now deposited in the Athenæum library. Sir Isaac Newton made use of Horrox's "Luuæ Theoria Nova," or new theory of Lunar observations, and held his talents in high estimation. In a letter written by Newton, dated 25th May, 1672, he says "the world will enjoy the writings of the excellent astronomers Horrox and Helvetius." He was cut off by the hand of death in 1641, at the early age of twenty-two.

EDWARD RUSHTON was born in John-street, Liverpool, on the 13th November, 1756, and at the early age of six years commenced his education at the free school of Liverpool. A desire to engage in the seafaring life was inspired by a perusal of Anson's voyage, and when little more than ten years of age, he was apprenticed to Messrs. Watt and Gregson, merchants, of this town. When only sixteen years old he was promoted to the rank of second mate for an act of intrepidity and courage, by which the ship in which he sailed was saved. At a period when the African slave trade was scarcely thought a crime, he was engaged as mate of a slaver bound for Guinea. When near Jamaica he was sent with a boat's crew on shore, and through some unknown cause, the boat was upset, and all were immersed in the boisterous element. A negro, whom he had treated with kindness and taught to read, seeing the perilous situation of Rushton, pushed towards him a cask, which he had seized for his own perservation, bade him good bye, and sunk to rise no more. This incident awakened the deepest emotions in the breast of Rushton when-

ever he related it.   For his earnest exertions in behalf
of the slaves he was frequently threatened with
imprisonment, but he persevered, and shortly afterwards became a victim to his philanthrophy, by los-
ing his sight in affording relief to a cargo of slaves
afflicted with ophthalmia;   medical aid was tried,
but in vain; and, on returning to Liverpool, the conduct of his step-mother banished him, in this helpless
state, from a father's home.   On the scanty allow-
ance of four shillings a week he managed to subsist
for seven years, paying threepence a week to a boy
for reading to him in the evening.   By this means he
became conversant with the best English poets and
essayists, Milton being his favourite.   In 1782, he
published a political poem against the American war,
and in 1787 his West India Eclogues. His father re-
lenting and wishing to befriend him, established him
and his sister in a tavern, a line of business which, of
all others, was most uncongenial to his pursuits.
He shortly quitted this, and became partner and
editor of the *Liverpool Herald.*   The candid statement of his sentiments regarding the impressment of
seamen, caused a dissension between himself and
partner, which obliged him to leave the concern; and
he opened a bookseller's shop in Paradise-street. Once
more his political opinions brought him into difficulties, but he ultimately succeeded, and gave to his
children the best of all endowments, a good education.
Mr. Rushton is maintained by Dr. Shepherd, his biographer, to have been the first projector of the Blind
Asylum.   He died in 1814 at the age of fifty-eight,
leaving behind him several poetical works.

GEORGE STUBBS, the celebrated animal painter, was the son of a currier, and born at Liverpool in 1724. He contributed annually to the exhibitions of the Metropolis, and in 1766 published a work on the anatomy of the horse, engraved by himself. He died at the advanced age of eighty-two, when in the course of preparing a work on "The Structure of the Human Body compared with that of a Tiger and a Fowl."

JOHN DEARE, an eminent Sculptor, was born at Liverpool, 17th October, 1759. The first indication which he gave of artistical talent, was his carving a miniature human skeleton with a penknife, when only ten years of age. This interesting specimen of youthful genius is still preserved. At the age of twenty he obtained the first gold prize medal from the Royal Academy, for a design, from Milton, executed in alto relievo. Under the patronage of George III., and of the Royal Academy, he was sent to Rome, where he prosecuted his studies with undiminished ardour and untiring enthusiasm, till death, (brought on by sleeping all night on a block of marble, under the superstitious idea that his dreaming fancy would enable him to display greater talent in the work about to be executed,) suddenly closed his career. In the gallery of art of the Royal Institution are two of his works, the subjects of which are, the Struggle of Satan with the Angel, and Eleanor sucking the Poison from the wound of her Husband.

FORTUNATUS WRIGHT was the son of a master mariner of Liverpool, who distinguished himself in

the defence of his country.   At an early age he
followed his father's profession.   Smollet, in his
History of England, in the reign of George II.,
records a heroic action between the St. George, a
privateer, equipped and commanded by Wright, and
a large French Xebeque, in which the former was
victorious.   He fell a victim to political interests
about the year 1760.

Sir William David Evans, a celebrated legal
practitioner, was sometime resident in Liverpool,
and was afterwards appointed as recorder of Bom-
bay, on which occasion he was knighted. He was
remarkable for an unusual degree of absence of mind.
When he arrived in India he found he had left his
despatches in England, and died before they arrived.
He was the author of numerous legal works, published about the beginning of this century.

Matthew Gregson, F.A.S., was one of those
humble individuals whom industry and frugality
have elevated to wealth and importance in society.
He was apprenticed to a paper-hanger and stationer,
and having gained the confidence of his employers,
he succeeded in commencing business for himself.
At an early period of life he devoted himself to
literary pursuits, and was elected fellow of the Anti-
quarian Society, and a member of several philosophical societies.   In 1817, he published the
" Antiquities of Lancashire," having for a long period
previously been collecting materials.   He died in
1824, from an injury sustained in reaching a book
from his library.

Mrs. Susannah Dobson, the wife of Dr. Dobson, was renowned as the authoress of the "Life of Petrarch," "Literary History of the Troubadours," "Memoirs of Ancient Chivalry," &c. She died in 1795.

James Currie, M.D., born in the year 1756, was a native of Dumfrieshire. At an early age, he proceeded to Virginia, in a mercantile capacity, but the breaking out of the American war caused him to return in 1776. He subsequently studied at Edinburgh University, and received his degree at Glasgow. He settled in Liverpool, and became an intimate friend of Roscoe. He published several miscellaneous works, and was a promoter of several literary and benevolent institutions in Liverpool; but when all these shall be forgotten, the name of Dr. Currie will go down to posterity, as the enlightened editor of "*The Life of Burns.*" He died in 1805, aged forty-nine years.

William Enfield, LL.D., was born on the 29th March, 1761, at Sudbury, Suffolk, of humble but respectable parents. At an early period he displayed considerable talent, and when aged seventeen, turned his attention to the ministry. In November 1763, he was ordained pastor of the congregation of Dissenters, meeting in Benn's Garden, Liverpool. He immediately commenced arranging materials for a history of Liverpool, which was published in 1773, and about the same period he published several other works. He afterwards received the degree of LL.D., from Edinburgh University. Besides the works he published during his lifetime, Dr. Aiken, his biographer, edited several others, which at the period of his death, in 1797, were in course of preparation.

———

RICHARD WATT, of Speke, came to Liverpool, when a boy, about the year 1750, and occupied the humble station of stable boy. His master finding him willing to learn, sent him to an evening school. Watt made such progress that he was speedily advanced to the counting-house, and he was ultimately sent as supercargo to Jamaica, where he amassed a fortune of upwards of half a million. On his return to Liverpool, he settled annuities on the survivors of his late master's family who were now in difficulties, and purchased the splendid estate of Speke Hall, which still belongs to his descendants.

———

WILLIAM HUTCHINSON, Dockmaster of the Port for upwards of forty years, kept an accurate tidal and meteorological register, which invaluable document is now deposited in the Liverpool library. In 1794 he published a treatise on Naval Architecture, &c. He was originally apprenticed in a small collier belonging to Newcastle, but he rose by his perseverance and integrity to the command of a government frigate in 1750, and was subsequently made dockmaster of Liverpool. He died in 1800.

———

REV. THOMAS SPENCER was born at Hertford on 21st January, 1791. In 1807 he was admitted into Hoxton Academy to study for the ministry. On the 3rd of February he accepted the pastoral charge of the Independent congregation meeting at Newington Chapel. His extraordinary talents and exemplary piety rendered him so acceptable that it was determined to erect a larger place of worship. The foundation of Great George-street Chapel was laid, and the work was rapidly progressing, when the beloved Spencer was suddenly snatched from his affectionate people, by the hand of death. On 5th August, 1811 he went, as was his practice, to the south shore to bathe in the Mersey. The tide had just turned and the spot was dangerous, but unapprehensive for his safety he plunged into the element, and was in a few minutes overwhelmed. His biographer, Dr. Raffles, thus describes him, "As a man he was generous, frank, independent, unaffected, unsuspecting and sincere; as a friend he was disinterested and affectionate; and as a christian fervent, holy, humble."

REV. LEGH RICHMOND, was born in St. Paul's-square, Liverpool, in 1772. At the age of seventeen he entered Trinity College, Cambridge, and there became intimately acquainted with John Singleton Copley, (now Lord Lyndhurst.) At college he was the projector, and an active member of several literary societies. In 1797 he entered on the curacies of Brading and Yaverland, in the Isle of Wight, where he discharged the duties of the pastoral office with faithfulness and zeal. He was the author of the well-known tracts of " *The Dairyman's Daughter,*" " *The Negro Servant,*" and " *The Young Cottager,*" of each of which millions of copies have been printed in many languages, and distributed over the face of the whole civilized world. He also published several larger works, which are held in high estimation. They breathe that fervour of spirit and amiability of character which was the ornament of his life. He died in 1827, and was interred in Turvey Church, Bedfordshire, of which he had been rector twenty-two years.

———

WILLIAM ROSCOE, who has been aptly styled the Lorenzo de Medici of Liverpool, deserves the most prominent place among its literati. He was born at a small cottage in Mount Pleasant, a few yards from the corner of Hope-street, in 1753, and at the age of twelve, was at his own request removed from school. For four years he employed himself in study and out door labour, after which he was apprenticed to an attorney. When engaged in legal pursuits, he acquired, during his leisure hours, a knowledge of several languages, and wrote a few pieces of poetry. When nineteen years of age, he published a long epic poem, entitled " Mount Pleasant," which is still read with pleasure. From a very early period he took a deep interest in the progress of the arts and literature in Liverpool, and a number of the institutions, noticed in the former part of this work, may be traced to his exertions in the cause of literature. His business required his attention until his forty-fourth year, after which he retired from the occupations of the desk to the more agreeable one of the study, with a competency sufficient to enable him to live an easy and respectable life. His most celebrated work is the " Life of Lorenzo de Medici," which has gained for him an enduring reputation, and caused him to be ranked among classic historians. " The Life and Pontificate of Leo X." in four volumes, was another of his great works, which succeeded the former

in about ten years. His other writings are numerous,
and are both of a political, scientific and classic
nature. Toward the close of his life, Roscoe was
chosen representative of the borough in parliament,
where he warmly supported the liberal interest. His
affluence was not destined to support him during his
old age, for the bank in which he was partner stop-
ped payment, and he was thus led into difficulties,
which obliged him to part with his valuable library
and costly collection of antiquities by auction, where
they realized upwards of £11,000. Eleven years afterwards, in 1831, this excellent man died of influenza,
leaving behind him a name which makes *" our own
Roscoe,"* dear to the heart of every friend of literature
in Liverpool.

The works of several members of his family, show
that the bright genius of the parent was stamped on
the minds of the children.

———

MRS. HEMANS, (Felicia Dorothea Browne) was one
of those bright gems in the literary world, of which any
place might be proud. She was born in Duke-street,
Liverpool, in 1794, and was the daughter of a respectable merchant. At an early age she discovered a
romantic turn of mind, and an extreme fondness for
poetry, and these feelings had freer scope for their
exercise, on the removal of the family to North Wales,
when Felicia was but a girl. Roaming amid the
mountains and woods of Cambria, she indulged her
fanciful imagination with every description of mental
luxury. Chivalry was her idol; by the recital of the
deeds of the gallant knights of old, her soul was
animated with a martial fire; and her enthusiasm

was kindled by the mention of the national prowess
of England. Heroism and patriotism filled her
heart. In the year 1812, she was married to Capt.
Hemans, who shortly afterwards was obliged to proceed to India, and leave her behind. At St. Asaph,
where she now took up her residence, were written
many of those beautiful pieces of poetry, that have
raised her to the eminence which she holds among
our female authors. They are too well known to
require to be particularized. Her writings are peen-
liarly sweet, and possess a power over the feelings
and affections of which few can boast. The plain
tive, melancholy strains in which she sometimes in-
dulges, render her still more endearing, and the feeling of sympathy which she displays in her writings,
brings her nearer to our hearts. The character of
her plaintive poems cannot be better described, than
by giving the well known lines of her beautiful poem
—" The Graves of a Household :"—

> They grew in beauty, side by side,
>   They filled one home with glee;
> Their graves are sever'd far and wide,
>   By mount, and stream, and sea,
>
> The same fond mother bent at night
>   O'er each fair sleeping brow;
> She had each folded flower in sight—
>   Where are those dreamers now ?
>
> One, 'midst the forest of the west
>   By the dark stream is laid—
> The Indian knows his place of rest,
>   Far in the cedar shade.
>
> The sea, the lone blue sea, hath one—
>   He lies where pearls lie deep,
> He was the loved of all, yet none
>   O'er his low bed may weep.
>
> One sleeps where southern vines are drest
>   Above the noble slain ;
> He wrapped his colours round his breast,
>   On a blood-red field of Spain.

And one—o'er her the myrtle showers
Its leaves, by soft winds fanned;
She faded 'midst Italian flowers—
The last of that bright band.

And parted thus they rest who played
Beneath the same green tree;
Whose voices mingled as they prayed
Around one parent knee!

They that with smiles lit up the hall,
And cheer'd with song the hearth—
Alas! for love, if thou wert all,
And nought beyond, O earth!

Mrs. Hemans spent the latter part of her life at Wavertree, near Liverpool, where she complains in a letter to a friend, of the annoyance she constantly received, in being requested to supply autographs to her friends. She concludes her letter with, " O the pleasures of fame! O that I were but the little girl on the top of the elm tree again,"—alluding to the romantic and playful habits of her childhood. She died at Dublin, where she had gone for the benefit of her health, in 1835, and the place of her burial is recorded by a monument, with the inscription, " In memory of Felicia Hemans, whose character is best pourtrayed in her writings.

Several other eminent characters may be claimed by Liverpool, but having already so far exceeded the space allotted for this department of the work, they are necessarily, though reluctantly, omitted.

NEWSPAPERS.

The earliest Liverpool newspaper on record is the *Liverpool Courant*, printed by S. Terry, Dale-street, No. 18, July 18th, 1712. The *Liverpool Advertiser* was commenced by Mr. Robert Williamson, on 28th May, 1756. It contained thirty advertisements. This paper has more than once changed its name, and is still published under the title of the *Liverpool Times*. On 27th December, 1765, *Gore's Liverpool Advertiser* was first published, and is still continued under the same name.

There are now ten newspapers published in Liverpool, viz:—

Newspapers.	*Days of Publication.*	*Political Bias.*
WEEKLY.		
Albion	Monday	Liberal.
Chronicle	Saturday	Liberal.
Courier..........	Wednesday	Conservative.
Gore's Advertiser..	Thursday	Mercantile.
Journal... ..	Saturday	Liberal.
Mercury .	Friday	Liberal.
Myers' Mercantile		Exclusively
Gazette........	Monday ..	mercantile.
Times	Tuesday	Liberal.
TWICE-A-WEEK.		
Standard	Tuesday & Friday.	Conservative.
THRICE-A-WEEK.		
Mail	Tuesday, Thursday and Saturday ..	Conservative.

ANTIQUITIES.

The reader who has perused the foregoing pages will have observed that there are few buildings in Liverpool which can lay claim to antiquity, modern improvement having caused the removal of nearly all the reliques of the days of yore.

BIRKENHEAD PRIORY, was founded in the reign of Henry II, by Hamo de Massey, for the accommoda.tion of sixteen Benedictine monks; and the right of carrying passengers by the ferry from Birkenhead to Liverpool, was claimed exclusively by the monks, who made what was in those days considered a very exorbitant charge. At the time of the dissolution of this monastery, in the reign of Henry VIII., the annual revenue amounted to £90 13s. In 1818, a grave stone, which is now placed in the wall of the chapel, was discovered, with an inscription signifying the spot to have been the burial place of Thomas Rayneford, formerly the good vicar of this house, who died 20th May, 1373. The ruins of this ancient gothic pile are beside the church of Birkenhead, and are well worthy of a visit.

PRINCE RUPERT'S COTTAGE.—This small cottage was the head quarters of the Prince during the siege of the town, mentioned in the ancient history, at the commencement of the volume. It is a small white-washed and thatched cottage, one story high, a little above Everton Brow, having still the same humble appearance which it had when occupied by the illustrious visitor. In the neighbourhood are several houses of considerable antiquity. Till the year 1803, a Beacon, erected probably in the reign of Henry III., stood on the site of St. George's Church, Everton. It was a square tower, two stories high, capable of holding a small garrison, and on the roof were placed combustible materials for the purpose of giving a signal of alarm to the beacons of Rivington Pike and Ashurst. When the country had ceased to be distracted by civil wars, the tower fell into decay, and was blown down during a storm in 1803.

Wavertree Well.—A little beyond the village of Wavertree, beside the lake, is an ancient well on which appears the following inscription:—

QVI. NON. DAT. QVOD. HABET.
DOEMON. INFRA. RIDET. ANNO.1414.

Above the arch there was formerly a cross on which were the additional words—

DEVS. DEDIT.
HOMO. BIBIT.

but it has been many years removed.

The Calder Stones, are four or five in number, placed irregularly at the junction of four roads near Allerton. They appear to be of considerable antiquity, and resemble what are generally considered Druidical remains. They bear traces of rude characters which have never been deciphered, but from the circumstance of finding coarse urns, containing human bones and dust, in digging about them, there is reason to believe that they indicate an ancient burial-place,—of what age or what people it has never been ascertained.

Speke Hall, although nine miles from Liverpool, may be noticed on account of its being an object of considerable attraction to the visitor. "It was built about 350 years ago, and is surrounded by a ditch or moat, and possesses every trait interesting to the lovers of antiquity. Gigantic yews shed their gloom over an antique court; the old hall is decorated with a wainscot mantel-piece, said to have been brought from Edinburgh Castle after the victory at Flodden Field; and Sir Wm. Norreys brought here a part of the Scotch king's library from Holyrood House. On the wainscoting is inscribed "SLEEP NOT TILL THOU HAST WELL CONSIDERED HOW THOU SPENT THE DAY PAST: IF THOU HAST DONE WELL, THANK GOD FOR IT; IF OTHERWISE, REPENT."

HALE HALL, nine miles south east of Liverpool, is the residence of John Blackburne, Esq., M.P. It has an ancient appearance and is partly covered with ivy. On the square tower in front is the date 1674, and the inscription "Built by Sir Gilbert Ireland, and Dame Margaret, his wife". In 1809 the south front was rebuilt in a style corresponding with the rest of the building. In this chapelry was born, in 1578, John Middleton, "THE CHILD OF HALE," who was possessed of extraordinary strength, and mea-sured 9 feet 3 inches in height! He visited the court of James I., and a portrait of him is preserved in Brazenose College, Oxford.

CHILDWALL CHURCH, four miles south east of Liverpool, is a building of considerable antiquity, of irregular form, with a low pointed spire. In the im-mediate vicinity, is Childwall Abbey, the property of the Marquis of Salisbury. The village of Childwall is a favourite place of holiday resort with the inhabi-tants of Liverpool.

Several FRAGMENTS OF ANCIENT BUILDINGS in the town have, from time to time, been met with in digging the foundations of modern erections. During the excavations made in Moor-street and Fenwick-street, a few years ago, several portions of arches and walls evidently, belonging to the ancient castle, were met with. A piece of a curious ancient pier was discovered during the recent alterations made in Canning-dock, which is supposed to have been a part of the harbour of the Pool, prior to the formation of the first dock. It was supported on oaken piles shod with iron, a number of which have been removed to the dock-offiee for preservation as reliques of the good old times.

THE RECORDS AND MANUSCRIPTS in possession of the town are, with a few exceptions, not of very great antiquity, as many valuable documents were destroyed by fire when the Town-hall was consumed.

The ORIGINAL SEAL OF KING JOHN is one of the few antiquities which have been preserved. It is silver, of an oval form, and has the "Lever," or Liver engraved upon it, with a sprig of sea-weed in its beak.

The SWORD OF STATE carried before Sir William Norreys, of Speke, during his embassy to the great Mogul, lies unnoticed among the civic treasures. It was presented in 1702 to the Corporation, by whom it was long used as the sword of state. Its handle was of silver. The scabbard is now so fixed on the blade by rust, that Herculean strength could not separate them.

ITINERARY.

For the convenience of Visitors, the following Routes are laid down, which will embrace the principal objects worthy the attention of Strangers in Liverpool.

ROUTE FIRST.

EXCHANGE, CASTLE-ST., SOUTH CASTLE-ST., CUSTOM-HOUSE, SALTHOUSE DOCK, DUKE'S DOCK, KING'S DOCK, QUEEN'S DOCK, COBURG DOCK, UNION DOCK, BRUNSWICK DOCK, TOXTETH DOCK, HARRINGTON DOCK, PARLIAMENT-ST., ST. JAMES'-PLACE, GREAT GEORGE-ST, DUKE-ST., CANNING DOCK, JAMES'-ST., FENWICK-ST., BRUNSWICK-ST., CASTLE-ST., EXCHANGE.

After visiting the *Town-hall, Exchange-buildings, and Nelson's Monument,* the visitor will accompany us along Castle-street, at the end of which is *St. George's Church,* in St. George's Crescent. Proceeding forward along South Castle-street, we arrive at the *Custom-house.* South Castle-street was formerly called Pool-lane, and it was narrow and irregular. Since the erection of the Custom-house, it has become a street of considerable importance. After walking completely round *Revenue-buildings,* and viewing the interior, we turn towards the shipping. Immediately opposite is the corner of *Canning Dock,* and adjoining it is *Salthouse Dock.* Between Salthouse Dock and the River, is a *new dock,* in course of erection. Proceeding along the side of Salthouse Dock, we arrive at *Duke's Dock.* A little further is a large pile of warehouses belonging to the Union Company, one side of which faces King's Dock, and the other Duke's Dock. By continuing along Wapping, we come to the *Railway Station* for goods. The tunnel proceeds from this point to Edge-hill, as formerly mentioned, and is 2,250 yards in

length. Turning to the right we arrive at *King's Dock*, on
the opposite side of which, is the *Tobacco Warehouse.*
Before reaching this building we pass the *Floating Chapel,*
in the north west corner of the dock. After leaving the
Tobacco Warehouse, we may proceed to the *Parade* between
it and the river, from which we have an excellent view of
the upper part of the Mersey, Birkenhead, where the spire
of the church stands in a picturesque manner among the
trees; Tranmere, Rock and New Ferries, with the numerous
marine villas on the margin of the river; Bebbington
Church in the distance; and still higher up, almost concealed in the thick wooded scenery, is the Ferry of Eastham.
From the Parade we proceed to *Queen's Dock*, along the
west side, and examine the Graving Docks. A little further
south is *Coburg Dock*, in which are the *North American
Steamers*, which ought by all means to be inspected. To
save trouble, the visitor should previously provide himself
with an order of admission from the agents, Messrs. Mac
Iver, in Water-street, near the Town-hall. On the south
side of this dock is the *Dock Yard.* Crossing the passage
between Union and Coburg Docks, we come to *Brunswick
Dock*, the largest in the port;—keeping along the west side
of it, and passing the basin, we arrive at the *Graving Docks.*
From this we cross the bridge to the east side of the Dock,
and still keep in a southward direction. *Toxteth Dock* is
the first dock we pass, and forms the boundary of the
Corporation property. The space on the left is entirely
occupied by *timber sheds*, which are situated here on account
of the proximity of the timber docks. A little further are
the *Harrington Docks*, adjoining which are the *Mersey Steel
and Iron Company's Works*, which shall be the southernmost
point of this route. After inspecting them we retrace our
steps to Brunswick Dock, keeping along the east side.
Nearly opposite the centre of this side is Warwick-street, at
the bottom of which is *St. Thomas's Church.* On the

eminence a little towards the south-east, appears the spire of
St. John the Baptist's Church. From Warwick-street, still
going north, we come to Parliament-street, at the bottom of
which is the handsome Church of *St. Barnabas.* The next
building above it is the *Southern and Toxteth Hospital.*
Proceeding up Parliament-street, and passing one or two
chemical, lime, and other manufactories, we cross Bedford-
street, in which there are several large *Chapels belonging to
the Welsh.* A little higher up the street is *St. James' Church*
on the right. We here turn to the left and see a spacious
triangular area, on the upper side of which is *St. James
Market.* Keeping along great George-street, we arrive at
Great George-street Chapel, a splendid building, at the angle
formed by this street and Nelson street. Opposite is the
Nelson Assembly Rooms, and from the end of the street we
see *St. Mark's Church,* in Duke-street, a little above where
we now are. Turning down Duke-street, which was
formerly the fashionable portion of the town, and in which
still many opulent families reside, we pass the *Union News-
room* on the right, and arrive at York-street, along which
we turn to *Messrs. Fawcett and Preston's Establishment.*
After inspecting these extensive premises, we return to Duke-
street, and pass the *Mates' Association-rooms,* and *Barracks,*
on the right-hand side of the street. In a few minutes we
reach the Custom-house, which we now pass, and proceed
to Canning Dock. On the west side of this dock is the *Life-
boat Station,* and the *Tide Surveyors' Office.* At the north
end of the dock is a large *stone building,* which is occupied
by the head-constable. We then turn along *James'-street,*
on the right-hand side of which, is the *Coalbrookedale
Company's* warehouse. At the top is *St. George's Church,*
on the right, and the *North and South Wales Bank* on the
left. Proceeding along Fenwick-street, which, from being
one of the narrowest and most irregular, has been recently
made a wide and elegant street, we see a number of hand-

some offices, and at the corners of Brunswick-street, are the *Union* and *Messrs. Heywood's Banks.* Turning up Brunswick-street, we find ourselves once more before the Exchange, where we conclude our first route.

————

ROUTE SECOND.

EXCHANGE, WATER-ST., PRINCE'S DOCK, WATERLOO DOCK, VICTORIA DOCK, TRAFALGAR DOCK, CLARENCE DOCK, NORTH BATTERY, WATERLOO-ROAD, OIL-ST., GREAT HOWARD-ST., NEPTUNE-ST., WATERLOO-ROAD, PRINCE'S PARADE, GEORGE'S DOCK, GEORGE'S PIER, CHAPEL-ST., EXCHANGE.

This route embraces all the north docks, after which, we will proceed to survey the town.

From the Exchange we pass down Water-street, in which most of the steam-packet offices are situated. Messrs. Bailey Brothers' iron warehouse at the bottom of the street occupies the site of the *Ancient Tower.* Turning to the right we pass *St. Nicholas' Church,* and arrive at *Prince's Dock.* We proceed along the east side and examine the *American Packets,* which are generally much superior in appearance to the vessels in the docks visited during the first route. Leaving Prince's Dock, we pass *Prince's Basin,* and arrive in succession, at *Waterloo, Victoria* and *Trafalgar Docks.* On the north side of Trafalgar Dock, is the *Corporation Crane,* at which some steamer will probably be receiving its engines. Beyond this, is *Clarence Dock,* in which lie the larger steamers. The *Glasgow packets* are most superbly fitted up, and will be readily shewn by the parties on board. Keeping along the south side of the dock and crossing a bridge we come to *Clarence Pier,* whence we have a view of Bootle Bay, the Rock Light-house, and the Ferries near

the mouth of the river. If it be near high water, we shall
probably be amused by watching the arrival of an Irish
steamer, and the curious scenes which occur when landing
the cargo of bipeds and quadrupeds.* If the gates of the
half-tide dock are closed, we cross them to the *Graving
Docks*, and afterwards proceed to the *Battery* at the north
extremity of the Docks. This Battery is about to be taken
down to make room for dock improvements, and another
building will be erected a little more to the eastward   A
little further is a *Windmill,* and beyond it the *North Shore,*
a considerable length of which is studded with *Bathing Machines,* and enlivened by the number of individuals of both
sexes to be seen floundering among the waves of the Mersey.
A little to the east is a large *Cotton Factory* ; and, surrounded by brick fields, and blackened by their smoke, stands *St.
Martin's-in-the-fields,* with its lofty spire. Returning along
Waterloo-road, we pass *Messrs. Wilson and Co's. Ship-building Yards,* the *St. George Steam-packet Company's Offices,*
and one or two manufacturies of various kinds. Turning to
the left along Oil-street, we pass the *Oil-mills* and several
large engineering establishments. Turning to the right,

* Our attention being drawn to the side of the river by a group
of steamers which had just arrived, we went over to them, and
were much amused by the odd scene their decks exhibited. The
stern part raised beyond the waist, as usual contained a freight of
bipeds old and young, some decently clothed, others in looped and
windowed garments, conversing in a jargon that, for what we knew,
might be Chaldee. The deck, from the waist forward, was crowded with sheep and pigs; so that it was difficult, without seeing it,
to conceive the medley of living creatures and disgusting filth.
While the animals on deck were slowly driven along a plank up to
the wharf, sailors were busily engaged at the windlass, and pre-
sently a large bullock emerged from the hatchway, like a lifeless
log, suspended in the air by a rope round his body. The poor
beast seemed paralyzed, for, on being lowered upon the dirty deck,
he sunk down as if he had never known the use of his legs ; but
on the sling, upon which he was raised, being pulled from under
him, he rose as if he recollected himself and "moved aft," as is
the sea phrase. A second animal then slowly ascended to the
light of day in the same manner, the sailors treating them all as
unceremoniously as if they had been bags of cotton.—*England
in the 19th century.*

when we come into Great Howard-street, we pass *St. Mat-thias' Church*, a short distance from the street, the *Borough Jail*, and several immense piles of warehouses. Proceeding towards the docks through Neptune-street, we are again in Waterloo-road. A few yards to the north is a hotel, called the *Rotunda Steam-packet Tavern*, which was formerly a windmill. Its interior having been destroyed by fire, it was converted to its present purpose, and is a place of favourite resort by "Tars," who, provided with a quantum of grog and tobacco, delight to " keep a good look out" on the roof, which is flat and fitted up with benches and other conveni-ences. Passing several slate-yards, and Prince's Basin, we cross the bridge beside Prince's Dock, and are on *Prince's Parade*. From this noble esplanade we have, at high water, a magnificent view of the Mersey with the Cheshire shore, and in the distance the blue mountains of Wales. The scenery is bounded by the Rock Light-house on the right, and we perceive, in succession, the fashionable villas of New Brighton, the Magazines, Egremont, and the populous neigh-bourhood of Seacombe. Still more to the left is Wallasey-pool, which seperates Seacombe from Woodside. On the hill behind Woodside is Bidston Light-house, with the tele-graph and numerous signal poles adjoining. The scene on the river is indescribably beautiful. Here and there are river steamers and ferry boats ploughing the smooth surface of the water. " Here is a vessel deeply laden just passing the dock gates, for a voyage to the Antipodes; there is ano-ther destined, perhaps, to the Indies, and afterwards to 'The Pole.' Now the weather-beaten rigging and patched sails of a ship preparing to enter, speak of tempests encountered beyond the equator, or amid the icebergs and snowy coves of Greenland."* Opposite to the parade is moored the *Floating Bath*, to which boats are constantly plying with passengers. Walking round the basin we come to *George's*

* England in the 19th century.

Dock, at the south end is the *Mariner's Church*. The east side is flanked by a range of lofty warehouses called the *Goree*, with piazzas on the ground story. On the west side between the dock and the river are the *Corporation Baths*. If the visitor is here at low water, he will observe at George's as well as at Prince's Pier, an ingenious *Floating Landing-stage* to enable steamers to land their passengers without the inconvenience of small boats. At the Egremont slip is a *Landing-stage* of a more improved construction, extending about 70 feet beyond the sea wall to a strong *floating-pier*, along side of which steamers can be moored. At this stage carriages can be landed at low water. Returning to St. Nicholas' Church, we perceive the *Telegraph* on the roof of a warehouse at the bottom of Chapel-street. Proceeding up Chapel-street, we arrive at the *Sessions-house* and *Bridewell*, from which we find our way to the Exchange area, our starting point.

ROUTE THIRD.

EXCHANGE, CASTLE-ST., LORD-ST., CHURCH-ST., PARKER-ST., CLAYTON-SQUARE, ELLIOT-ST., MARKETS, ROE-ST., MURRAY-ST., WILLIAMSON-SQUARE, ROE-ST., HAY-MARKET-LORD NELSON-ST., HOTHAM-ST., GLOUCESTER-ST., RUSSEL-ST., BROWNLOW-HILL, EDGE-HILL, EDGE-LANE, RAKE-LANE, WAVERTREE-ROAD, DUKE-ST., CHATHAM-PLACE, GRINFIELD-ST., OXFORD-ST., MOUNT PLEASANT, RENSHAW-ST., NEWINGTON, BOLD-ST., CHURCH-ST., SCHOOL-LANE, PARADISE-ST., LORD-ST., CASTLE-ST., EXCHANGE.

After proceeding along Castle-street, we turn to the left and have a full view of Lord-street, which is now one of the handsomest in the town. Passing through it we enter Church-street, in which is situated *St. Peter's Church*.

A little further on the same side is *Messrs. Promoli and Hausburg's Bazaar*, and the *Exhibition-rooms* in old Post-office Place. On the same side of the street is the *Athenæum* and the *Liver Theatre*, the latter of which will scarcely be recognised, except by the Liver, which is placed in front, as the lower story is occupied by shops. Turning up Parker-street, we are in Clayton-square, which is chiefly appropriated to *Hotels*. Passing forward we reach *St. John's Market*. On the right is the *Pedler's Market*, and on the left the general market, which we enter. After proceeding from end to end we leave it by one of the side gates, leading to Great Charlotte-street, and there see the *Fish Market* and the *Amphitheatre*. Walking towards Queen-square, and then turning to the left, we pass the end of the market and the *Fish Hall* in Roe-street, in which fish is sold in wholesale quantities. A little further is Williamson-square, in which is the *Theatre Royal*. From this we retrace our steps along Murray-street and Roe-street, to the spacious area formerly occupied as a *Haymarket,* and see before us the *Railway Station,* and on the left *St. John's Church* and the new building of the *Assize Courts and St. George's Hall.* At the south angle of the Haymarket is a *Baptist Chapel.* We pass the Railway Station and turn up Lord Nelson-street. The first building on our right is the *Church of the School for the Blind,* and that on the left, the *Blind Asylum,* which we will visit in a subsequent walk. Nearly opposite the church is the *Nelson Assembly-rooms.* We pass along Hotham-street till we arrive at Gloucester-street, in which is *St. Simon's Church.* In Copperas-hill, the next street beyond Gloucester-street, is *St. Nicholas' Catholic Chapel.* We continue in Gloucester-street till we arrive at Russel-street, in which are the *Welsh Charity Schools* and the *New Jerusalem Chapel.* Behind Russel-street are the *Public Slaughter-houses and Abbatoir Company's premises.* From Russel-street, which is one of a principal line of streets, we turn into Brownlow-hill, and some distance higher up, we pass the *Workhouse*, the *House of Recovery*, and the *Lunatic Asylum*. In Brownlow-street, which we cross, the *Infirmary* is situated. Keeping up Brownlow-hill, we pass a *Welsh Chapel* on the left, and see *Edge-hill Church* before us. Leaving this and turning a little to the left, we get into Edge-lane, which leads us to the *Botanic Garden*. We pass several mansions before we arrive at it, and if we continue our walk further in the same direction, we meet with many more of the residences of the wealthy inhabitants. After inspecting the garden we turn towards town, till we arrive at Rake-lane, which leads to Wavertree-road, and to the *Edge-hill Railway Station and Tunnel*. We proceed along Wavertree-road, towards town, till we arrive at Duke-street, (Edge-hill,) through which we pass into Chatham-place, nearly opposite which is the site of the new *Catholic Chapel and Convent*. Turning down Chatham-place and Grinfield-street, to Oxford-street, and passing a small *Chapel* in Sidney-place, we come to the *School for the Deaf and Dumb*, behind which it the *South Haymarket*. Below this is Abercromby-square, in which is *St. Catharine's Church*, and a little to the left of the bottom of Oxford-street, are the *Alms-houses* and the *Parochial Cemetery*. At the corner of Hope-street are the *Medical Institution* and *St. John the Evangelist's Church;* and nearly opposite are the back of the *Workhouse*, the *Scotch Secession Chapel*, and the *Wellington-rooms*. Behind the latter, by passing along Great Orford-street we come to *two Chapels* in Pleasant-street. We continue our walk down Mount Pleasant, and pass on the left, Rodney-street, in which is *St. Andrew's Scotch Church*, and a little lower on the same side is the *Catholic Orphan House*, and on the right, a *Methodist Chapel*, and the *Eye and Ear Institution*. At the bottom of the street is the *Adelphi Hotel*, which is the largest establishment of the kind in the town. In Brownlow-hill, a little above the Adelphi Hotel, is the *Welsh Church*. From the Adelphi six streets proceed in different directions. We choose Renshaw-street, and find on our right *Newington Chapel*, and *St. Andrew's Church*, and on the left a *Unitarian Chapel*. Beyond this on the same side is Oldham-street, in which is the *Oldest Scotch Church*. Turning along Newington, we pass on the left the *Portico* and a *Billiard-room*, (intended to be appropriated for a junior club-house,) and on the right the *Arcade;* and we arrive in Bold-street, the Regent-street of Liverpool, in which the beauty and fashion of this wealthy town are, about the middle of the day, to be seen promenading. We walk down Bold-street, near the top of which is the *Savings' Bank*, passing the *Music-hall* on the left, and the *Palatine Club-house*, the *Rotunda*, and the *Lycæum* on the right; and are then in Church-street. Walking forward till we arrive at *St. Peter's Church*, we there turn to the large building behind the church, which is the *Blue Coat Hospital*. Leaving this interesting institution, we pass the *Unitarian Chapel* in Paradise-street, and by turning to the right, find ourselves in Lord-street, from which we once more proceed to the Exchange and complete our third route.

ROUTE FOURTH.

EXCHANGE, CASTLE-ST., SOUTH CASTLE-ST., PRICE-ST., CLEVELAND-SQUARE, PITT-ST., GREAT GEORGE-SQUARE, GREAT GEORGE-ST., ALFRED-ST., MOUNT, CEMETERY, MOUNT-ST., KNIGHT-ST., BERRY-ST., SEEL-ST., COLQUITT-ST., SEEL-ST., HANOVER-ST., CHURCH-ST., LORD-ST., NORTH JOHN-ST., COOK-ST., CASTLE-ST., EXCHANGE.

Passing from the Exchange through Castle-street and South Castle-street, and under the portico of the Custom-house, we arrive at Price-street by which we enter Cleveland-square. On the right through a small opening we see *St. Thomas' Church*, in Park-lane. We pass through the square into Pitt-street, which is of considerable length. On the right is a *Wesleyan Chapel*, and in Upper Frederick-street, the next street behind Pitt-street, are situated the *Corporation Wash-house and Baths*. On the left in the upper part of the street is *St. Michael's Church*, and Great George-square still higher up; crossing Great George-street we enter Alfred-street, at the top of which is St. James'-road with *St. James' Walk*, (or the Mount,) before us. From this agreeable promenade we obtain a fine view of the town below, and of the opposite parts of Cheshire and the mountains of Wales in the distance. Leaving it at the north end we enter the *Cemetery*, and after spending half an hour among the habitations of the dead, we leave it by the same entrance. Above the Cemetery is Gambier-terrace, a noble range of buildings, behind which is Percy-street, which, although a retired street, contains some of the most elegant private dwellings in the town, together with *St. Brides' Church*. From the lower corner of the Cemetery in Duke-street we perceive the back of the *Mechanics' Institution*, in Mount-street, to which we proceed. After having surveyed this extensive building, we go downwards, crossing Rodney-street, through Knight-street, till we arrive in Berry-street, in which is *St. Luke's Church*. We enter Seel-street, and the first building which attracts our attention, on the right, is the *Jews' Synagogue*. On the left is the *Police Hall* and the *Royal Institution Schools*. In Colquitt-street are the *Apothecaries' Hall*, the *Royal Institution*, the *Permanent Gallery of Art*, and *Harrison's Gymnasium*. Further down Seel-street is *St. Peter's Catholic Chapel* and *Messrs. Samuel and James Holmes' Works* on the left, and the *Liverpool Sawmills* on the right. We cross Slater-street, in which the *Bible Depository* and *Charitable Institution House*, are situated. Seel-street terminates at Hanover-street, at the corner of which is the the *Bank of England*. From this we turn to the right into Church-street, and from that to Lord-street. About the middle of Lord-street, is North John-street, along which we proceed. In Temple-court, on the right is the *Fire Engine Station*, and most of the coffee roasters' premises. Cook-street is on the left, in which we find a small piece of *Wood Pavement* and *Monsieur Huguenin's Gymnasium*. After inspecting these, we turn into Castle-street, and are once more at the Exchange.

ROUTE FIFTH.

EXCHANGE, OLDHALL-STREET, LEEDS-ST., VAUXHALL-ROAD, NAYLOR-ST., BEVINGTON BUSH, BEVINGTON HILL, SCOT-LAND-ROAD, RICHMOND-ROW, SONO-ST., STAFFORD-ST., LON-DON-ROAD, PRESCOT-ROAD, MOUNT VERNON, EDGEHILL, IRVINE-ST., WEST DERBY-ST., PEMBROKE-PLACE, LONDON-ROAD, SHAW'S BROW, DALE-ST., EXCHANGE.

Part of this route is through the more disagreeable portion of the town, but it is nevertheless worthy the attention of those who wish to make a complete survey of Liverpool.

We pass through the area of the Exchange into Oldhall-street, and on the left see the *Ship Masters' Association Rooms*. In Union-street, a little further on, is the *Government Emigration* and *Irish Pass-office*. Edmund-street, on the right, contains the *Catholic Chapel* and *Reformed Presbyterian Chapel*; and Prussia-street on the same side leads us to *St. Paul's Church*. Returning to Oldhall-street, we pass Messrs. Bartons, Irlam and Higginson's office, formerly "the *Old-hall*," from which the street derives its name. At the end of the street is the *Leeds and Liverpool Canal Basin*, on the right of which is the *Northern Hospital*. Proceeding along Leeds-street we pass *Leeds-street Chapel and School*, and enter Vauxhall-road nearly opposite the *North Dispen-*

sary. Further north are the *Gas Works,* a number of *Wind-mills,* and lime, soap, starch, and a variety of other *Manu-factories.* In the south direction are the *Clarence Foundry,* and Br*idewell.* We proceed through Naylor-street, in which are *St.* B*artholomew's Church* and Mr. Logan's *Veneer Mills,* to Bevington Bush; on the west side of which is the No*rth Corporation School.* Passing along Bevington Hill we enter *St. Martin's Market,* from which we proceed to Scot-land-road. Proceeding north we pass the new *Scotch Church* and *St. Anthony's Catholic Chapel* on the right, and a little distance to the left is *St. Martin's-in-the-fields.* Returning towards town we pass the end of Nelson-street (north,) at the other end of which is a *New Wesleyan Chapel.* We then turn up Richmond-row, and leave on our right the B*aptist Chapel,* in Byron-street, and *Queen's Theatre,* Christian-street; and on the left the *Two Chapels* in Comus-street, *All Saint's Church* and *St. Annes' Church.* Turning along Soho-street we pass a B*aptist Chapel* on the left, and see *St. Au-gustine's Church,* on the eminence above, and *Trinity Church* on the right. Crossing Islington we enter Stafford-street, at the end of which is the *Monument of King George III.* The statue was executed by Westmacott; and the figure, the countenance of which is an excellent likeness of his late majesty, sits gracefully on his horse. This monu-ment was intended to have been placed in Great George-square, but the present situation was chosen in con-sequence of the inhabitants of the square not agreeing in which direction the horse's head was to be placed. We are now in London-road the great thoroughfare for vehicles previous to the opening of the Railways. Proceeding in the direction from the town we pass the *Methodist Chapel* in Moss-street, and *St. Jude's Church* on the left. A little above the church on the other side is Harper-street, in which the West Derby P*ublic Offices* are situated, under which are cells capable of confining two hundred prisoners. In Low-hill the old *West Darby (Derby) Workhouse* faces us. The inmates have been removed to the more spacious premises in Everton, and it is now occupied by the children belonging to the Liverpool workhouse. From this point we turn to the right, along Mount Vernon, from which we have a good view of the town. In the next street below, the *Catholic Convent* for the Sisters of Mercy is now erecting. At the end of Mount Vernon on the left is an antiquated building called *The Piory*, the residence of the Rev. F. Barker. We now leave Edgehill and turn towards town, along Irvine-street, which leads us to West Derby-street and Pembroke-place, at the corner of which is *Pembroke Chapel*, (Baptist.) The next street we pass is Ashton-street, in which are situated the *Lunatic Asylum* and *Lock Hospital*. Brownlow-street already noticed is also passed, as well as Pembroke-street, in which are the *Albion Oil Mills*. Nearly opposite this is *St. Silas' Church*. Below, on the left, is Gill-street, in which is the *Sandemanian Chapel*, the *Market*, now building, the *Soup Kitchen, &c.* We are once more at the monument, whence we continue our walk downwards past the *Blind Asylum*. After leaving this interesting institution, we come to *Islington Market* on the right, having on our left the *Railway Station*, the *Assize Courts*, and *St. John's Church*. Shaw's Brow, (a steep and narrow declivity through which all the coaches, in former days, used to pass prior to the opening of Manchester-street,) is our next object; and this leads us, after crossing Byrom-street, at the end of which is *St. Stephen's Church*, to Dale-street, in which the principal *Inns* and *Coach Offices* are situated. This street we may always recognize by the bustle of porters and the rattling of omnibuses. Formerly we should, perhaps, have been interrupted in our walk by the sudden exit of four fiery greys, with a loaded coach at their heels, from the yard of the Saracen's Head, or by the luggage landing from the roof of a London coach at the door of the Angel; now, though still a busy scene, the "High Flyer," and "L'Hirondelle," with their splendid teams, are changed for the cumbrous omnibus and its hacks; and Dale-street possesses only three coaches, a miserable remnant of its former number! On the right is the gas works, whence we perceive the Exchange, to which we hasten, after viewing the *Royal Bank Buildings*, on the left, glad to conclude our fifth route.

ROUTE SIXTH.

EXCHANGE, DALE-ST., MANCHESTER-ST., ST. JOHN'S-LANE, HAY-MARKET, COMMUTATION-ROW, ISLINGTON, SHAW-ST., EVERTON-VILLAGE, EVERTON-TERRACE, ST. GEORGE'S-HILL, NORTHUMBERLAND-TERRACE, ST. DOMINGO-LANE, CHURCH-ST., (EVERTON,) EVERTON-ROAD, DERBY-ROAD, ZOOLOGICAL GARDENS, EXCHANGE.

Leaving our usual starting place, we pass along Dale-street to Manchester-street, on the left side of which is the principal office of the *Bootle Water-works*. We then proceed from this point across the old haymarket, up St. John's-lane, leaving Queen's-square, in which is the office of the *New Gasworks* on the right. This brings us to the Haymarket whence we turn to *Islington Market* in London-road. Proceeding along Commutation-row, we arrive at Islington, and find on our right the *Catholic Blind Asylum*, and on the left the *Eastern Dispensary*. Keeping straight up this street we pass on the left Salisbury-street, in which *St. Francis' Xavier's Catholic Chapel* is about to be built. A little above this, is Shaw-street, along which we turn, passing the *Collegiate Institution* and *St Augustine's Church*. About half way down Everton-brow is *Crescent Chapel*. and a little above Shaw-street is the *Round-house* and the celebrated *Everton Toffee Shop*. Turning upwards here, through Everton-village we pass *Prince Rupert's Cottage* on the right with

P

several other buildings of antiquity. We next proceed along
Everton-terrace, and then ascend St. George's-hill, whence
we have a noble view of the mouth of the river. From this
we go through Northumberland-terrace into St. Domingo-
lane, close to which is *St. Domingo-house.* This elegant
mansion was built by Mr. Sparling with the proceeds of a
French prize ship from St. Domingo, whence it derived its
name. It was occupied for a short period as the residence
of the Duke of Gloucester when on a visit to Liverpool, and
was afterwards purchased by government. It was latterly
used as a boarding school, and very recently was purchased
for a comparatively small sum, for a Roman Catholic College.
In the neighbourhood of Everton are some of the most
fashionable residences of the Liverpool merchants. A little
past St. Domingo is the *Bootle Water Works* reservoir, and
further on is the village of Kirkdale. Returning along St.
Domingo-lane we pass *Messrs. Whalley's Nursery,* which is
well worthy of a visit, and arrive at *St. George's Church.*
Passing again through the village of Everton, we go along
Everton-road and perceive on our left the chimney of Hy-
geia-street *Glass-works,* (at present disused,) and in Mill-lane,
the *Everton National School.* Further south in Everton-
road we come to the old *Baptist Burial-ground* on the
right, and at the angle formed by this and Derby-road, we
find the *Necropolis.* Having walked round this "city of the
dead," we proceed along Derby-road and perceive before us the
Zoological Gardens on the right, together with "*The Derby*"
Hotel, a *Zoological Museum,* &c. On the left we see the
West Derby Union Workhouse, which is approached by Mill-
lane. This extensive building was opened in 1841, for the
reception of the poor of West Derby Union, which consists
of twenty-one parishes, and at present contains four hundred
individuals, although there is accommodation for five hundred. The building is of brick and has all the modern improvements. It consists of an octangular centre, in which

is the governor's house, with front, back, and side wings of considerable extent. From the octagon, all the parts of the building may be seen, by which arrangement the inmates are constantly under the eye of the governor. The east wing is appropriated to females and the west to males. The ground-floor of the back wing is occupied as school-rooms, the story above as a dining-room, and on the upper floor is a chapel capable of containing six hundred individuals. On the roof are spacious reservoirs for supplying the apartments, to which the water is forced by a small steam-engine, which also performs several culinary and other domestic operations. The entire area of the ground on which the building is situated is about two acres. We then enter the *Zoological Gardens* where we will probably stay several hours, after which we will find it more agreeable to return to the Exchange in an omnibus or car, than to trudge the distance, after so long a previous walk.

ROUTE SEVENTH.

EXCHANGE, CASTLE-ST., LORD-ST., CHURCH-ST., BOLD-ST., LEECE-ST., HARDMAN-ST., HOPE-ST., FALKNER-ST., CROWN-STREET, UPPER STANHOPE-ST., LODGE-LANE, ULLET-LANE, DINGLE, PARK-ROAD, ST. JAMES'-PLACE, ST. JAMES'-ST., PARK-LANE, SOUTH CASTLE-ST., CASTLE-ST., EXCHANGE.

Leaving the Exchange for the seventh time, we arrive by way of Castle-street, Lord-street, Church-street and Bold-street, at *St Luke's Church* in Berry-street, opposite which is the *New Arcade*. We proceed along Leece-street, and Hardman-street, crossing Rodney-street, past *St. Philip's Church* to Hope-street, and turning to our right we come to Falkner-street. From Falkner-street we pass into Canning-street, in which is the *Church of the Holy Apostles*, and return to Falkner-street a little below the *Female Penitentiary*.

In Mulberry-street, a short distance from this, is a *Welsh Chapel*. We continue in Falkner-street keeping *St. Saviour's Church* to the right till we come to Crown-street, in which the old *Railway Station* is situated. This street leads us across Parliament-street to Upper Stanhope-street, in which is *St. Clement's Church*, and a little above it at the corner of Lodge-lane, the new *Reservoir &c.* of the *Liverpool and Harrington Water-works*. From near this point a pathway leads across a field on the left to the *Railway Station at Edgehill*. Turning to the right at the Waterworks we walk the whole length of Lodge-lane, passing several handsome dwellings, till we arrive at Ullet-lane which leads us past the ground allotted to the *New Park*, to the *Dingle-lodge*. After wandering through these delightful grounds, we turn into Park-road and pass on the right *Park Chapel*, the oldest dissenting chapel in the neighbourhood, and on the left a handsome *Independent Chapel* in South Hill-place. As we approach town we leave, at some distance on the left, the place where the *Herculanæum Potteries* formerly stood, and we pass in succession *St. John the Baptist's Church, a New Connexion Methodist Chapel*, and *St. Patrick's Catholic Chapel*. A little above Park-road is a *Wesleyan* and a *Welsh Chapel*, and at the corner of Warwick-street and Mill-street is *Hanover (an Independent) Chapel*. From the Catholic Chapel we proceed along St. James'-place, St. James'-street and Park-lane, in the latter of which are the *North Corporation School* and *St. Thomas's Church*, to the Custom-house, whence we easily find our way to the Exchange.

THE ENVIRONS.

The following are the principal villages and hamlets in the neighbourhood of Liverpool, arranged according to their relative position, commencing with those to the north of the town.—

BOOTLE is a village about three miles distant, much frequented during summer months for sea bathing. The principal objects of attraction are the Church, which has two towers, the Water-works, and the Land-marks on the sands.

SEAFORTH is about a mile beyond Bootle and contains a number of delightful residences.

WATERLOO is a newly established, but much frequented watering place, disposed in the form of a crescent with a large hotel in the centre. A handsome church has been recently erected. Near this are the villages of LITHERLAND and CROSBY, the latter of which has a church and grammar-school, and four miles farther north is the village of INCE BLUNDELL, in which is the Hall, long the residence of the Blundell family, containing an extensive and rare collection of casts, pictures, sculptures, and other curiosities. The property of this estate was the occasion of the celebrated law-suit Blundell *versus* Weld, by which it was alienated from the heirs to a son of Cardinal Weld.

SEFTON is a township seven miles north of Liverpool. The parish church is dedicated to St. Helen, and the beauty of its interior, perhaps, exceeds that of any church in the county. The ancient church was erected in the year 1111, but the present edifice is of the time of Henry VIII., built by Anthony Molyneux, rector of the place. The chancel is divided by a magnificent screen from the body of the church, and contains sixteen stalls of elegant sculpture. The sepulture of the "noble and knightly family of Molyneux," as

Camden styles them, has been here for a succession of ages. A monument records that Sir, Wm. Molyneux distinguished himself in the battle of Agincourt, and received the honour of knighthood from Henry V.

CROXTETH-PARK is the residence of the Earl of Sefton, four miles south east of Liverpool.

KNOWSLEY HALL is the seat of the Earl of Derby, eight miles east of Liverpool.

WALTON is three miles from Liverpool, and is the parish to which Liverpool originally belonged. The church is of great antiquity and of an irregular form; it has recently had a handsome steeple added, together with a large and powerful new organ. At Spellow Mount a short distance from this, are the beautiful nurseries of Mr. Skirving.

KIRKDALE is a large suburb of the town, with which it is now connected by a continuous line of streets. It contains a neat church, St Mary's Cemetery, several chapels, and the county House of Correction, previously noticed.

WEST DERBY, the greatest part of which is the property of the Earl of Derby, is an old and picturesque village, four miles north east, surrounded by a thickly wooded country.

OLD SWAN is a small hamlet on Prescot-road, near which is the cattle-market, a church, a new Catholic chapel, and a Wesleyan chapel.

A short distance from the Old Swan is BROAD GREEN railway station, and a little further in the southerly direction is the romantic village of CHILDWALL, with its abbey and church.

ALLERTON is five miles south east of Liverpool. In its neighbourhood are the calder stones, formerly noticed, and Allerton Hall, the residence of Roscoe, till the reverses of fortune obliged him to quit it in the decline of life.

GATEACRE and WOOLTON are delightful villages, the latter of which contains a neat church. They are much visited by the inhabitants of the town during summer.

WAVERTREE is a large village containing numerous residences of the more opulent classes, together with an old church and an Independent and Wesleyan chapel. In the village is a large sheet of water called Wavertree lake, near which are the bridewell and an ancient well. The cutting for the railway at Olive Mount, is a little distance from this place. This is a stupendous excavation, in one place 70 feet below the level of the ground, and is well worthy the notice of the visitor.

Between Wavertree and Aigburth are numerous elegant villas and suburban residences. The village of AIGBURTH is beautifully situated three miles south of Liverpool, on the Mersey. In the neighbourhood is a handsome modern church in the Norman style of architecture, in which is a fine painted window representing "Christ healing the leper There is also a Catholic chapel; and a Catholic Magdalen asylum is shortly to be built.

Returning towards town we come into Toxteth-park, in which is situated St. Michael's church, a handsome Gothic erection; and the whole of the neighbourhood through which we pass is thickly studded with gentlemen's seats.

Till the visitor has made the tour of the environs, he will have no idea of the splendour of the private dwellings of the opulent Liverpool merchants, and of the taste which is displayed in the arrangement of the grounds. In making this survey he will find much to interest, as well as to amuse; and, had not this little work been already considerably extended beyond the limits at first proposed, he would have been assisted in his perambulations by a more detailed account of the environs than is now given.

THE CHESHIRE SHORE OF THE MERSEY

has become so thoroughly identified with the interests of Liverpool, that, to omit a short description of the numerous populous villages opposite Liverpool, would be to render this Strangers' *vade mecum* incomplete.

Although there are many places worthy of particular notice on the Cheshire side of the Mersey, two routes will be sufficient to enable the stranger to see the principal objects of attention.

ROUTE FIRST.

WOODSIDE, BIRKENHEAD, ROCK FERRY, NEW FERRY, BEBBINGTON, AND EASTHAM.

Proceeding to George's Pier, we make our way to the Woodside steamer,* by which we are in a few minutes conveyed to the slip at the other side.

WOODSIDE

is the most ancient of the ferries on the Mersey, and it has been in the family of Mr. Price, the present proprietor, for upwards of 500 years. Though formerly merely a ferry house it is now a densely populated neighbourhood, laid out with a considerable degree of elegance and taste. The principal streets are wide and regular, the houses being generally of stone; and it is evident that considerable attention has been paid to effect in their construction. Hamilton-square, designed by G. Graham, Esq., of Edinburgh, contains a num-

* The names of the ferries to which the steamers ply are painted on the paddle boxes; but in addition to this, passengers are assisted in distinguishing the different boats by a *Ball* at the mast head of the Birkenhead steamer, a *W* at that of the Woodside boat, a *Star* at that for Rock Ferry, and the representation of a *Locomotive Engine* at that of the Railway steamer.

ber of elegant dwellings of the Doric style of architecture, and the centre is occupied by a spacious shrubbery. The principal buildings worthy of notice are the *Town-hall, Prison,* and *Market,* which is an extensive erection one story high with a stone front, the centre part of which rests on six columns. The right wing is used as the Jail, and the left as the Town-hall and Parish-offices. The rear of the building which is continued to form a square, is fitted up conveniently as a Market, and is well supplied with provisions, &c. The building was designed by Mr. Rampling, of Liverpool, and erected by Messrs. J. and W. Walker, for less than £4,000. *Trinity Church* is a splendid Norman edifice, recently opened, constructed entirely of white freestone, and the workmanship is of the richest and most costly description. The tower, which is square, is at the west end, and under it is the principal entrance, enriched by carved heads and other ornaments. The *Independent Chapel,* Hamilton-square, is a handsome building in the Gothic style, with lancet windows between the buttresses. The entrance is by a porch, supported on Gothic arches. *The Scotch Church,* also in the Gothic style, has a stone front with projecting turrets, which are carried up above the walls of the building, and terminated by pinnacles. The sides are stuccoed, and have buttresses, each of which is finished with a pinnacle. The principal entrance is by a pointed arched doorway, ascended by a broad flight of steps. *Brunswick Chapel,* belonging to the Wesleyans, situated in Brunswick-terrace, is a neat building with an Ionic portico, and the date of erection, A.D. MDCCCXXX, inscribed over the entrance. The *Catholic Chapel* (St. Werburg's) is a large substantial building of red stone, with a cross at each end. The *Chester and Birkenhead Railway Station,* in Grange-lane, has nothing in its appearance to render it worthy of notice. At a little distance from it are two handsome lodges, forming the entrance to that part of the neighbourhood called *Clifton Park,* which is laid out in villas.

In the hollow below Holt-hill, on ground recovered from a pool, caused by the influx of the tide, are situated the *Gasworks*, from which the whole of this part of Cheshire is lighted. There are several large hotels in different parts of the village, as well as those in the neighbourhood of the ferry.

A little beyond MONKS' FERRY, which is at present chiefly used by the railway passengers is

BIRKENHEAD.

The *Church of St. Mary*, built in the Gothic style of architecture, with a lofty spire, is a prominent object from Liverpool, and its position in connexion with the *Old Abbey*, renders it an interesting object to the visitor. The abbey has been already noticed under the head *Antiquities*. The church is cruciform, and was erected by F. R. Price, Esq., the lord of the manor, in 1819, since which period it has been enlarged, by the addition of the transepts. The Inn at Birkenhead is very commodious, and there are tastefully arranged gardens adjoining, overlooking the river, and commanding an excellent view of the town of Liverpool. From Birkenhead we proceed to TRANMERE, a ferry which is not now in use, and crossing the bridge over Tranmere Pool, we direct our steps to the next ferry up the river, which is

THE ROYAL ROCK FERRY.

This is a delightful neighbourhood, thickly studded with elegant villas and mansions, all of which are of modern erection. A splendid esplanade connects this with the New Ferry. Near the slip is a neat edifice containing hot and cold baths, and above this, is a good hotel. The park, which is open to the public, contains some of the best houses; and a handsome *New Church*, dedicated to *St. Peter* has just been built by subscription, on ground presented by R. W. Barton, Esq. The foundation stone was laid on the 14th April, 1841, and the work completed by Messrs. Samuel

and Walker, from the designs of Messrs. Hurst and Moffat.
The building is of the old Norman style of architecture,
with a spire rising 68 feet above the roof of the church.
The interior is appropriately fitted up, without galleries,
although they may easily be added if necessary, and it will
accommodate 750 individuals. Half a mile higher up the
river is

NEW FERRY,

from which only small sailing-boats ply to Liverpool. Modern
improvement and taste has not done so much for this ferry
as for the one last named, although there are many beautiful cottages near the shore. There are also comfortable
baths, and bathing-machines to be had in summer. Leaving
New Ferry, and proceeding from the river across the Chester
road, we pass under the railway, and shortly arrive at

LOWER BEBBINGTON.

This is a retired hamlet, having a fine *Old Church*, with an
ivy-mantled spire, a glimpse of which can be caught from
the Liverpool side of the Mersey. A little before arriving
at the church we pass a curiously ornamented house, and
find in the wall of the garden several stones with curious inscriptions. From Bebbington we make will our way
across or round Bromboro' Pool to

EASTHAM,

a small village situated among the richly wooded property
of Sir Thomas Stanley. *The Church* is of great antiquity,
and the architect is said to have been Inigo Jones. Half a
mile from the village, and entirely concealed by the luxu-
riant plantations, is the *Ferry of Eastham*, which is the
most picturesque on the river. The gardens of the hotel
are delightfully laid out, and will form a pleasant resting

place after the long route which we have taken. After we
have partaken sufficiently of the choice things provided by
'mine host' of the Inn, we return to Liverpool by one of
the steamers.

ROUTE SECOND.

WOODSIDE, BIDSTON, WALLASEY, LEASOWE, NEW BRIGH-
TON, FORT AND LIGHTHOUSE, MAGAZINES, EGREMONT,
LISCARD, SEACOMBE.

Once more at Woodside, we turn to the right, after leaving
the ferry, and pass *Mr. Laird's iron ship-building yard* and
patent-slip, on the margin of Wallasey Pool. This pool
is a large inlet of the river, proceeding several miles into
the interior, preventing us from getting directly to the next
ferry in the southward direction. A handsome bridge is about
to be built over the pool by the inhabitants of the neighbourhood. It will be a draw-bridge, working on stone piers
at a height of 30 feet above the present surface, having seven
wooden arches of 20 feet span each, leaving a waterway of
nearly 200 feet. The bridge will be approached by a new
road across Bidston-moss. The architect is Mr. Alfred
Yarrow, and the contractors are Messrs. Walker and Craven.
From Woodside we make for B*idston Lighthouse* on Bidston
hill, about three miles distant, from which we have a splendid
view of the Mersey and the Dee, and the neighbouring
mountains of Flintshire and Denbighshire. The lighthouse
was erected in 1770, and the internal arrangements are
worthy of inspection. At the top of the pool is the village
of WALLASEY, which was at one time a formidable rival of
Liverpool. The *Church* stands on an eminence above the
village. Not far from Wallasey, in the direction of Seacombe, is a *Monument* with a small spire, on the road side,

in memory of Mrs. Boode, of Leasowe Castle, who was killed near the spot, by a fall from her pony carriage, in 1826. About two miles from Wallasey is

LEASOWE CASTLE,

to which an omnibus runs daily from Woodside, at twelve o'clock. Some parts of the building are of modern construction, while other parts are of considerable antiquity. One of the apartments contains the wainscotting of the celebrated Star Chamber, which was transferred to this place from St. Stephen's Chapel, in 1834, by Sir Edward Cust, the proprietor of the castle. A part of the castle is used as an Inn, and is a favourite place of resort by the inhabitants of Liverpool. *Leasowe Lighthouse* is on the shore opposite the Inn, and is a prominent object from the sea. From Leasowe we proceed to

NEW BRIGHTON,

a watering place, which at no very distant period, promises to become one of the most fashionable and delightful places of resort in this part of the kingdom. It was projected by James Atherton, Esq., of Liverpool, who purchased 170 acres of land, about seven years ago, and immediately commenced erecting marine villas. The situation has considerable advantages, it rises in a succession of ridges of a convex semicircular form, from the margin of the sea, and is capable of being arranged in terraces, so that none will intercept each other's view. The shore is admirably adapted for bathing, and there is an abundant supply of fresh water, which is received in a reservoir, capable of containing 1,600 gallons. Spacious streets, nearly a mile in length, are laid out, and numerous villas, and a commodious hotel, have been already erected ; shewing the spirited manner in which the project of the proprietor is being carried out, and the gigantic nature of his plans.

THE FORT, AND LIGHTHOUSE

described in a previous part of this volume, are situated at the entrance to the Mersey, below New Brighton. The *Fort* will accommodate 100 men, and has all the necessary conveniences. The west front is 200 feet in length, and mounts six thirty-two pounders, and the north front has four guns, which with those at the west front and at the angles, will give a direct fire of fourteen guns on an enemy attempting to pass up the Rock channel, which he is compelled by the nature of the sand-banks to do within 900 yards of the fort. The approach is by a stone bridge of three arches, and the interior of the building is elevated $14\frac{1}{2}$ feet above the surface of the rock. The entire area is upwards of 3,000 square yards, and it mounts eighteen thirty-two pounders. It was planned by Captain Kitson, of the Royal Engineers.

THE MAGAZINES.

The village is so named from the circumstance of all the gunpowder arriving at the port being deposited in a building in the neighbourhood. It is situated on the margin of a sand-hill, and the rustic simplicity of the cottages strongly contrasts with the appearance of the elegant villas of the neighbouring ferries.

EGREMONT

is the next ferry southward. At the slip is a large hotel, and at a little distance are numerous elegant residences. Westward of the hotel is a handsome *Church*, erected by Sir John Tobin, for the joint convenience of the inhabitants of Egremont and Seacombe.

LISCARD

is a neat hamlet, a short distance from Egremont ferry, in which there is a *Wesleyan* and an *Independent Chapel*.

SEACOMBE

is a populous village pleasantly situated on the rising ground on the north side of Wallasey Pool, having a comfortable hotel, the gardens of which are neatly laid out as a tea-garden. In the neighbourhood are many agreeably situated marine villas. From this ferry we cross in the steamer, and once more reach Liverpool.

APPENDIX

POST OFFICE, LIVERPOOL.

WILLIAM BANNING, ESQ., POSTMASTER.

THE DELIVERIES.

The office opens for the FIRST DELIVERY about 8 15 every morning, and continues open until 9 p.m. The letters in the first delivery are those (brought by the Grand Junction Railway Mails) from London and the line of road, the East, South, and West of England, Falmouth, Exeter, Bristol, Gloucester, Worcester, South Wales, Birmingham, Bilston, Wolverhampton, Stafford, Eccleshall, Stone, Rugely, Newcastle, the Potteries, and Warrington: and from Chester, North Wales, Shropshire, and Cheshire; the East and West Indies, North and South America, and the Mediterranean; (by the Carlisle Mail) from Ormskirk, Preston, Blackburn, Burnley, Garstang, Lancaster, Kendal, Penrith, Carlisle, Westmoreland, Cumberland, and all Scotland; (by the Dublin Packet) from all Ireland, and (by the first Manchester and first York Mails) from Manchester, Stockport, Rochdale, Macclesfield, all Yorkshire, Durham, Northumberland, Lincolnshire, Nottinghamshire, and Derbyshire.

The SECOND DELIVERY commences about 11 a.m. and includes letters from Kenyon, Newton, Bolton, and Manchester (per Second Manchester Mail).

The THIRD DELIVERY includes the letters by the second Dublin Packet, due at 11 30 a.m. which will be ready for delivery in half an hour after arrival.

The FOURTH DELIVERY commences about 1 30 p.m. (the third Manchester Mail) with letters from Manchester, Prescot, and St. Helens.

The FIFTH DELIVERY commences at 3 30 a.m. and includes letters from Chester, Neston, Eastham, and New Ferry.

The SIXTH DELIVERY commences about 4 30 p.m. and includes letters (brought by the third Manchester and second York Mails) from Newton, and Manchester, Rochdale, Halifax, Bradford, Wetherby, Leeds, and York, and (by the second Grand Junction Railway Mail) from Birmingham, Walsall, Wolverhampton, Stafford, Newcastle, Middlewich, Winsford, Northwich, Warrington and Huyton.

The SEVENTH DELIVERY commences at 6 30 p.m., and includes letters from Southport, Ormskirk, Maghull, Crosby,¡ Bootle, Walton, West Derby, Old Swan, Wavertree, Woolton, Upton, Birkenhead, Seacombe, and New Brighton.

The EIGHTH DELIVERY commences at 7 45 p.m., including letters from Manchester, and (by the second London and third Grand Junction Railway Mails) from London and the towns beyond London, and Foreign Parts passing through London, and the line of road from London and Birmingham.

₊ *When any delay occurs in the arrival of the Mails, a corresponding one must unavoidably take place in the commencement of the deliveries.*

N.B.—The post-office is not open for the delivery of letters on Sundays between the hours of nine and two, on which day it finally closes at 8 p.m.

The BOX DELIVERY is closed daily (Sundays excepted) at 9 p.m. Letters addressed to the post-office, " Until called for," are not delivered after 9 p.m. ; and letters to be post-paid, are received until twelve at midnight, and on Sundays from 9 to 10 15 a.m.

There are three deliveries daily by the letter carriers, commencing about 8 15 a.m., 2 p.m. and 6 p.m. On Sundays only the first.

THE DESPATCHES.

The following are the hours at which the letter box is closed for making up the several mails, and the hour at which each mail is despatched :—

Box closed at		Mail despatched at
1 30 A.M.	For Warrington, Bolton, Wigan, Chorley, Sandbach, Congleton, Macclesfield, Stafford, Wolverhampton, Birmingham, London; Foreign (via London), Preston, Garstang, Lancaster, Burton, Kendal, Penrith, Carlisle, Edinburgh, Glasgow, and all Scotland; for Chester, and the line of road to Holyhead, and for Wrexham, Ruabon, Ruthin, Denbigh, and Carnarvon..........	3 0 A.M.
	For Dublin, and all Ireland	5 0 A.M.
6 15 A.M.	For Manchester and York line of road..	6 45 A.M.
6 65 A.M.	For New Ferry, Eastham, Neston, and Chester	7 15 A.M.
7 30 A.M.	For Maghull, Ormskirk and Southport	8 0 A.M.
9 15 A.M.	For Warrington, Northwich, Middlewich, Newcastle, Stafford, Wolverhampton, Walsall and Birmingham	10 15 A.M.
10 0 A.M.	For Prescot, St. Helens and Manchester.	10 45 A.M.
1 0 P.M.	For Kenyon, Newton and Manchester.	1 45 P.M.

Box closed at		Mail despatched at
3 0 P.M.	For Birkenhead, Eastham and Chester.	3 45 P.M.
3 30 P.M.	For Wigan, Bolton, Manchester, Rochdale, Halifax, Huddersfield, Bradford, Preston, the North Road, Westmoreland, Cumberland, and all Scotland..	4 30 P.M.
5 30 P.M.	For Birkenhead, Chester, Wrexham, and North Wales; Warrington, Wolverhampton, Sheffield, Nottingham, and Birmingham; the counties of Rutland, Lincoln, Northampton, Bedford, Berks, Suffolk, Herts, Warwick, Worcester, Huntingdon, Cambridge, Norfolk, and Oxford; for London, Bristol, Exeter, Falmouth, all parts of the South and Southwest of England and South Wales; also South America, and the West Indies	6 45 P.M.
	For Rochdale, Halifax, Bradford, Leeds, York, and all Durham........	7 15 P.M.
	For Dublin and all Ireland	7 15 P.M.

MONEY ORDER OFFICE.

To prevent the loss of money sent in letters by post, *for which the Post Office is not accountable*, and for the convenience of persons remitting small sums not exceeding five pounds, a clerk attends at the Money-order Office, Post Office, from ten in the morning until three in the afternoon, and from half-past five to seven in the evening, (Sunday excepted), to pay orders drawn upon the Post Master, Liverpool, and to give orders payable at sight, on the Post Masters where the remittances are required to be paid, in any part of the United Kingdom,

THE LOCAL POST OFFICES.

Time of Despatch from Liverpool.	Places.	Receivers.	Time of Despatch to Liverpool.
8 30 A.M.& 1 45 P.M.	Newton ....Mr. Saile ....9 15 A.M. & 2 15 P.M.		
8 0 A.M.	Maghull.... — Watkinson, Saddler .... 4 30 —		
	Walton ..... — Musker, Schoolmaster ... 5 15 —		
8 20 A.M.	Bootle ...... — Peters, Shopkeeper...... 3 40 —		
	Crosby......Miss Gilles, Repository . 3 0 —		
	Wavertree...Mr. Rigby, Shopkeeper ...... 4 0 —		
	Woolton .... — Ball, Shopkeeper ......3 0 —		
	Old Swan ... — Hoult, Old Swan Inn ... 3 45 —		
	West Derby.. — Westmore, Shopkeeper .. 3 15 —		
8 15 A.M.	N. Brighton.. — Williams, Albion House, 2 45 —		
	Egremont ... — Dewhurst, Church-street, 3 30 —		
	Seacombe ... Hill, Victoria-road...... 3 55 —		
	Aigburth .... — Cockburn.............. 3 30 —		
1 45 P.M.	Kenyon .... Leather, Lane-end ...... 9 0 A.M.		
8 30 A.M.	Huyton .... Broadhurst, Shopkeeper, 3 15 P.M.		

THE POST OFFICE RECEIVING HOUSES.

Situations.	Receivers.	Letters sent to Gen. Office at
		P.M. P.M.
4, Gt. Howard-street.	Mr. Bark	11 45 A.M. ... 4 0 & 8 0
1, Regent-road	— Sharrock....	12 0 — .. 4 15 & 8 15
97, New Scotland-rd.	— Hardisty	12 15 .. 4 30 & 8 30
1, Vauxhall-road	— Mucklow....	12 30 P.M. ... 4 45 & 8 45
Exchange-buildings..	The News Room..	12 45 .. 3 0 & 5 0
Kirkdale,37,Castle-st.	Mr. Walker	11 45 A.M. ... 4 0 & 8 0
Everton,33,Church-st.	— Walsh	12 0 — .. 4 15 & 8 15
83, Low-hill	— Watson......	12 15 P.M ... 4 30 & 8 30
68, London-road	— Underhill ...	12 30 — .. 4 45 & 8 45
Lime-street	The Railway Stn.	12 35 .. 4 50 & 8 50
67, Church-street....	Mr. H. Marcus ..	12 45 — 3 0 5 0 & 9 0
Edge-hill, ... } (op. the Church) }	— French....	11 45 A.M. ... 4 0 & 8 0
256, Falkner-street ..	Garlick	12 0 .. 4 15 & 8 15
30, Oxford-street ..	Titherington.	12 15 P.M. ... 4 30 & 8 30
Harrington, 2 Mill-st.	— Balderston ..	12 30 4 45 & 8 45
42,Berry-street....	— Davies	12 45 5 0 & 9 0
73, Park-road	— Pearson	3 45

The Post-Office Receiving Houses are Closed on Sundays.
Postage Stamps are sold at the General Post Office, and at the Penny Post Offices, and Post Office Receiving Houses, Labels at 1d. and 2d. each, Covers at 1¼d. and 2¼d. each.

STEAM NAVIGATION.

When the hour of sailing is not specified, it is generally a short time before high water. The most accurate and cheapest Liverpool Tide Tables, are in the Liverpool Commercial Almanack, published annually, at 74, South Castle-street, containing 72 pages, price 6d.

STEAM BOATS SAIL FROM GEORGE'S PIER, FOR

Runcorn.—Daily, 2½ hours before high water. Offices, Mann Island.

Eastham.—Summer, at 6, 8, and 11, a.m.; ½-past 1, 3, 5, and 7, p.m. Winter, 8 and 11, a.m.; 3 and 5, p.m. Office, Mrs. Dod's, James'-street.

Monk's Ferry.—Twenty minutes before the starting of the trains of the Birkenhead and Chester Railway.

Rock Ferry, Birkenhead, and Woodside.—Every half hour.

FROM SOUTH END PRINCE'S PARADE OR NORTH PIER OF GEORGE'S BASIN, FOR

Seacombe and Egremont.—Every half hour.

New Brighton —Every hour during the summer.

Amlwch.—Windermere, every Tuesday morning, from George's Pier. Elizabeth Winder, Upper Pownall-street.

Annan, Dumfries, Carlisle, and Whitehaven.—Royal Victoria three times a fortnight, from Clarence Dock. J. D. Thompson, 35, Water-street.

Beaumaris, Bangor, and Menai Bridge.—Erin go Bragh, Tuesday, Thursday, and Saturday.   Samuel Perry, Water-street.

Beaumaris, Bangor, Menai Bridge and Carnarvon.—Snowdon and Benledi, in summer, Mon., Wed., and Friday, at ½-past 10 ; winter, twice a week.   R. Roberts, Canton-buildings, Water-street.

Belfast.—Athlone, Wednesday, two hours before high water. Samuel Perry, Water-street.

Belfast.—Reindeer and Falcon, Monday and Friday, from Clarence Dock.   Langtrys and Co., 20, Water-street.

Carlisle and Annan.—Newcastle, three times a fortnight, calling off Whitehaven and Maryport.   H. Halton, 31, Water-street.

Chester.—Dairy Maid, Wednesday and Saturday, from Trafalgar Dock.   Charles Davison, 9, James'-street.

Coleraine.—Coleraine, Monday, to Port Rush, Larne, and Giant's Causeway.   J. A. and R. Forshaw, 6, Goree Piazzas.

Conway.—The Oswald, Monday and Thurs., from George's Pier.

Cork.—Prince of Wales, every Wednesday, from Clarence Basin. J. Brebner, 20, Water-street.

Cork.—Ocean and Erin, Tuesday and Saturday, St. George Steam-packet Company, Clarence Dock.

Down Patrick and Strangford Lough.—Eclipse, every Sat., from Trafalgar Dock, T. M'Tear, 15, Water-street.

Down Patrick and Strangford Lough.—Warrington, once a fortnight.   Glover and Thorpe, India-buildings, Water-street.

Douglas.—H. M. Royal Mail Steam Packets, King Orry, Queen of the Isle, and Mona's Isle, twice a week in winter, about high water ; in summer, daily, at half-past 10 o'clock, from George's Pier.   Moore and Christian, 7, Strand-street.

Drogheda.—Grana Ueile, Irishman, Green Isle, Fair Trader, and Town of Drogheda, daily, from the Clarence Dock.   Patrick Ternan, 25, Water-street.

Dublin.—H. M. Royal Mail Steam-packets, Medusa, Merlin, Urgent, and Medina, for Kingstown, every morning, at 6, from Birkenhead, to which passengers are conveyed by the tender Redwing, at ½-past 5 ; Com. T. Bevis, 5, India-buildings., Water-st.

Dublin.—The City of Dublin Steam-packet Company's first class vessels, Queen Victoria, Prince, and Princess, every evening at 7 o'clock, from George's Pier to Kingstown Harbour, with *Her Majesty's Mail and Cabin Passengers only;* and second-class Steam-packets, with goods and passengers, about 2 hours before high water, daily, (Sunday excepted.)   Samuel Perry, Water-st.

Dumfries, direct.—Nithsdale, twice a week in summer, and once in winter.   John Rae, Rhodes'-buildings, South Castle-street,

Dundalk.—Fin M'Coul, and Glasgow, Wednesday and Saturday, James Metge, 31, Water-street.

Galloway.—Countess of Galloway, summer twice, and winter once a week, for Kirkcudbright, Garliestown, and Wigtown, alternately.   A. Laurie and Co., 11, King-street.

Greenock & Glasgow.—Admiral and Commodore, from Clarence Dock, three times a fortnight.   D. M'Iver and Co., 12, Water-st.

Greenock and Glasgow.—Achilles and Fire King, from Clarence Dock, three times a fortnight.   Martin and Co., 7, Water-st.

Greenock & Glasgow.—Princess Royal, and Royal George, from Clarence Dock, three times a fortnight.   J Brebner, 20, Water-st.

Lancaster.—Duchess of Lancaster, from Clarence Dock, twice a week. William Dowson and Son, 8, Goree Piazzas.

Londonderry.—Robert Napier and Isabella Napier, and Maiden City, Tuesday and Friday, at the morning tide, from the Clarence Dock. W. Moore, 35, Water-street.

Maryport, Kirkcudbright, and Isle of Whithorn.—Warrington, twice a week. Glover and Thorpe, India Buildings, Water-street.

Maryport.—See Carlisle.

Mostyn.—Taliesin and Black Diamond, Tuesday, Thursday, and Saturday. Office, Holyhead Tavern, Chapel-street.

Newry.—Lee and Severn, Tuesday, Thursday, and Saturday, from Clarence Dock. St. George Steam Packet Company, Clarence Dock ; or T. M'Tear, 15, Water-street.

Preston.—Tuesday, Thursday, and Saturday, from George's Dock Basin. J. M. Nelson, 4, George's Dock Gates.

Rhyl.—The Benledi, in summer, thrice, and in winter, once a week. R. Roberts, Canton-buildings, 13, Water-street.

Swansea, Milford, and Bristol.—Troubadour, every Saturday. T. M'Tear, Water-street.

Ulverston.—Windermere, with passengers only, summer thrice, and winter, once a week. E. Winder, Upper Pownall-street.

Waterford.—William Penn or Gipsy, from Clarence Dock, every Tuesday. Archer, Daly and Co., 2, Cook-street.

Wexford.—Warrington, on Tuesday and Wednesday, alternately. Glover and Thorp, India-buildings, Water-street.

Wexford.—Town of Wexford, from Trafalgar Dock, every Tuesday. T. M'Tear, 15, Water-street.

Whitehaven.—Earl of Lonsdale and Countess of Lonsdale, summer, three times, and winter, twice a week from Trafalgar Dock. William Dowson and Son, 8, Goree Piazzas.

Boston and Halifax.—The Hibernia, Britannia, Acadia, Caledonia, or Columbia, the 4th and 19th of every month, except in Dec., Jan., Feb., and March, when they sail on the 4th only. D. and C. M'Iver, 12, Water-street.

New York.—The Great Western, alternately from this port and Bristol.

RAILWAY INFORMATION.

GRAND JUNCTION.

From Liverpool and Manchester to Birmingham.

H. M.			H. M.
3	30 a.m.	First Class joins London Train at......	8 30 a.m.
6	0 a.m.	Mixed Class joins London Train at	12 0 noon
8	15 a.m.	First Class joins London Train at......	1 15 p.m.
		and Derby Train at	1 0 p.m.
10	30 a.m.	First Class joins London Train at......	4 0 p.m.
		and Derby Train at	3 30 p.m.
1	0 p.m.	First Class.	
4	45 p.m.	Mixed.	
*7	0 p.m.	First Class joins London Train at......	12 0 night
		and Derby Train at	12 40 a.m.

The 3h 30m a.m. Train from Liverpool starts from the Station at Edge-hill only.

On Sundays the Departures will be

3	30 a.m.	First Class joins London Train at......	8	30 a.m.
8	15 a.m.	Mixed Class joins London Train at	1	30 a.m.
10	30 a.m.	Mixed Class		
*7	0 p.m.	Mixed Class joins London Train at	12	0night

To Derby, First Class passengers only.

The Trains on Sundays stop at the First Class Stations only

* No private carriages or horses can be conveyed by the 7 p.m. departure from Liverpool and Manchester.

TO LONDON.

By the Trains 8 15 a.m. } on week { and at 8 15a.m. } on
    ,,   ,, 10 30 a.m. } days {   ,,   7 0p m. } Sundays
    ,,   ,,   7 0 p.m. }

TO DERBY, NOTTINGHAM, AND THE MIDLAND COUNTIES
FROM LIVERPOOL.

3 30 a.m.	Mail Train.		10 30 a.m.	Mail Train
6 0 a.m.	2nd Class Train		4 0 p.m.	Mixed Train
8 15 a.m.	1st Class Train		7 0 p.m.	Mail Train

FARES.—1st Class, 28s.; 2nd Class, 20s. 6d.; one horse, £2 18s.; two, £4 11s.; three, £6 4s. Carriages, £4 4s. each.

First Class Passengers, Horses and Carriages, will, if required be booked *throughout from Liverpool and Manchester only*, to London, without change of carriage at Birmingham.

Fares between Liverpool or Manchester and Birmingham.

Four Inside Coach...£1	7	6	One Horse £2	0	
Six Inside 1st Class do. 1	6	0	Two Horses............ 3	0	
2nd Class close Carriage 0	18	0	Three Ditto............ 4	0	
3rd Class open Carriage			Dogs, each 0	3	
by 6 a.m. Train from			Carriages, four wheels .. 3	0	
L'pl. or Man., *(book-*			Ditto, two wheels... 2	0	
ing to 1st Class Sta-			Grooms in Charge of Horses,		
tions only) 0	13	0	if with them in the box. 0	14	
Passengers in Private			Servants in attendance on		
Carriages 0	18	0	their employers, may go		
Children under 10 yrs. half price.			in First Class Trains at		
Children in arms, free.			Second Class Fares 0	18	

Fares from Liverpool or Manchester to London, when booked throughout as above.

	G. J.	L. & B.	TOTAL.
MAIL TRAINS.—Six Inside Coach £1 6 0	—£1 10 0	—£2 16 0	
Ditto. Four Inside do. 1 7 6	— 1 10 0	— 2 17 6	
Ditto. *night.* Six Inside do. 1 6 0	— 1 12 6	— 2 18 6	
Ditto. ,, Four] Inside do. 1 7 6	— 1 12 6	— 3 0 0	
OTHER TRAINS.—Six Inside do. 1 4 6	— 1 10 0	— 2 14 6	
Ditto. Four Inside do. 1 7 6	— 1 10 0	— 2 17 6	
Ditto. *night.* Six Inside do. 1 4 6	— 1 12 6	— 2 17 0	
Ditto. Four Inside do. 1 7 6	— 1 12 6	— 3 0 0	

LIVERPOOL AND MANCHESTER RAILWAY.

The following are the times of departure from Lime-street, Liverpool, and from Liverpool-road, Manchester:—

From Liverpool to Manchester.	From Manchester to Liverpool,
First Class. Second Class.	*First Class. Second Class.*
3 15 Morning.. 7 0 Morning	3 30 Morning.. 7 15 Morning
8 45 ,, .. 9 45 ,,	9 0 ,, ..10 0 ,,
11 0 ,, .. 2 15 Aftern.	11 15 ,, .. 2 30 Aftern.
3 30 Aftern., .. 5 15 ,,	3 45 Aftern., .. 5 30 ,,
7 30 Evening .. 7 30 Mixed.	7 30 ,. .. 7 30 Mixed.
Stopping only at Huyton Gate, Rainhill, St. Helens' Junction, Newton, Parkside, and Kenyon Junction.	Stopping only at Patricroft, Bury-lane, Bolton Junction, Parkside, Newton, and St. Helens' Junction.

On Sundays.

From Liverpool to Manchester.	From Manchester to Liverpool.
First Class. Second Class,	*First Class. Second Class.*
3 15 Morning, by Parkside.	3 30 Morning, by Parkside.
7 30 Morning.	7 30 Morning.
5 15 Afternoon.	5 30 Afternoon
7 30 Evening.. 7 30 Mixed.	7 30 Evening.. 7 30 Mixed.
Stopping as on other days.	Stopping as on other days.

FARES.

By First Class Train, Four Inside, Royal Mail.......... 6s. 6d.
Ditto, Six Inside Glass Coaches........ 6 0
By Second Class Train, Glass Coaches 6 0
Ditto Open Carriages................ 4 6
Four-wheeled Carriages, 20s. each.—Two-wheeled ditto, 15s. each.
HORSES. — For One Horse, 14s,—Two Horses, 20s.—Three Horses, 24s.

TO PRESTON AND WIGAN.

From Liverpool.	From Manchester.
3 15 Morning, 1st Class Train	3 30 Morning, 1st Class Train
8 45 ,, Mixed do.	9 0 ,, Mixed do.
11 0 ,, First Class do.	11 15 ,, First Class do.
2 30 Aftern. Second Class do.	2 45 Aftern. Second Class do.
4 45 ,, Mixed do.	5 0 ,, Mixed do.
7 30 ,, First Class do.	7 30 First Class do.

On Sundays.

3 15 Morning, 1st Class Train	3 30 Morning, 1st Class Train
7 30 ,, Mixed do.	7 30 ,, Mixed do.
4 45 Afternoon, do. do.	4 45 Afternoon, do. do.
7 30 ,, First Class do.	7 30 ,, First Class do.

FARES to Preston—First Class, 7s. 6d.—Second Class, 5s. 0d.
,, Wigan 5s. 0d. 3s. 6d.

TO FLEETWOOD AND POULTON.

From Liverpool.   From Manchester.
8 45 Morning, Mixed Train.   9 0 Morning, Mixed Train.
2 30 Afternoon,   do.   2 45 Afternoon,   do.

On Sundays.

7 30 Morning, Mixed. | 7 30 Morning, Mixed.

FARES to Fleetwood—First Class, 12s. 6d.—Second Class, 8s. 6d.
 Poulton „ 11s. 6d.   8s. 0d.

TO LANCASTER.

From Liverpool.   From Manchester.
3 15 Morning, 1st Class Train   3 30 Morning, 1st Class Train
8 45 „ Mixed do.   9 0 Mixed do.
11 0 „ First Class do.   11 15 „ First Class do.
2 30 Aftern. Second Class do.   2 45 Aftern. Second Class do.
4 45 „ Mixed do.   5 0 „ Mixed do.

FARES.—First Class, 13s. 6d.—Second Class, 9s. 0d.
CARRIAGES. — Four wheels, 42s. 6d. —Two wheels, 30s. each·
HORSES.—For one Horse, 21s.—Two Horses, 40s.
Three Horses, 48s.

TO BOLTON.

From Liverpool.   From Manchester.
8 45 Morning, 1st Class Train   9 0 Morning, 1st Class Train
2 30 Afternoon, Second do.   2 45 Afternoon, Second do.
5 30 „ do. do.   5 30 „ do. do.

On Sundays.

7 30 Morning 2nd Class Train   7 30 Morning, 2nd Class Train
4 45 Afternoon, do. do.   4 45 Afternoon, do. do.

FARES from Liverpool—Inside, 5s. 6d.—Outside, 4s.; and from
Manchester, 2s. 6d. and 2s.

TO ST. HELENS.

From Liverpool.   From Manchester.
7 0 Morning, 2nd Class Train   7 15 Morning, 2nd Class Train
9 45 „ do   10 0 „ do.
2 0 Afternoon do   2 0 Afternoon, do.
5 30 „ do   2 45   do.
         5 30 „ do.

On Sundays.

7 30 Morning, 2nd Class Train   7 30 Morning, 2nd Class Train
4 45 Afternoon, do.   4 45 Afternoon, do.

FARES from Liverpool—Inside, 2s. 6d.—Outside, 2s.; and from
Manchester, 4s. and 3s.

CHESTER AND BIRKENHEAD.

TO CHESTER.

From Grange Lane Station, Birkenhead.

MORNING.	AFTERNOON.
At †7 o'clock.	10 minutes before 1 o'clock.
20 minutes past 8 o'clock.	10 ,, ,, 4 ,,
20 ,, ,, 10 ,,	15 ,, ,, 7 ,, or
	immediately on arrival of mail.
	†10 minutes before 8 oclock.

On Sundays.

10 minutes before 9 o'clock.	15 minutes before 7 o'clock, or
	immediately on arrival of mail.

The Steamer sails from George's Pier for the Railway, twenty minutes before the starting of the train.

TO BIRKENHEAD.

From Brook-street Station, Chester.

MORNING.	AFTERNOON.
†* At 5 o'clock.	At 1 o'clock.
Half-past 8	Half-past 3 ,,
Half-past 10	15 minutes past 6 ,, or
	immediately on arrival of mail.
	at †8 o'clock.

On Sundays.

* At 5 o'clock.	At 8 o'clock.
,, 10 ,,	

* Mail Trains will not stop on the Road.

All the above Trains, except those marked *, are Mixed Trains, and will stop at Sutton, Hooton, Bebbington, and Mollington Stations.

The departures of 3rd Class Carriages will be confined to trains marked thus (†) except on Sundays, when they will be attached to all the trains.

A Steam-packet will wait the arrival of the Train to convey Passengers and Produce to Liverpool.

FARES.

	1st Class.		2nd Class.		3rd Class.	
From Birkenhead						
To Chester	3s.	6d.	2s.	6d.	1s.	6d.
Bebbington	1	0	0	9	0	6
Hooton	1	6	1	0	0	9
Sutton	1	9	1	3	0	9
Mollington	3	6	2	6	1	6
From Chester						
To Mollington	1	0	0	9	0	6
Birkenhead	3	6	2	6	1	6
Sutton	1	9	1	3	0	9
Hooton	2	0	1	6	1	0
Bebbington	3	6	2	6	1	6

Children above Three Years old, and under Ten, Half Fare.

Carriages, 4 wheels, 15s. —2 wheels, 10s.—1 Horse, 6s.—2 Horses, 10s.

The charge for the Ferry, in addition to the above, is 2d., for passengers of all classes. Omnibuses are provided between Monks' Ferry and Grange Lane, fare 3d. each.

Passengers and Parcels booked at the Railway-office, James'-street, Liverpool, or at Grange Lane Station, Birkenhead.

CHESTER AND CREWE.

FROM CHESTER.

*Mail	4 15 a.m., to meet	3 30 a.m. train from L'pl. & Man.
FirstClass	11 30 ,,	,,	10 30 ,,	,,
Mixed	5 0 p.m. ,,	4 0p.m. Train frm. do. & 4 30p.m. Train from Birm.
*Mail	7 50 p.m. ,,	7 0p.m. Train from L'pl. & Man.

FROM CREWE.

*Mail	4 15 a.m. on arriv. of	1 45 a.m. Train from Birming.
Mixed	9 0 ,, ,,	6 0 ., Trains from L'pool. Man. & Birmingham.
First Class	2 0 p.m. ,,	11 30 ,, Train from Birming.
Mail	5 15 ,, ,,	2 45 p.m.

Horses and Carriages will not be conveyed by the Trains marked thus *.

The Mail Trains only run on Sundays.

FARES—Chester to Crewe, 5s. and 4s. —Chester to Birmingham, 18s. and 14s.—Chester to Manchester, 10s. and 7s.

COACHES·

ORMSKIRK.—From the Mitre Inn, Dale-street, every afternoon at 5 p.m. summer, and 4 p.m. in winter, except on Sundays and Thursdays.

ORMSKIRK AND PRESTON.—From Atkinson's, Scotland-road, at 7 a.m., Sundays excepted.

ORMSKIRK AND SOUTHPORT.—From the Saracen's Head, Dale-street, daily, at 4 p.m., Sundays excepted.

SOUTHPORT Royal Mail, from the Saracen's Head, Dale-street, at a quarter before 8 every morning.

ST. HELENS.—From the Crown Vaults, London-road, at 5 p.m., daily.

OMNIBUSES.

AIGBURTH AND TOXTETH PARK.—From the Exchange at $9\frac{3}{4}$, 10, and 12 a m., and $12\frac{1}{2}$, $1\frac{1}{2}$, 2, 3, 4, $4\frac{1}{4}$, $4\frac{1}{2}$, $4\frac{3}{4}$, 5, $5\frac{1}{2}$, $7\frac{3}{4}$, and 8 p.m. On Sundays at $1\frac{3}{4}$, 2, 3, 8, and $8\frac{1}{4}$ p.m.

BOOTLE, SEAFORTH, WATERLOO, AND CROSBY. — From the Angel Hotel, Dale-street, every half-hour during summer, and every hour during winter, from 9 in the morning to 9 in the evening, (Sudays excepted.)

EDGE HILL.—From the Exchange at $9\frac{1}{2}$ a.m., 1, $4\frac{1}{2}$, and $5\frac{1}{4}$ p.m., (Sundays excepted.)

EVERTON.—From the Exchange at 9½ a.m , and 4½, and 5½ p.m., (Sundays excepted.)

EVERTON AND KIRKDALE.—From the Exchange at 9½ a.m., 4, 5, and 7 p.m.

KIRKDALE AND WALTON.—From the Exchange at 9½ a.m., 4¾, and 7 p.m.

OLD SWAN AND KNOTTY ASH.—From the Angel Hotel, Dale-street, and the Exchange, at 11 a.m., 2, 4½, 5, 7, and 8 p.m.

PRESCOT.—From the Grapes Inn, Lime-street, every evening at 5 p.m.

PRESCOT.—From the Stanley Arms, London-road, every evening at 5 p.m.

WAVERTREE, WOOLTON, AND GATEACRE.—From the Exchange though Clayton-square, at 9¾ a.m., 2, 4½, 5½, and 7½ p.m. On Sundays, from Clayton-square, at 10 a.m., 2, 2½, 7, and 9 p.m.

WAVERTREE.—From the Exchange at 9¾ a.m., 2, 5, and 7 p.m.

WEST DERBY AND ZOOLOGICAL GARDENS.—From the George Inn, Dale-street, at 10½ a m., 4½, and 8 p.m. On Sundays at 11 a.m., and 8 p.m.

There are also omnibuses from the principal hotels to the Railway and Steam-packets.

CANAL PACKETS.

BOOTLE, CROSBY, &c., from the Canal Basin, back Leeds-street, during the summer at 8 a.m., and at 1, 4½, and 6 p.m., daily, except Sundays, when they go at 8 a.m., and 2 p.m. During winter at 1½, 4¼ and 6 p.m., daily.

AINTREE every evening at 6, in summer; in winter at 4¼ p.m., except Sundays.

LIST OF PRINCIPAL HOTELS IN LIVERPOOL.

Adelphi, Ranelagh-place; Angel, Dale-street; British, Moor-fields; Belvedere, South Castle-street; Brunswick, Hanover-st., Castle, Clayton-square; Clayton Arms, Clayton-square; "The Derby," West Derby-road; Dolphin, Clayton-square; Feathers, Clayton-square; George, Dale-street; Grecian, Dale-street; Mersey, Old Church-yard; Neptune, Clayton-square; Rainbow, Basnett-street; Royal, Moorfields; Stork, Queen-square; Talbot, Great Charlotte-street; Union, Clayton-square; Waterloo, Ranelagh-street; Wellington, Dale-street.

Besides these, there are many other highly respectable establishments in the neighbourhood of the railway station and coach-offices.

COACH AND CAR FARES,

CAR FARE TWO-THIRDS OF COACH.

Coach Fares.

s d

Abercromby-sq. (east end)..2 6
Adelphi hotel..............1 6
Angel hotel 1 0
Bedford-st.,Brownlow-hill..2 0
　　　　Falkner-street..2 6
Botanic garden...........3 6
Boundary-place, London-rd.2 6
Byrom-street.............1 6
Canal-packet Sta., Leeds-st.1 6
Cattle Market ....,...4 6
Cemetery (St. James') north
　　entrance.............2 0
Clarence Dock 2 0
Clayton-square...........1 6
Cleveland-square 1 6
Coburg Dock 2 6
Crown-street, Brownlow-hill2 6
　　Up. Parliament-st.3 0
Custom-house 1 0
Duke-street, end Suffolk-st..1 0
　　end Gt. George st..2 0
Duke's-place, Wapping 1 6
Edge-hill Coffee-house.....3 0
Everton village, (centre)....2 6
　　St. Domingo house ..3 6
　　St. George's Church..3 6
Fairfield.................3 6
Falkner-terrace, Upper Par-
　liament-street 2 6
Gilead-house, Kensington ..3 0
Great George-square 2 0
Hope-street, Hardman-st ..2 0
Infirmary 2 6
Islington Market.........1 6
King's Monmt., London-rd.1 6
Kirkdale, (Stretch's) 3 6
Lodge-lane, Smithdown-lane3 0
　　to Roperies 3 6
Low-hill 2 6
Marybone,top Gt.Crosshl.-st.1 6
Moss-street, London-road ..2 0
Mount Vernon, Prescot-st ..2 6
Necropolis, Low-hill 3 0
Newsham-house 3 6
North Sh. (Townson's-mill)2 6

Coach Fares.

s d

Old Swan 5 0
Parliament-st., Queen's Dk.2 0
Plumbe's-hall 3 6
Railway Station, Lime-street1 6
　　　　Wapping..1 6
Richmond-row,Scotland-pla.2 0
　　end St. Anne-street2 0
Rodney-st., Mount-pleasant.2 0
Roscommon-st., Gt. Hom.-st.2 6
　　upper end....3 0
Royal hotel 1 0
Russell-st , Brownlow-hill ..2 0
Sandhills Bridge 4 0
Saracen's-head Inn 1 6
Scotland-rd.,to St. Anthony's
　　Chapel.................2 6
Shaw-street, Islington 2 0
Soho-street, Richmond-row.2 0
　　　Islington......2 0
Spekelands (west gate) 3 0
St. Anne-street, Islington ..2 0
　　　Richmond-row..2 0
St. James' Market 2 0
St. Luke's Church 2 0
St. Martin's Market 2 0
St. Michael's Church,Pitt-st.1 6
St. Patrick's Ch., St. James'2 6
Town-hall 1 0
Toxteth-park, High-park
　　Coffee-house 3 0
　　St. John Baptist's Ch.3 0
　　Alfred-place 3 6
　　Park Chapel 3 6
　　St. Michael's Church4 6
　　Otterspool 5 0
Tue-brook 5 0
Up. Parlmt.-st.,end Hope-st.2 6
　　end Crown-st.3 0
Vauxhall-rd end Gt.Oxfd.-st.3 0
Walton-road, to Skirving's..4 6
Wapping, Duke's-place 1 6
Waterloo hotel 1 6
Williamson-square 1 6
Zoological Gardens 3 0

FROM RAILWAY STATION, LIME-STREET, TO	Coach Fares. s d
Abercromby-square	1 6
Adelphi hotel	1 0
Allerton (Mr. Clegg's)	5 6
Angel hotel	1 0
Beacon's-gutter	2 6
Bedford-street, north of Abercromby-square	1 6
south of ditto	2 0
Bold-street	1 0
Bootle lower road, south end	3 0
First Toll-bar	3 6
Rimrose hotel	5 6
Botanic garden	2 6
Boundary-st.,Kirkdale-road, end of	2 6
Breck-la., end Whitefield-la.	2 6
Broad-green	5 6
Brook-house, Smithdown-la.	3 6
Brownlow-st., end Brownlow-hill	1 6
Brunswick dock (centre)	2 6
Canal-packetStation,Leeds-st	1 6
Cattle Market	3 6
Chatham-street	2 0
Childwall	6 0
Clarence dock (centre gate)	2 6
Clayton-square	1 0
Custom-house	1 6
Duke-st., end Hanover-st.	1 0
end Berry-st.	1 6
Edge-hill Coffee-house	2 0
Everton-village, west end	1 6
Brow, end of Netherfield road South	1 6
Crescent	1 6
Netherfield-road, S. end	2 0
Ditto, North end	2 6
Falkner-st., end Bedford-st.	1 6
Fox-st., end Gt. Homer-st.	1 6
George's-pier	1 6
Gilead-house, Kensington	2 0
Grinfield-st., Smithdown-la.	2 0
Great George-st., St. Jas.-st.	1 6
Gt. Homer-st., end of Fox-st.	1 6
Great Mersey-st., Kirkdale	2 6

FROM RAILWAY STATION, LIME-STREET, TO	Coach Fares. s d
Gt. Oxford-st. N., south end	2 0
north end	2 0
Highfield-house, Old-swan	5 0
Hope-street to Canning-st.	1 6
to Up. Parliament-st.	2 0
Kensington, to Mr. Carver's	1 6
Kirkdale (Stretch's)	2 6
Knotty-ash	5 0
Low-hill	1 6
Moss-st., Islington-square	1 0
Mount-pleasant,endHope-st.	1 6
Necropolis, Low-hill	1 6
Old Swan	4 0
Oxford-street, Crown-street	2 0
Park-lane, end Kent-street	1 6
Pembroke-pl., end Ashton-st.	1 0
Prince's Dock, (centre gate)	2 0
Queen's Arms hotel	1 6
Queen's Dock, Norfolk-st.	2 0
Railway Station, Wapping	2 0
Rodney-street, Duke-street.	1 6
Roscommon-st., bottom end.	1 6
Netherfield road South	2 0
Scotland-place	1 0
Seacombe-slip	1 6
Shaw-street, Islington	1 6
Smithdown-la.,end Lodge-la.	2 6
Spekelands	2 6
St. James' Market	1 6
St. Martin's Market	1 6
St. Michael's Church, Pitt-st.	1 6
Town-hall	1 6
Toxteth-park, High-park Coffee-house	2 6
The Dingle	3 6
St. Michael's Church	4 0
Tue-brook	3 6
Walton-road, to Skirving's	3 6
Walton Village	4 0
Warwick-street, Park-road	2 0
Waterloo hotel	1 0
Wavertree	4 0
West Derby Chapel	5 0
Williamson-square	1 0
Zoological Gardens	2 0

COUNTRY FARES, FROM THE STAND IN CASTLE-STREET.

Names of Places.	Miles.	Coach Fares. s d	Names of Places.	Miles.	Coach Fares. s d
Aigburth-hall	4½	6 0	Lark-hill or Mill-hill	3¼	4 6
Allerton-hall	5¾	8 0	Linacre	4½	5 6
Anfield	3	4 6	Linacre Toll-bar	3½	5 0
Ashfield	4½	6 6	Litherland	5	7 0
Barlow's Strawberry			Livesley's house&Breck	2	3 0
Garden	2½	3 6	Lowhill	1½	2 0
Black Bull, Warbreck			Maghull	7½	10 0
Moor	4½	6 6	May-place		5 0
Bootle Coffee-house	3¾	5 0	Melling		12 0
Bootle Toll-bar	2½	3 6	Mosley-hill	4	5 6
Broad-green	4¼	6 6	Newsham-house	2½	3 6
Brook-farm	2¾	3 6	Norris-green	4	6 0
Childwall	5	7 0	Oak-hill		5 6
Crosby, Little		14 0	Old Roan	6	8 0
Crosby, Great		12 0	Old Swan	3½	5 0
Croxteth	5¾	8 0	Orrell	4¾	6 6
Derby-road, Bibby's-lane		5 6	Park Coffee-house	2¼	3 0
Derby Town	4½	6 0	Park Chapel	2½	3 6
Eaton-house or Lodge	4½	6 0	Plumbe's-hall		3 6
Everton Coffee-house	1½	2 6	Prescot	8¼	11 0
Fairfield	2½	3 0	Roby	5¾	8 0
Fazakerly	5¾	8 0	Rock-house	2½	3 6
Finch-House	5¾	8 0	Round-house	4¼	6 6
Fir-grove	4	6 0	Seaforth-house	4½	6 6
Garston	5¾	8 0	Sephton	8	11 0
Gilead-house		3 0	Speke	9	12 0
Green-bank	3¼	4 6	Spekelands		3 0
Halewood-green		10 0	St. Domingo	2	3 6
Hazels	7½	10 0	Summer-hill		7 0
Highfield-house	4½	6 0	Vernon's-hall	1¾	3 0
Huyton	7½	10 0	Walton, Town	3¼	4 0
Ince-hall		16 0	Walton-hall	4¼	5 6
Jericho	3½	5 0	Waterloo		7 6
Kirkby Chapel		12 0	Wavertree Coffee-house	3½	4 6
Kirkdale Coffee-house		3 0	Wheat-hill		8 6
Knowsley-hall	8½	11 0	Woolton	6	8 0

CAR FARES TWO-THIRDS OF THE ABOVE.

LIST OF

THE PLACES OF WORSHIP, CLERGYMEN, &c.,

IN LIVERPOOL AND ITS ENVIRONS.

ESTABLISHED CHURCH,

In the Order of the Date of Consecration.

CHURCHES.	CLERGYMEN.	CURATES, ETC.	HOURS OF SERVICE.		
			M.	A.	E.
St. Nicholas', Chapel-st.	Rev. A. Campbell, A.M., Rector.	Rev. C.T. Wilson. A. M. T. Macgill.	10¾	2¾	—
St. Peter's, Church-st.	Jonathan Brooks, A.M., Rector.	T. Halton, & J.G. Headlam, A.M.	10½	3	6½
St. George's, Castle-st.	J. B. Monk, A.M.	T. G. Leigh, A.M.	11	3	
St. Thomas', Park-lane.	J.C. Prince, A.M.	T. L. Pain, A.M.	11	—	6½
St. Paul's, St.Paul's-sq.	J.H.Stafford, A.M R. Davies, A.M.	J. Jackson, evening lecturer. W. Hughes, do.	11 Welsh,	3 6	
St. Anne's, Gt. Richmond-st.	. . . .	W. D. Blundell, A.M.	10½	—	6½
St. John's, Haymarket.	R. Loxham, A.M. T. Moss, A.M.	T. Stringer, A.M. J. E. Wentworth,	11	3	
Trinity St. Anne-st.	Thos. Bibby, A.M.	A.M.	10¾	3½	
St. Stephen's, Byrom-st.	T.S.Ackland, A.B.	. . . .	10¾	—	6½
St. Mathew's, Key-st.	J.L.Figgins, A.B.	. . . .	10½	—	6½
Christ, Hunter-st.	F. Ould, A.M.	— Hill, A.M.	10¾	—	6½
St James', Upr. Parliament-st	H.Hampton, A.M	H. Berkeley, A.B.	11	—	6½
All Saints, Grosvenor-st.	A.M'Conkey, A.M	J. N. Peill, B.D.	10½	—	6½
St. Mark's, Duke-st.	Rd. Blacow, A.M.	B. A. Marshall, A.B.	10¾	—	6½
St. Mary's, Edgehill.	F. Barker, A.M.	. . . .	10½	3	6½
St. George's, Everton.	Wm. W. Ewbank, A.B.	J. Bush, A.B.	10¾	—	6½

ESTABLISHED CHURCH.

CHURCHES.	CLERGYMEN.	CURATES, ETC.	HOURS OF SERVICE.		
			M.	A.	E.
National school in con. with St. George's.	....	— Crowther, A.B.	10½	3½	—
St. Andrew's, Renshaw-st.	John Jones, A.M.	D. H. Morice, A.B.	11	—	6½
St. Philip's, Hardman-st.	Rd.L.Townsend, A.M.	....	11	3	—
St. Mary's school for the Blind. Hotham-st.	E. Hull, A.M.	....	11	—	6½
St.Michael's, Up. Pitt-st.	H. Carpenter, A.B. Cyrus Morrall, A.M.	E. Whitley, A.B.	10¾	—	6½
St. David's, Brownlow-h.	....	R. P. Jones.	Welsh 9&3 Eng.11,6½		
St. Martin's in the Fields, Gt.Oxford-st.	C. T. Gladwin, LL.B. Cecil Wray, A.M.	J. Blair, A.M.	10¾	—	6½
St. Augustine's, Shaw-st.	T. Tattershall, D.D.	....	11	—	6½
St. Bride's, Percy-st.	Jas. H. Stewart, A.M.	A. Townsend, A.M.	11	—	6½
St. Luke's, Berry-st.	T. Hornby, A.M. C. W. Lawrence, A.M.	....	11	3	—
St. Jude's, Low hill.	Hugh M'Neile, A.M.	W. Faloon, A.B.	10¾	—	6½
St. Catharine's, Abercromby-sq	J. North, A. M.	....	11	3	—
St. John the Baptist, Park road.	J. Hassall, A.M.	....	11	-	6½
St. Matthias, Love-la., Gt, Howard-st.	E. Spencer, A.M.	....	10½	—	6½
St. Simon's, Gloucester-st.	John B. Connor, A.M.	....	10¾	—	6½
St. Saviour's, Falkner-sq.	Prince Crawford, A.M.	....	11	—	6½
St. Barnabas, Parliament-st	T. Nolan, A.M.	C. Badham, A.B.	10¼	—	6½
St. Silas, Pembroke-pl.	John Cordeaux, A.M.	....	11	—	6½
St. Thomas, Warwick-st.	Walter Butler, A.M.	....	11	3	6½

ESTABLISHED CHURCH.

CHURCHES.	CLERGYMEN.	CURATES, ETC.	HOURS OF SERVICE.		
			M.	A.	E.
St. John Evan. *Hope-st.*	R. Cargill, LL.B.	....	10¾	—	6½
St. Clement's *Up.Stanhope-st*	F. Parry, B.D.	....	10¾	—	6½
St. Bartholomew's, *Naylor-st.*	G. Dover, A.M.	....	10½	—	6½
Mariner's, *George's-dk.*	Wm. Maynard, A.M.	....	10½	3	—
Workhouse, *Brownlow-h.*	Stephen Cragg, A.M.	....	11	—	6½
Borough Gaol. *GtHoward-st.*	T. Carter, A.M.	....	11	3	—
West Derby U. Workhouse. *Mill-lane.*	T. Dwyer, A.M.	....			
In the Neighbourhood.					
St. Mary's, *Kirkdale.*	D. James, A.M.	....			
St. Mary's *Bootle.*	John Gladstone, A.M.	....			
St. Thomas', *Seaforth.*	W. Rawson, A.M.	....			
St. Michael's, *Crosby.*	E. B. Chalmer.	....			
Christ Church, *Waterloo.*	J. E. Bates, A.M.	....	10½	2½	·
St. Mary's, *Walton.*	T. Moss, A.M.	R. Wilson, A.B.			
St. Ann's, *Old Swan.*	T. Gardner, A.M.	....	10½	—	6
St.John Evang. *Knotty Ash.*	F. Green, A.B.	....			
Derby Chapel. *Woolton.*	Rd. Blacow, A.M.	W.Moriarty,A.M.			
Childwall.	R. Leicester, A.M.	....			
Trinity, *Wavertree.*	A.Campbell,A.M. W. Badnall, A.M.	A. J. Douglas, A.M.			
St. Ann's, *Aigburth.*	Wm. J. Purdon.	....			
St. Michael's, *Toxteth Park*	Wm. Hesketh, A.M.	....	11	3	—
St. Mary's, *Birkenhead.*	Andrew Knox, A.B.	C. J. Hamilton, A.M.	11	—	6

ESTABLISHED CHURCH.

CHURCHES.	CLERGYMEN.	CURATES, ETC.	HOURS OF SERVICE.		
			M.	A.	E.
Trinity, *North Birkenhead.*	Joseph Baylee, A.M.	....	11	—	6½
St. Catherine's *U. Tranmere.*	Wm. Cleminson, A.B.	M. Spencer, A.B.	11	3	
St. Peter's, *Rock Ferry.*	T. F. Redhead.	....	11	3	
Bebbington.	R. M. Fielden, A.M.	C. Bickmore.			
Bidston	Joshua Gate,				
Wallasey	T. Byrth, D.D.				
St. John's, *Egremont.*	J. Tobin, A.M.	....	11	3	

CHURCHES IN CONNEXION WITH THE

ESTABLISHED CHURCH OF SCOTLAND.

CHURCHES.	MINISTERS.	HOURS OF SERVICE.		
		M.	A.	E.
Oldham-street.	Rev. Jos. R. Welsh.	11	3	
St. Andrew's, *Rodney-st.*	„ John Parke, A.M.	11	—	6½
St. Peter's, *Scotland-rd.*	„ John Ferries.	11	—	6½
Woodside.	„ John Gardner.	11	3	

ROMAN CATHOLICS.

CHAPELS.	CLERGY.	HOURS OF SERVICE.				
		Sundays & Holidays.				Daily.
		MORN.			VESP.	A.M.
St. Mary's Edmund-st.	Rev. T. Fisher. James Wilkinson. William Dale.	7¼	8½	10½	3	8½ —
St. Peter's, Seel-street	J.F.Appleton,DD George Caldwell. Thos. Margieson. Richard Croft.	7½	8½	10½	3	7½ 8½
St. Nicholas', Copperas-hill.	T. Youens, D.D., V.G. Robert Gillow. — Gillow.	8	9	10½	3	8½ —
St. Patrick's, Park-place.	William Parker. Wm. Grayston. J. Walmsley.	8	9	11	4	8½ —
St. Anthony's, Scotland-rd.	Peter Wilcock. Ambrose Lennan. Patrick Phelan. Jas. Fleetwood.	7 8 9		11	6½	8½ —
St. Werburg's, Birkenhead.	Wm. Henderson.					
St. Oswald's Old Swan.	John Maddocks.					
Aigburth Chap.	Robert Prest.					
Crosby, do.	J. H. Dowding.					
Woolton, do.	. . . .					
Workhouse, In-firmary, &c.	John Dawber.					

CATHOLICS.

CHURCHES.	CLERGY.	HOURS OF SERVICE.			
		Sun. & Hol.		Daily	
		A.M.	P.M.	A.M.	P.M.
Church of the Holy Apostles, Canning-street.	Rev.J.Houghton, A.M.	6 9	3 5	6 Wed.&F. at 9 a.m.	5

DISSENTERS' CHAPELS.

INDEPENDENTS.

PLACES OF WORSHIP.	MINISTERS.	HOURS OF SERVICE.	
		M.	E.
Great George-street.	Rev. T. Raffles, D.D., LLD.	$10\frac{3}{4}$	$6\frac{1}{4}$
Crescent, *Everton.*	„ John Kelly.	$10\frac{1}{2}$	$6\frac{1}{2}$
Newington, *Renshaw-st.*	„ William Bevan.	$10\frac{1}{2}$	$6\frac{1}{2}$
Hanover, *Mill-street.*	„ George Pridie, B.A.	$10\frac{1}{2}$	$6\frac{1}{2}$
Toxteth, *South Hill-place.*	„ William P. Appleford.	$10\frac{1}{2}$	$6\frac{1}{2}$
Providence, *Pleasant-st.*	„ Charles Farnsworth.	$10\frac{1}{2}$	$6\frac{1}{2}$
Claremont, *Kirkdale.*	„ Joshua Tunstall.	$10\frac{1}{2}$	$6\frac{1}{2}$
Hamilton-sq., *Woodside.*	„ W. M. O'Hanlon.	$10\frac{1}{2}$	$6\frac{1}{2}$
Trinity, *Wavertree.*	„ Thomas Sleigh.	$10\frac{1}{2}$	$6\frac{1}{2}$
Liscard, *Cheshire.*			

BAPTISTS.

PLACES OF WORSHIP.	MINISTERS.	HOURS OF SERVICE.		
		M.	A.	E.
Pembroke, *Pembroke-pl.*	Rev. C. M. Birrell.	$10\frac{1}{2}$	—	$6\frac{1}{2}$
Soho-street.	„ R. B. Lancaster	$10\frac{1}{2}$	—	$6\frac{1}{2}$
Byrom-street.	„ D. H. Giles.	$10\frac{1}{2}$	—	$6\frac{1}{2}$
Lime-street.	„ James Lister.	$10\frac{1}{2}$	$2\frac{1}{2}$	—
Comus-street.	„ William Guyton.	$10\frac{1}{2}$	$2\frac{1}{2}$	—
Sidney-place, *Edge-hill.*	„ D. S. Wylie, A.M.	$10\frac{1}{2}$	$2\frac{1}{2}$	—

SCOTCH SECESSION CHURCH.

PLACES OF WORSHIP.	MINISTERS.	HOURS OF SERVICE.		
		M.	A.	E.
Mount Pleasant.	Rev. Hugh Crichton, D.D.	11	—	$6\frac{1}{2}$
Bond-street.	„ John Riddel.	11	—	$6\frac{1}{2}$

WESLEYAN METHODISTS.

PLACES OF WORSHIP.	MINS.	HOURS OF SERVICE.		
		M.	A.	E.
Mount Pleasant		$10\frac{1}{2}$	—	6
Pitt-street		7	$10\frac{1}{2}$	6
Brunswick, *Moss-street*..................		$1\frac{1}{2}$	—	6
Wesley, *Stanhope-street*		$1\frac{1}{2}$	$2\frac{1}{2}$	6
Great Homer-street......................		$10\frac{1}{2}$	3	6
Windsor.................................		$1\frac{1}{2}$	—	6
Wavertree		$1\frac{1}{2}$	—	—
Woolton................................		$1\frac{1}{2}$	—	6
Garston		$1\frac{1}{2}$	—	6
Old Swan		$10\frac{1}{2}$	—	6
Aigburth		—	—	$6\frac{1}{2}$
Brunswick, *North Birkenhead*..........		$10\frac{1}{2}$	—	6
Queen-street, *Tranmere*..................		—	2	—
Seacombe		$10\frac{1}{2}$	—	6
West Derby		—	—	$6\frac{1}{2}$
Walton		$10\frac{1}{2}$	—	$6\frac{1}{2}$
Lower Bebbington		10	3	—
Upper Tranmere.........................		$10\frac{1}{2}$	—	$6\frac{1}{2}$

MINS. column (spanning): Supplied by the Circuit preachers in rotation.

WESLEYAN ASSOCIATION.

PLACES OF WORSHIP.	MINISTERS.	HOURS OF SERVICE.	
		M.	E.
Pleasant-street.	Rev. J. Molyneux, Jos.	$10\frac{1}{2}$	6
Tabernacle, *Bispham-st.*	Saul, and R. Rutherford,	$10\frac{1}{2}$	6
Heath-st., *Toxteth Park.*	in rotation.	$10\frac{1}{2}$	6
Scotland-road.		$10\frac{1}{2}$	6

METHODIST NEW CONNEXION.

PLACES OF WORSHIP.	MINISTERS.	HOURS OF SERVICE.	
		M.	E.
Hotham-street.	Rev. Wm. Burrows, Wm.	$10\frac{1}{2}$	6
Bevington-hill.	Cook, and J. Candelet,	$10\frac{1}{2}$	6
St. James's-road.	in rotation.	$10\frac{1}{2}$	6

PRIMITIVE METHODISTS.

PLACES OF WORSHIP.	MINISTERS.	HOURS OF SERVICE.
		M. A. E.
Maguire-street.		10½ — 6
Walnut-street.	Various.	10½ — 6
Liscard, *Cheshire*.		

INDEPENDENT METHODISTS.

Seamen's Church, *Rathbone-street*.	Rev. Edward Loxdale.	10½ 3 6½

UNITARIANS.

Paradise-street.	Rev. James Martineau.	11 — 6½
Renshaw-street.	J H. Thom.	11 3
Park, *Park-road*.	John Robberds.	11 3

REFORMED PRESBYTERIANS.

Edmund-street.	Rev. John Nevin.	10½ — 6½

NEW JERUSALEM CHURCH.

Russel-street.	....	10¾ — 6½
Rose-place.	....	11 — 6½

SANDEMANIANS.

Gill-street.	Rev. Abraham Banks.	11 3

BEREAN UNIVERSALISTS.

Bold-street.	Rev. David Thom.	11 — 6½

FLOATING CHAPEL.

King's Dock.	Supplied by Dissenting ministers of different denominations.	10½ 2½

FRIENDS' MEETING HOUSE.

Hunter-street.	....	10 — 6 Winter, 3
Woodside.	....	— 4 —

JEWS' SYNAGOGUE.

Seel-street.	M. S. Oppenheim. M. D. Isaac, lecturer.	Summer. Friday, 7½ Winter, 4½ Saturday, 8 A.M.

WELSH CHAPELS.

INDEPENDENTS.

PLACES OF WORSHIP.	MINISTERS.	HOURS OF SERVICE.		
		M.	A.	E.
Tabernacle, *Great Crosshall-street.*	Rev. Wm. Rees.	$10\frac{1}{2}$	2	6
Bethel, *Bedford-street.*	„ T. Pierce.	$10\frac{1}{2}$	2	
Salem, *Brownlow-hill.*	„ R. Thomas.	$10\frac{3}{4}$	2	
Seacombe.		—	2	6

CALVINISTIC METHODISTS.

		M.	A.	E.
Pall Mall.		9	2	6
Bedford-street.		9	2	6
Rose-place.		9	2	6
Burlington-street.	Rev. H. Rees, J. Hughes, and John Roberts, in rotation.	9	2	6
Mulberry-street.		10	—	6
Comus-street.		9	2	6
Woodside.		—	2	6
Seacombe.		—	2	6

WESLEYAN METHODISTS.

		M.	A.	E.
Benn's Gardens.	Rev. T. Aubrey, and — Jones, in rotation.	$10\frac{1}{2}$	2	6
Chester-street.		$10\frac{1}{2}$	2	6
Borroughs' Gardens.		$10\frac{1}{2}$	2	6

INDEPENDENT METHODISTS.

		M.	A.	E.
Brick-street.	....	$10\frac{1}{2}$	2	6

BAPTISTS.

		M.	A.	E.
Great Crosshall-street.	Rev. ———	10	2	6
Stanhope-street.	„ W. Roberts.	10	2	6
Sir Thomas's-buildings.	„ D. Jones.	10	2	6
Great Howard-street.	„ J. Roberts.	10	2	6

B. SMITH, PRINTER, SOUTH CASTLE-STREET, LIVERPOOL.

Lightning Source UK Ltd.
Milton Keynes UK
UKOW06f1245020916

282047UK00017B/486/P